The Persons of the Godhead

Children's Bible Studies
Volume Three

R. B. THIEME, JR., BIBLE MINISTRIES
HOUSTON, TEXAS

A catalogue of available audio recordings and publications will be provided upon request.

R. B. Thieme, Jr., Bible Ministries
P. O. Box 460829, Houston, Texas 77056-8829
www.rbthieme.org

Printed in the United States of America

ISBN 1-55764-404-7

Contents

Preface

Before you begin your Bible study, if you are a believer in the Lord Jesus Christ, be sure you have named your sins privately to God the Father.

> If we confess our [known] sins, He is faithful and righteous to forgive us our [known] sins and to cleanse us from all [unknown, or forgotten sins] unrighteousness. (1 John 1:9)

You will then be in fellowship with God, filled with the Holy Spirit, and ready to learn Bible doctrine from the Word of God.

> "God is spirit, and those who worship Him must worship in [the filling of the] spirit and [biblical] truth." (John 4:24)

If you have never personally believed in the Lord Jesus Christ as your Savior, the issue is not naming your sins. The issue is faith alone in Christ alone.

> "He who believes in the Son has eternal life; but he who does not obey [the command to believe in] the Son shall not see life, but the wrath of God abides on him." (John 3:36)

THE WORD OF GOD is alive and powerful, sharper than any two-edged sword, piercing even to the dividing asunder of the soul and the spirit, and of the joints and the marrow, and is a critic of thoughts and intents of the heart. (Heb. 4:12)

All Scripture is God-breathed, and is profitable for doctrine, for reproof, for correction, for instruction in righteousness; that the man of God might be mature, thoroughly furnished unto all good works. (2 Tim. 3:16–17)

Study to show thyself approved unto God, a workman that needeth not to be ashamed, rightly dividing the word of truth. (2 Tim. 2:15)

History of *Children's Bible Studies*

Children's Bible Studies were originally published in the 1960s as the *Doctrinal Bible Studies*, a compilation of Bible lessons taught to children in Berachah Church Sunday School. Affectionately referred to as "The Quarterlies," the series comprised thirty-two books addressing eight age levels. Each level was divided into the Quarterlies: Fall, Winter, Spring, and Summer. The series begins with basic doctrines for the very young child and progresses toward more advanced doctrines for the older child.

In 1972, Pastor R. B. Thieme, Jr., replaced Berachah Church Sunday School with Prep School and a new system of teaching. From the Bible doctrine resident in their souls, teachers would prepare their own Bible lessons to teach the children. However, the Quarterlies have remained a treasure-trove of ideas for parents and teachers looking for ways to communicate Bible doctrine at a child's level of understanding. When complete, *Children's Bible Studies* will contain all of the original material in eight volumes: *What God Wants Me to Know*; *What Is God Like?*; *The Persons of the Godhead*; *God's Plan of Salvation*; *The Christian Way of Life*; *The Life of Moses*; *The Mental Attitudes*; and *The Dispensations*.

Children's Bible Studies complement the lesson formats and research guide from *Train Up a Child...Children's Bible Studies Source Book*. The lessons are organized into chapters with an overview outlining the subject, titles of the lessons, story objective, vocabulary and doctrinal concepts, *Source Book* keywords, and activities. New visual aids pertinent to the lessons are included in the back of the book for use in making training aids. The lessons in the *Children's Bible Studies* are easily incorporated into the extensive curriculum found in the *Source Book* enabling parents and teachers to master lesson preparation while providing creative ways to teach Bible doctrine.

The Persons of the Godhead, the third volume in the series, begins with a review of the essence of God as taught by the animals. These stories from the Bible use animal behavior, instinct, and characteristics to also teach the lessons of salvation, humility, obedience, and faithfulness to God's Word. With these doctrines refreshed in his mind, the child is ready to learn about the Trinity. Each member of the Godhead is presented from His distinct role and His relation to the eternal will and plan of God. Understanding God the Father's plan explains the child's destiny in time and eternity; the study of the person and work of Jesus Christ illuminates the child's so-great salvation; and knowledge of the ministries of God the Holy Spirit focuses the child on the divine power he has for living the Christian way of life. Girded with this knowledge, the child will come to love God, grow spiritually, and reflect the glory of our God-man-Savior, the Lord Jesus Christ.

To the Parents

God mandates you, the parent, to study and learn Bible doctrine. With Bible doctrine in your soul, you are the best teacher in the world for your children. From your own doctrinal frame of reference, personality, and approach, you can then fulfill your responsibility to God to teach your children the Word of God.

> "And these words, which I am commanding you today, shall be on your heart; and you shall teach them diligently to your sons and shall talk of them when you sit in your house and when you walk by the way and when you lie down and when you rise up." (Deut. 6:6–7)

Teach your children Bible doctrine the way you teach them to play ball, to make a bed, to wash their hands, to use table manners. Teach them over and over. Then, check them. Repeat and repeat, until they know Bible doctrine as readily as they know their own name. When the time comes for them to leave home, you can rest confidently in God's promise:

> Train up a child in the way he should go,
> Even when he is old he will not depart from it.
> (Prov. 22:6)

Consider how much time you already spend training your children how to live as well-mannered, responsible citizens. How much more time are you willing to spend to ensure that they know how to live as believers in the Lord Jesus Christ who reflect the glory of God? You have the privilege of teaching your children that learning and applying Bible doctrine is the most wonderful blessing in life. In fact, Bible doctrine is the most valuable heritage you can give your children.

> I was very glad to find *some* of your children walking in truth, just as we have received commandment *to do* from the Father. (2 John 4)

How to Use This Book

Teaching the Word of God requires careful preparation. You cannot teach what you do not know. To facilitate your preparation, each chapter of the *Children's Bible Studies* begins with an Overview, the plan for developing the subject of that particular chapter. The Overview provides a solid foundation on which you can build your own lesson plans, tailored to your setting, teaching style, and the children's age levels.

THE CHAPTER OVERVIEW:

Subject: The chapter title summarizes the primary doctrinal emphasis and the biblical reference upon which each story is based.

Lesson Titles: The lesson titles reflect a further delineation of the doctrinal concepts taught in each story.

Story Objective: The story objective is a synopsis, from an adult frame of reference, of the doctrines to be taught in each chapter. Each primary doctrine is documented with Scripture references. The story objective includes teaching pointers regarding specifics for presentation of the doctrine in that particular chapter.

Vocabulary and Doctrinal Concepts: Each chapter has a list of specific, technical vocabulary words that are used in the stories. It is important that the child understand the definitions of these words as the story progresses. The list of doctrinal concepts extrapolated from the stories is provided with Scripture references for preparation.

***Source Book* Keywords:** Keywords provide a link to the corresponding subject in the Research Guide in *Train Up a Child...Children's Bible Studies Source Book*. The Research Guide provides Scripture references, book titles, and audio recordings on keyword subjects taught by R. B. Thieme, Jr. These resources are available upon request at no charge from R. B. Thieme, Jr., Bible Ministries, P.O. Box 460829, Houston, Texas 77056-8829, USA.

Activities: A list of suggested activities is provided to enhance and reinforce the biblical concepts of the lesson. For a comprehensive list of teaching aids and resources, consult the *Source Book*.

Suggested Visuals: Most of the lessons have diagrams that illustrate the doctrinal concepts in the story as it unfolds. These diagrams may be used in any number of applications, including: flannel boards, worksheets, craft projects. The visuals used in assembling these diagrams are located in the back of this book. They may be copied, traced, or scanned and are intended to be colored, glued, glittered, used for models, mobiles, or backed with flannel fabric for use on a flannel board (a piece of board covered with flannel fabric).

Games, Songs, Worksheets: Any or all of these activities can be utilized to enhance the doctrinal concepts in the lessons. Many memory type games can be modified to challenge recall of doctrinal principles and vocabulary. Singing doctrinal lyrics fitted to familiar tunes reinforces biblical concepts. Worksheets provide an effective way to review the key points of each lesson.

Memory Verse: A Scripture verse pertinent to the subject is woven throughout the entire chapter and is for review at the end of each lesson.

Opening and Closing Prayer: Each lesson must begin with the private confession of sin (1 John 1:9). Opening prayer is time for soul preparation, time to request help from God the Holy Spirit for concentration and understanding of the Bible lesson to be taught. Each lesson should end with closing prayer, thanking God for His Son and His gift of our so-great salvation, thanking Him for the opportunity to learn His Word, and asking Him to challenge us in the application of His Word in our lives.

THE LESSONS:

Learning comes by repetition. Teach these lessons repeatedly, drawing the many different applications for the child from them. The lessons are organized so that doctrine is built upon doctrine, from the basic concepts to the more complex. Each lesson has three sections: The Story, What God Wants Me to Know, and the Lesson Review.

The Story illustrates how Bible doctrine can be learned, stored, and applied. The story is presented for a child's frame of reference and can be adjusted to any age level. Each story incorporates the chapter memory verse, weaving it throughout and tying it to the story objective.

What God Wants Me to Know gives the application of the doctrinal concepts to the child's life. In this section, the Gospel is also presented. That a child is saved cannot be taken for granted. Therefore, the need for and the way of salvation can never be presented too often.

Lesson Reviews are specifically designed for a categorical review of the doctrinal concepts, vocabulary words, and memory verse presented in each story. Utilizing the review not only ensures that the key points of the lesson are covered, but leaves the children with something to anticipate in the next lesson.

GENERAL SUGGESTIONS:

Whether you teach in the classroom or in the home, formally or informally, with complex lessons and many activities or with simple, concise presentations, always make learning Bible doctrine enjoyable for the children. Never bore your children with the Word of God. Remember, "The word of God is alive and powerful" (Heb. 4:12)! Captivate their imaginations with God's truth. Hold their attention so that they eagerly look forward to learning more and more Bible doctrine. Let your children have an active part in the lessons. Encourage their natural curiosity, individual thought, expressions, and questions. For the effective communication of God's Word, the following guidance is provided for your consideration.

Reinforce the lesson subject in different ways. Use whatever methods are comfortable for you and effective with your children: sing songs, use puppets, play games, have surprises, use a variety of teaching aids. Many different teaching aids are readily available such as flannel graph stories, coloring books, recordings, CDs, and storybooks found in Bible bookstores and toy stores. Stores that provide materials for public school teachers are also an excellent source of teaching aids. Chalk or dry erase boards, worksheets, puppets, or craft projects for your children to make can all be adapted to enhance any lesson. Do not limit yourself to your classroom; go on a picnic, or to the zoo, or visit a museum.

Begin each lesson with the private confession of sin. Teach the children that the only way to approach the Word of God is after restoration of fellowship with Him through the filling ministry of God the Holy Spirit. Remind them that the Holy Spirit is the real teacher of God's Word (John 14:26).

Devote part of each lesson to learning the memory verse. Then, make reference to it as it applies to the subject. Help the children look up the verse in the Bible and impress on their minds that God's written Word is the source of all truth. For younger children, paraphrase or shorten verses for easier memorization. Most importantly, make memorizing verses a delightful part of the lesson.

Present the Gospel in every lesson. You never want to take the salvation of your children for granted. Even though you may feel certain your children are born again, repeat the Gospel. Find the opportunity to talk to each child individually about his eternal relationship with the Lord. Provide for those who want to believe in the Lord Jesus Christ as their Savior the time and opportunity to make the decision.

Define the vocabulary words. Understanding the doctrinal concepts depends upon understanding the meaning of the technical vocabulary words. Never assume the child already knows the meaning of a word, or is necessarily hearing the word correctly. You need to enunciate the word clearly, and define it in terms of the child's frame of reference.

Review, review, review. The doctrinal concepts, vocabulary words, and memory verses all need to be reviewed, and then reviewed again. When asking questions, provide hints that will help the children to recall the correct answers. Encourage them to express, in their own vocabulary, what they have learned. Make the reviews enjoyable by playing games, singing songs, reviewing teaching aids, and having contests. Always leave your children with Bible doctrine to consider and Bible doctrine to anticipate.

Chapter One

God's Plan for His Animals

OVERVIEW

A. Subject: God's Plan for His Animals—Genesis 1:26–30; 2:19–20; 9:3

B. Lesson Title: How the Animals Became Our Teachers

C. Story Objective:

Relatively little is taught about the animals mentioned in the Bible. They have a very definite part in God's plan; otherwise, God would not have created them (Gen. 1:20–26). We are told that God brought the animals to the first man to see what he would name them, and that He gave man dominion over them (Gen. 2:19–20; Ps. 8:4–8). This rulership of man over lower creation was reaffirmed to Noah and his descendants (Gen. 9:2). However, because of the curse of sin, many of the animals lost their gentleness and trusting confidence in man; some became shy and fearful, others even ferocious.

But according to God's plan, the animals have become man's servants and companions down through the years. They have provided food and clothing, labor and transportation. More than that, the 'dumb animals' have often taught mankind invaluable lessons. For this series, we want to take up the challenge of Job 12:7–8b, "But now ask the beasts, and let them teach you; And the birds of the heavens, and let them tell you . . . And let the fish of the sea declare to you," and see what lessons of spiritual value we can glean from the animal kingdom. Since most children are fond of animals, these chapters should prove enjoyable to them.

The aim of these lessons is to show that God has a special plan for all the works of His hands (Ps. 115:3; 135:6). He always makes known His purposes to the animals and inanimate creation. Thus the heavens declare His glory—the outer manifestation of His essence, with emphasis on His power and sovereignty; and as a result, His excellence is seen universally (Ps. 19:1–6; Rom. 1:20). To this day, the vegetable kingdom perpetuates itself within its species, providing food for man and beast alike according to God's command (Gen 1:11–12; Isa. 55:10b).

The animal kingdom, once created, was blessed of God and told to "be fruitful and multiply" (Gen. 1:20–25), and man was given rulership over all this (Gen. 1:26; Ps. 8:4–8). It is tragic that the most intelligent of God's creatures—be they angelic (Ezek. 28:12–15) or human (Gen. 1:26–27; 2:19–20)—should rebel against their Maker's perfect plan for them and choose their own imperfect plan instead. "Professing to be wise, they became fools" (Rom. 1:22; cf. 1 Cor. 3:19–20).

We should do well to learn from the truly wise creatures of God how to find happiness and fulfillment within the framework of God's plan and purpose for our lives. Were the 'dumb animals' to speak, as they have been known to on occasion, how they would rebuke many of us! It is these wise creatures to which we shall refer mainly in these lessons.

D. Vocabulary and Doctrinal Concepts:
  1. Vocabulary: crafty, garments, Lucifer, serpent, straightforward
  2. Doctrinal Concepts:
     a. God's excellence manifested in creation, power, and purpose (Ps. 8; 19:1–6)
     b. The categories of God's will and their effect on the believer's life (Ps. 19:7–11):

1) Law—Pentateuch, teaching of doctrine
2) Testimony—principles of action
3) Statutes—regulations for social conduct
4) Commandments—God's orders, military emphasis
5) Fear—reverential trust; here directed toward God's nature, discipline, and judgments
6) Judgments—rule of administration, or how God performs His will

E. *Source Book* Keywords: Adam and Eve, creation/restoration, Garden of Eden

F. Activities:
1. Suggested Visuals: Adam and Eve after the Fall
2. Games, Songs, Worksheets
3. Memory Verse: "But now ask the beasts, and let them teach you." (Job 12:7*a*)
4. Opening and Closing Prayer

LESSON
HOW THE ANIMALS BECAME OUR TEACHERS

*H*ow would you like to go to a school where all the teachers are animals, either cattle or birds or fish or reptiles or insects? "Oh boy, I'd love it," you say, "only there is no school like that!" Well, you are wrong—there is! God has such a school, and it's found right here in His Word. His school has many classrooms; some are indoors, some outdoors, others are up in the sky, and still others are under the earth or in the waters.

You may doubt my word, but you must never doubt God's Word; it is true from cover to cover, and it was written for our learning (Rom. 15:4). Do you want to see where we are told about our animal teachers? Turn to the Book of Job, in the middle of your Bible, just before the Book of Psalms. Did you find it? Very good! Now turn to chapter twelve, verses 7 and 8*b*. Let's read them together. "But now ask the beasts, and let them teach you; And the birds of the heavens, and let them tell you . . . And let the fish of the sea declare to you." Our memory verse is, "But now ask the beasts, and let them teach you" (Job 12:7*a*).

We shall attend God's "Little Red School House" together to see what we can learn from the animal kingdom. Now when I say "animal kingdom," I mean everything that goes on two or more legs, everything that flies, and everything that wiggles, crawls, or swims—no matter how small or large. Come along with me to our first classroom, way back to the beginning of time on the earth.

God Makes the Animals

God had finished making the heavens and the earth, the seas and the sky. Already the sun, moon, and stars twinkled in the heavens and gave their light by day and by night, exactly as God had told them (Gen. 1:14–18; Jer. 31:35). Flowers and trees had come up on the grassy slopes, and seeds were beginning to ripen so that there would always be growing things upon the earth. The waters of the rivers and seas rippled gently in the soft breeze. What a lovely sight it all was!

Then God said, "Let the waters teem with swarms of living creatures, and let birds fly above the earth in the open expanse of the heavens. And God created the great sea monsters, and every living creature that moves, with which the waters swarmed after their kind, and every winged bird after its kind" (Gen. 1:20–21*a*). What a whirring and flapping of wings that must have been as birds of all colors soared through the sky; what gay songs of praise they must have sung to God! What a splashing of water, as the fish jumped and swam back and forth through the rivers, lakes, and seas! Why, if we are really still, we can almost hear what it must have been like.

But God was not through yet. "Then God said, 'Let the earth bring forth living creatures after their kind: cattle and creeping things and beasts of the earth after their kind'; and it was so" (Gen. 1:24). When God had said those words, all kinds of animals began to move about. They nibbled on the juicy grass as if they had always known how; they played tag and darted in and out among the bushes and trees. Wouldn't it have been fun to watch them?

God Declares His Purpose for the Animals

But what was that? Suddenly all animals stopped what they were doing and raised their heads to listen. God was speaking to them; He was blessing them or declaring them blessed. This means that God was saying that all would be well with them. This was a promise backed by the very essence of God, by all that God is and can do. And now God was telling them all why He had made them and what His plan was for their lives. "And God blessed them, saying, 'Be fruitful and multiply, and fill the waters in the seas, and let birds multiply on the earth'" (Gen. 1:22). Eat "every green plant for food," God told them (Gen. 1:30); and perhaps all the animals and birds, all the fish and creeping things, bowed their heads and thanked God in their own way.

School Begins

The very next day, school began for the animals when God sent a teacher into their outdoor classroom. Who was that teacher? Yes, Adam was the wisest man who ever lived, apart from the Lord Jesus, of course. Adam had never been to school himself, but then, God had made him in His own image and after His own likeness (Gen. 1:26–27). It was God's plan from the very beginning of time on earth that man should rule over the animals. This way man would teach the animals. And what do you think was their first lesson? God's Word tells us what it was in Genesis 2:19. The Lord brought all the animals to Adam to see what he would call them. "And whatever the man called a living creature, that was its name" (Gen. 2:19*b*).

Did you know that this is how the animals got their names? Perhaps Adam watched them walk by, one by one; perhaps he watched them fly or creep, climb or crawl. Then Adam decided what they were to be called. "And the man gave names to all the cattle, and to the birds of the sky, and to every beast of the field" (Gen. 2:20*a*).

The next time the animals went to 'school' they learned something new: They learned that God had made Adam and all mankind to rule over them (Gen. 1:28; Ps. 8:6–8). That meant all the animals must obey mankind and serve him. And would you believe it? Not one of the animals stamped his foot and said, "But I won't!" They were content with God's will for them, and that's more than we can say for ourselves! How nice it would have been had things continued as God intended. But they did not. The cleverest angel, Lucifer or Satan, and the cleverest human being, Adam, went against God's perfect will, and sin came into the world (Gen. 3).

The First Animal Teachers

It was true, man would still have the use and ownership of the animals, but the curse of sin had the animals fearful of mankind instead of trusting him (Gen. 9:2). And from the time of Adam's sin, not only would man continue to show the animals what to do, but often the animals would teach mankind very important lessons. Would you like to know who the first animal teachers were? Listen and see if you can guess.

After Adam and Eve believed God's promise of a Savior from sin, we read of something God did for them: "And the LORD God made garments of skin for Adam and his wife, and clothed them" (Gen. 3:21). Did the first man and his wife understand what these garments of skins taught them? I am sure they did. They knew well that the punishment for sin was death—first spiritual, then physical (Gen.

2:17). But God had told them that He would send a Savior to die in their place (Gen. 3:15). Would they believe this? Indeed they did (Gen. 3:20)! That was when the first man and his wife learned their lesson from their animal teachers. What kind of animals were they? Right, lambs (John 1:29)! Sinless lambs had given their lives that the first sinners' sinfulness might be covered from God's sight.

What God Wants Me to Know

You have learned that God is perfect righteousness and perfect justice. He insists that sin be punished wherever it is found. Well, then, had the little lambs sinned so that they had to die? They had not! Adam's sin had brought suffering, sadness, and death into the world (Rom. 5:12), to the animals as well as to human beings. The lambs only taught what would happen when God's promised Savior came into the world. He would die for the sins of the world. Then all who believed in Him would be clothed in Christ's own righteousness; that is, they would be made good enough to come into God's presence (2 Cor. 5:21).

And the Savior did come! No longer did the little lambs need to die to teach God's lesson of salvation. God's own perfect Lamb had come to take away the sins of the world. When John the Baptist saw the Lord Jesus, he called out, "Behold, the Lamb of God" (John 1:29*a*)! "Behold" means look! That is exactly what the Lord Jesus wants every one of us to do. He said, "Turn to Me, and be saved . . . For I am God, and there is no other" (Isa. 45:22). "And there is salvation in no one else; for there is no other name under heaven that has been given among men, by which we must be saved" (Acts 4:12). "Looking" to the Lord Jesus is the same as believing or trusting in Him. Will you believe in the Lord Jesus right now? "Believe in the Lord Jesus, and you shall be saved" (Acts 16:31*a*).

But there was another lesson Adam and Eve would never forget—a lesson they had learned the hard way. It was the lesson of the serpent. "And just what was that lesson?" you may wonder.

Did you notice what the Bible said about the serpent in Genesis 3:1*a*? Let me read it to you: "Now the serpent was more crafty [more clever, more intelligent] than any beast of the field which the LORD God had made." It could very well be that Eve had taken the serpent for her pet. It could even be that because the serpent was so wise, he could actually speak some words, for Eve was not one bit surprised when those tempting words came out of the animal's mouth. What Eve did not know was that they were not the serpent's words but Satan's, the devil's words, and oh my, they sounded like a good thing to her—good enough to obey Satan and to disobey God!

Have you ever seen how crooked a serpent is? That's what the devil is like (Rev. 12:9). There is nothing straightforward or honest about him (John 8:44b). He makes wrong look right, and right look wrong. He would love for us to want to play, read, or just 'goof off' rather than take time for God and His Word. Next time you are tempted to have your way instead of God's way, will you remember what you have learned today? Will you think of this verse, "But now ask the beasts, and let them teach you" (Job 12:7a)? They will teach you that God's way is best for you! In our next lesson you will hear of another animal that actually spoke in a human voice.

Lesson Review

The first lesson we learned in God's school with the animals was that the animals really do teach us. What Bible verse told us so? "But now ask the beasts, and let them teach you" (Job 12:7a). God first made the animals; then He made man. He blessed them all and told them to fill the earth, to be fruitful and multiply. God wanted Adam to rule over all things on the earth, but there was one thing God did not want Adam to do. What was it? To eat of the tree of the knowledge of good and evil.

Can you tell me why God brought the animals to Adam? To name them. Two of these animals were especially mentioned in our lesson: The first is said to have been the most clever of all the animals; the second is known to be very, very gentle. The serpent and the lamb. What two lessons did these animals teach the first man and woman? Serpent—sin; lamb—salvation.

Memory Verse

"But now ask the beasts, and let them teach you." (Job 12:7a)

Chapter Two

A Lesson in Faithful Obedience

OVERVIEW

A. Subject: A Lesson in Faithful Obedience—Numbers 22:1–35

B. Lesson Titles:
  1. Lesson One: Balaam and the Donkey
  2. Lesson Two: A Lesson for Balaam

C. Story Objective:
  By contrasting the faithful obedience, service, and devotion of a donkey to her master with the believer's disregard of the Lord's expressed will for his life, we learn that true happiness can only be realized in the center of God's will (John 13:17).

D. Vocabulary and Doctrinal Concepts:
  1. Vocabulary: abound, Angel of the Lord, beasts of burden, captivity, cliff, herd, mockery, perverse, plains, ravine, sorcerer, two-by-four, yoke
  2. Doctrinal Concepts:
   a. General principles:
    1) Disobedience to God is called acting "foolishly" (1 Sam. 13:13*a*).
    2) "To obey is better than sacrifice" (1 Sam. 15:22*b*).
    3) Serve God with a willing mind (1 Chron. 28:9; Eph. 6:6).
    4) We belong to Him, not to ourselves (Ps. 100:3; 1 Cor. 6:19–20).
    5) Love for the Lord motivates obedience (John 14:15; cf. Rom. 6:17).
    6) Rules of conduct for the believer's life (Eph. 5:15–17).
    7) Motivation for the believer's production (Phil. 2:13).
    8) Do all things faithfully, be trustworthy (3 John 5; cf. 1 Cor. 4:2).
   b. Information regarding Balaam:
    1) Balaam was converted (Num. 22:8, 13, 18–19, 38; 23:12).
    2) He would not leave Mesopotamia without divine permission (Num. 22:13, 20).
    3) He met and conversed with Christ (Num. 22:22, 32–34).
    4) The Lord put words in Balaam's mouth (Num. 23:5, 12, 16).
    5) Balaam refers to God as "the LORD my God" (Num. 22:18).
    6) The Holy Spirit "came upon him" (Num. 24:2).
   c. Balaam's carnality:
    1) The "way of Balaam"—his love of wealth and prestige; he would do anything for money (2 Pet. 2:15)
    2) The "error of Balaam"—materialism and power lust; he knew doctrine but did not apply it to experience (Jude 11)
    3) The "teaching of Balaam"—giving advice contrary to God's Word; hypocrisy and compromise neutralize believers (Num. 25:1–2; 31:15–16; cf. Deut. 5:7, 9; 1 Cor. 10:8; Rev. 2:14)
   d. The will of God for Balaam:
    1) Directive (Num. 22:12)
    2) Permissive (Num. 22:20, 35)
    3) Overruling (Num. 22:22; 31:8)

E. *Source Book* Keywords: divine guidance, obedience and happiness

F. Activities:
   1. Suggested Visuals: Angel of the Lord, Balaam, Balaam's donkey

2. Games, Songs, Worksheets
3. Memory Verse: "If you know these things, you are blessed if you do them." (John 13:17)
4. Opening and Closing Prayer

LESSON ONE
BALAAM AND THE DONKEY

God made known His will to all of His creatures. As long as Adam obeyed God all was well, but once he decided to disobey, sin and sorrow, pain and death, came into the world. It was the same with the serpent. Had Satan not used him, the serpent would still be the most beautiful and the most clever of all the animals—not a slithering, crawling snake!

God's Word tells us that if we know and do God's will, we shall be truly happy. "If you know these things [the things God wants us to know, to do, or not to do], you are blessed if you do them [if you obey]" (John 13:17). In our lesson, we will see two of God's creatures, a man and his donkey, and learn how faithfully one of them did what God intended, while the other did not. Who was the obedient one, the man or the donkey? Well, listen carefully and you will find out.

Balaam Introduced

Our 'classroom' is the twenty-second chapter of the Book of Numbers. Remember: Genesis, Exodus, Leviticus, Numbers. We shall be both indoors and outdoors for our lesson. Right now we want to meet the man to whom this lesson was first taught; then we will meet his teacher; and last of all, we will see what we can learn from this story to use in our own lives.

Balaam lived in those long-ago days when Moses was leading the Israelites toward the land God had promised to give them. At the time Balaam's lesson begins, the Israelites had set up their tents in the plains or flat lands of Moab.

The Moabites had heard how strong the armies of the Israelites were, and they feared for their lives. Really, they need not have feared, for God had told His people not to trouble the Moabites (Deut. 2:9); only the Moabites did not know this. Quickly, the Moabites sent word of the approaching Israelites to their friends, the Midianites.

Just then, Balak, the king of the Moabites, had an idea. He would send for Balaam. Balaam was a well-known sorcerer, something like a wizard or witch doctor, a real magician! If Balaam blessed someone, all went well for that person; but if Balaam cursed—wow, could he ever make that curse stick! Perhaps if Balak offered Balaam great rewards, Balaam would do as he wished, thought the king. So King Balak sent high-ranking, important messengers bearing gifts and this special message: "Please come, curse this people [the Israelites] for me" (Num. 22:6*a*).

What King Balak did not know was that Balaam had since come to believe in the true God of heaven and earth. Balaam had learned that God hated wizards and their lying wonders and tricks of magic (Deut. 18:10–12). God no longer wanted him to do those things. Besides, Balaam had learned that it would never do to curse what God has blessed (Gen. 12:3; Num. 23:8). You see, Balaam *knew these things*, and now the question was, would he *do* them? Would he obey God's will or the will of the king of Moab? Think of your memory verse and tell me which would bring happiness to Balaam. Right—*doing* God's will. "If you know these things, you are blessed if you do them" (John 13:17).

Balaam looked longingly at the rewards the king had sent him. My, but they looked tempting! Balaam wanted to be rich, for he thought that having great sums of money along with his fame would surely make him happy. And he began to wonder, should he or shouldn't he go?

While Balaam thinks about that, let me ask you a question. I know that no one will come to offer you great riches for cursing people. But let's just suppose that this was your day to go to Bible class and you are also invited to spend the night with some unbelieving friends instead. They promise you great fun and tell you that skipping class "just once" won't matter. Do *you* know what God would want *you* to do? Job 23:12 says that learning the doctrines of the Word is even more important than eating food. Now God will neither make you go to class nor to your friend's house. He gave you volition and leaves the choice up to you. Think of your memory verse before you decide; then you will know where *your* real happiness would be!

God's Will for Balaam

That night, while the king's messengers slept, God told Balaam, "Do not go with them; you shall not curse the people; for they are blessed" (Num. 22:12). Balaam had to send away the messengers. "Go back to your land," he said, and maybe he sighed just a little, "for the LORD has refused to let me go with you" (Num. 22:13). But King Balak would not accept no for an answer. He sent even more important messengers and costlier gifts; he promised Balaam greater honors (Num. 22:15–17). That was too much for greedy Balaam. He kept thinking wishfully, "Oh, if God would only let me go!"

God knew that Balaam had in fact already made up his mind to go against God's will. That night God said, "Rise up *and* go with them; but only the word which I speak to you shall you do" (Num. 22:20*b*). I am sure that Balaam hardly slept a wink that night. Early the next morning, he got ready for the journey, and this is where we meet the real hero, or rather "heroine," of our lesson, Balaam's teacher—the donkey. "So Balaam arose in the morning, and saddled his donkey, and went with the leaders of Moab" (Num. 22:21).

Introducing the Donkey

Do you think of donkeys as stupid, stubborn animals that won't budge unless they are hit with a two-by-four? Why do you think so? Because 'they' say so? You cannot always go by what people say, but you can always go by "Thus says the Lord"! I want to tell you some facts about this animal and show you from God's Word who the real donkey was in this story!

Did you know that the donkey is one of the most frequently mentioned animals in the Bible? We know donkeys as beasts of burden (Gen. 42:26; Matt. 21:5). We know that they were used to plow the ground (Isa. 30:24). They carried riders on their backs, and for all their hard work, they are satisfied with plain food—some chopped straw, barley, a few beans, thistles, and grass. Even today, donkeys are used where no other animal can travel. Perhaps you have ridden one down into the Grand Canyon!

At one time, the donkeys were free. They roamed in herds of nearly twenty animals through southern India, Iran—the "Persia" of the Bible, and some parts of Africa. They lived in the deserts near Palestine. Each herd had its own chief and appointed one of their numbers to see to the safety of them all. You see, donkeys can sense approaching danger quite easily. They were large, strong, and stately animals, some measuring fifteen hands high, about the size of a horse. They were swift as horses and far more surefooted and healthy. They walked fearlessly along dangerous paths, with rocky cliffs on one side and deep ravines on the other. And though they were gentle and shy, if attacked they could defend themselves with their mouths and kicking heels without even missing a pace. Nothing but the purest water would do for their thirst, and they stepped around muddy spots in the road in order not to soil themselves.

Man began to watch this proud creature. He caught a few of them to train to serve him. He found the donkey to be useful, patient, sturdy, and oh, so willing to work. He made a splendid animal to ride, and some donkeys were so costly that only kings and high-ranking nobles could afford them. Balaam had such a donkey, which tells us that he must have been a rich and important man in his day. It is said that the remarkable thing about donkeys is that once the donkey has been made to carry a heavy burden, he takes on a dull and stupid look, which has earned him his bad name. Why, it's just as if the donkey no longer cares now that he has lost his freedom.

Over the years, the donkeys in captivity increased in number and kind. Now even the poor could afford to own them. Some owners neglected to care for their donkeys as they should and often mistreated them. The only way the donkey knew to complain was to refuse to work faithfully and obediently. Only once in history did a donkey answer back in a human voice. We will hear all about it in our next lesson.

What God Wants Me to Know

We are told in God's Word that "An ox knows its owner, And a donkey its master's manger [feed bin]," but only too often God's people forget, or else do not care who owns them (Isa. 1:3*a*). The donkey knew she belonged to Balaam; she stood still and let Balaam saddle her. Do you know to whom you belong? If you have believed in the Lord Jesus Christ, you belong to Him. He made you and saved you (John 1:3; 1 Cor. 6:19). Should you not serve Him willingly?

Think of what a good master He is! Even if you disobey, He still keeps right on loving you. When you confess your sins, you are forgiven. He supplies all your needs (Phil. 4:19) and promises to give you many good things besides

(Ps. 34:10b). He will never give you a burden that is too heavy for you to carry. "My yoke is easy [My burden is light]," He promises (Matt. 11:30). And should you think it too heavy for you, why, you always can cast "all your care upon him; for he careth for you" (1 Pet. 5:7, KJV). All He asks of us who are His own is, "If you love Me, you will keep My commandments" (John 14:15).

Maybe you have never come to the Lord Jesus in faith, believing what He did for you. Then hear this: Once there was a young donkey. He had never been ridden, and he had kept close to his mother who was securely tied, perhaps to a fence post, in a little village just outside Jerusalem. Yet, when the Lord Jesus sent for him, he came willingly, never even bucking once. Happily he trod all the way to Jerusalem. To think that the Lord Jesus, God Himself, had need of him (Mark 11:3)! What a rider to carry! Surely the little donkey never forgot that wonderful day!

You are still young, but even this minute the Lord wants you to know that He has need of *you*. Why? Because He loves you and wants you to serve Him. Once sin kept you from coming to God. Sin is the heaviest burden man could bear (Ps. 38:4); in fact, a burden much too heavy for any of us. That's why the Lord Jesus came down from heaven to take our sins in His own body on the cross (1 Pet. 2:24). The only sin He could not die for is the sin of unbelief. That sin makes us dull and stupid to God and His Word (1 Cor. 2:14). Use your volition to believe in the Lord Jesus Christ. Don't wait stubbornly for another day. Right now is the best time (2 Cor. 6:2), while you are very young, to "serve the LORD with gladness" (Ps. 100:2).

Lesson Review

Answer these questions "true" or "false." Balaam was a king. False, he was a sorcerer. The Moabites were friends of the Midianites. True. Balak, the king of Moab, sent messengers to invite Balaam to a party. False, to ask him to come and curse Israel. God told Balaam to go and curse the Israelites. False, God told him not to go and not to curse them. The king sent fewer messengers and fewer rewards the second time. False, he sent more important messengers and more rewards. Balaam had decided to go before God said he could. True. God made one condition: He said Balaam could go, but he must do as God said. True. Balaam saddled his horse. False, Balaam saddled his donkey. In those days only poor people rode donkeys. False, only kings and the very rich. The donkey knew that she belonged to Balaam. True. The Lord Jesus Christ owns us; therefore we should do as He says. True. Our memory verse says that we can only be truly happy when we do what God wants us to do. True.

Memory Verse

"If you know these things, you are blessed if you do them." (John 13:17)

LESSON TWO
A LESSON FOR BALAAM

*D*id you ever ask your parents' permission to do something you wanted to do very badly, and they said "No"? Why, of course you did; we all have done it. Why do you think they said "No"? Because they knew best what was good for you. Now, instead of forgetting about the whole thing, you kept right on begging and nagging them day after day until your parents finally gave in. "All right," they answered at last. Then followed the condition—*but*! Sure enough, even though you had your way, it brought you nothing but unhappiness. Perhaps, if you were really honest, you'd have to admit it would have been better if you had listened and obeyed.

That's the way it was with Balaam. God's will and answer was a firm "No." But since God knows all your thoughts, and Balaam's thoughts, God knew that in his mind Balaam was halfway to Moab already. So God let Balaam have his way, though it most certainly displeased Him!

Balaam had his selfish wish; he never gave God another thought along the way until—well, we shall get to that shortly. Open your Bible to Numbers 22, where we will continue with verse 22.

God Blocks the Way

Balaam was on his way to Moab and, as he thought, to riches and honors. The donkey trotted along smartly, but surely not nearly so fast as Balaam would have liked. Poor, foolish, and selfish fellow! Do you know why I say "foolish"? Hold your place and turn to 1 Samuel 13:13a, where we read what a prophet of God told a disobedient king:

"You have acted foolishly: you have not kept the commandment of the LORD your God."

Still holding your place, go to Proverbs 28:20. Poor, selfish Balaam was in for a disappointment. Had he faithfully obeyed God, the first part of this verse would have come true for him: "A faithful man will abound with [have plenty of] blessings." Sad to say, only the last part of the verse fits Balaam: "But he who makes haste to be rich will not go unpunished." Balaam was quickly moving away from God's will for his life.

God was terribly angry with Balaam, yet in His grace He would give Balaam what Balaam did not deserve—another warning. "But," you ask, "hadn't God said Balaam could go? Why then should He be angry?" Think back: What had been God's perfect will for Balaam in the first place? That he *not* go. Had Balaam really loved God, he would have dropped the matter and left well enough alone. I have an idea that if you went against your parents' better judgment they'd be quite cross with you—for your own good—don't you think so?

The Donkey Saves Balaam's Life

Do you remember that I told you the donkey is very quick to sense danger? For that matter, so are most members of the animal kingdom. For instance, did you know that birds and squirrels are the first to sound the alarm in the forest? Did you know that miners take canaries down into the mineshaft with them to make sure that there are no harmful gases present? Did you know that geese and dogs are the finest watchmen and can detect burglars or fire, long before persons can?

Balaam's faithful donkey raised her head. She sniffed the air, and perhaps she snorted. Let's read the Bible account as it happened. "When the donkey saw the angel of the LORD standing in the way with his drawn sword in his hand, the donkey turned off from the way and went into the field; but Balaam struck the donkey to turn her back into the way. Then the angel of the LORD stood in a narrow path of the vineyards, *with* a wall on this side and a wall on that side. When the donkey saw the angel of the LORD, she pressed herself to the wall and pressed Balaam's foot against the wall, so he struck her again. And the angel of the LORD went further, and stood in a narrow place where there was no way to turn to the right hand or the left. When the donkey saw the angel of the LORD, she lay down under

Balaam; so Balaam was angry and struck the donkey with his stick" (Num. 22:23–27). The Angel of the Lord *is* the Lord and He was the one who blocked the way. The donkey saw Him but instead of braying, or whinnying, she spoke in a human voice. "And she said to Balaam, 'What have I done to you, that you have struck me these three times?'" (Num. 22:28*b*).

Would you be surprised to hear an animal speak? I would! But look, Balaam was not surprised at all. He didn't ask, "How can you speak?" Not Balaam—he was used to magic tricks, and perhaps he thought this was all part of it. He never ever dreamed that God might have worked a miracle. So, just as if this sort of thing happened all the time, Balaam carried on a conversation with his donkey. He answered the donkey's question and said, "Because you have made a mockery of me! If there had been a sword in my hand, I would have killed you by now" (Num. 22:29).

A Lesson from the Donkey

God did not want the donkey to die; He wanted her to teach Balaam a lesson instead. See if you can find out what lesson this was, while I read you what she said. "And the donkey said to Balaam, 'Am I not your donkey on which you have ridden all your life to this day? Have I ever been accustomed to do so to you [have I ever done anything like this to you before]?'" (Num. 22:30). That made Balaam think! He had to admit that this was the first time the donkey had ever done such a thing. How faithfully she had served him all these years! He really had been unfair to her. What lesson had Balaam just been taught? If you want another clue, you may look up 2 Peter 2:15–16. These verses tell you the reason why the Lord let the donkey talk back to Balaam and 'tell him off.'

You are right! The donkey taught her master a real lesson in faithful obedience. How well she had served him by always doing what he wanted her to do! And why do you think she did this? I am sure there are several reasons: (1) he owned her; (2) he looked after her and fed her; (3) he expected her to obey; and (4) she was doing what God wanted her to do. Did Balaam understand the lesson? He should have! Just as he owned the donkey, so the Lord owned him and looked after him. The Lord had every right to expect Balaam to serve and obey Him, not just once, but *always*!

Now, I am afraid Balaam missed the point. He did not turn around and head back home, as he should have done.

That's why God let another miracle happen—He allowed Balaam to see why the donkey had done what she did. Balaam's eyes opened wide in amazement; was that what the donkey had seen? The Lord stood in the way, ready to do battle, a drawn sword in His hand. Had He come to kill him, Balaam wondered? He bowed his head and fell flat on his face before the Lord (Num. 22:31).

Now the Lord said sternly, "Why have you struck your donkey these three times? Behold, I have come out as an adversary, because your way was contrary to me [I stood in the way to keep you from going to Moab, for it is not My will for you to do what you plan!]. But the donkey saw me and turned aside from me these three times. If she had not turned aside from me, I would surely have killed you just now, and let her live" (Num. 22:32–33).

Balaam's Confession and Failure

At last Balaam saw how wrong he was. "I have sinned," he confessed, "for I did not know that you were standing in the way against me" (Num 22:34a). Now you know, as soon as a believer confesses his sins, he is forgiven (1 John 1:9). What should Balaam do now? Yes, go back home and be more obedient next time.

For a moment it looked as though Balaam would do just that. Listen to what he told the Lord: "Now then, if it is displeasing to you, I will turn back" (Num. 22:34b). Wait a minute, Balaam, didn't the Lord make it plain enough that He was very much displeased indeed? Why ask Him again? Didn't he know that God would not force him to go home, although He could well have done so? "If you know these things, you are blessed if you do them" (John 13:17).

Balaam knew well enough, but in spite of this, he still wanted to go on. How good God is, and how very patient with His own! "Go with the men [you've gone this far; you might as well go on]," God said. "But you shall speak only the word which I shall tell you" (Num. 22:35). Balaam got back up on the donkey, and patiently and faithfully the donkey trotted after the princes of Moab.

Now I'll let you in on a secret: Balaam ended up blessing God's people rather than cursing them, and for it, he had to flee for his life. He never saw the riches and honors which he had hoped would bring him happiness (Num. 24:10–11).

What God Wants Me to Know

What a difference between those two, the man and the donkey! God had made them both, and both knew His will. You would expect the man, a believer at that, to obey and the 'dumb' donkey not to know any better than to stubbornly disobey! Far from it! There are many, many faithful animals, "But who can find a trustworthy man?" (Prov. 20:6b).

What about faithful boys and girls who claim they love the Lord? Faithfulness and obedience begin in the little things we are expected to do every day! The donkey carried her master on her back year after year before God let her do something really big for Balaam—saving his life three times. Do you even *know* what God expects of you? Look in His Word! That's where He tells you what He wants you to know and to do. Shall we look up some of the places and find out His will for you? (1) 1 John 1:7—staying in the bottom circle in fellowship; (2) 1 Thessalonians 5:18—thankfulness "in everything"; (3) 1 John 5:14—prayer in accordance with His will; (4) John 6:38—to do His will, not our own.

Do you know what God's will for you is like? Let's read Romans 12:2 and find the three words which describe it. "And do not be conformed to this world, but be transformed by the renewing of your mind, that you may prove what the will of God is, that which is good and acceptable and perfect." Yes—good, acceptable, and perfect. Could anyone wish for anything better than the best? So let me remind you just once more that "if you know these things, you are blessed if you do them" (John 13:17).

The same Lord Jesus Christ, who once stood in the way to keep Balaam from doing wrong, came down from heaven to take all the wrong we have done out of the way. He came to do the Father's will—to save us (Heb. 10:9). Now the Father's will for all mankind is "that we believe in the name of His Son Jesus Christ" (1 John 3:23). The choice is up to you. Faithful and obedient though animals are, Jesus Christ did not come to save them, but us. Will you let Him save you? "Believe in the Lord Jesus, and you shall be saved" (Acts 16:31a).

Lesson Review

"If you know these things, you are blessed if you do them" (John 13:17). God had told *who* His will? Balaam. Did God want him to go to Moab? No. God did not want him to *what* the Israelites? Curse. Balak, the king of the Moabites, promised Balaam *what*? Rewards and honors. How many times did the king send messengers to Balaam? Twice. Once God knew that Balaam was planning to go to Moab, what condition did God put on him? Balaam must only say what God told him to say.

The donkey had always obeyed Balaam, but on the way to Moab she suddenly stopped and went off the road into a *what*? A field. *What* did she see? The Lord blocking the path. She saved her master's life how many times that day? Three. But instead of thanking her, Balaam did *what* to her three times? Beat her. Balaam was not surprised when the donkey spoke in the voice of *what*? A man. What lesson did she teach Balaam? To faithfully obey God. The same lesson applies to us: We, too, can only be truly happy when we do God's will.

Memory Verse

"If you know these things, you are blessed if you do them." (John 13:17)

Chapter Three

A Lesson on God's Loving Care

A. Subject: A Lesson on God's Loving Care—Luke 12:6–7, 22–31; 1 Kings 17:1–6

B. Lesson Title: How God Supplied Elijah's Needs

C. Story Objective:

God's creatures are the recipients of His grace (Ps. 145:9) in that He supplies their daily needs (Ps. 68:19; Matt. 6:11). God's loving care stems from His love (1 Pet. 5:7), His sovereignty (Ps. 24:1; 50:10), His omniscience (Matt. 6:32b), His omnipotence (Luke 1:37), His omnipresence (Isa. 41:10; Heb. 13:5b), and His immutability (Ps. 89:1; Lam. 3:21–24). Encourage your child to look to the Lord as the giver of every good and perfect gift (James 1:17) in the full expectation that He will do what He has promised (Ps. 34:10b; Heb. 10:23).

D. Vocabulary and Doctrinal Concepts:
1. Vocabulary: brook, drought, famine, idols, plumage, ravens, worrywart
2. Doctrinal Concepts:
   a. "In famine He will redeem you from death" (Job 5:20a).
   b. "I have not seen the righteous forsaken, Or his descendants begging bread" (Ps. 37:25).
   c. "He will sustain you" (Ps. 55:22).
   d. "The God who workest wonders" (Ps. 77:14).
   e. He "satisfies your years with good things" (Ps. 103:5).
   f. "He causes the grass to grow for the cattle" (Ps. 104:14).
   g. Provision of sufficient food (Ps. 104:27–28; Prov. 30:8b).
   h. He is kind to the ungrateful (Matt. 5:45; Luke 6:35).
   i. By Him all things exist (Col. 1:17; Heb. 1:3).

E. *Source Book* Keywords: Elijah, essence of God, grace (logistical)

F. Activities:
1. Suggested Visuals: Elijah, Essence Box, ravens
2. Games, Songs, Worksheets
3. Memory Verse: "And my God shall supply all your needs according to His riches in glory in Christ Jesus." (Phil 4:19)
4. Opening and Closing Prayer

LESSON
HOW GOD SUPPLIED ELIJAH'S NEEDS

*W*hile we learned last time about something we can do to please the Lord, today we want to learn of one of the many, many things God does for us daily. What might that be? His faithful care of us day after day, week after week, year after year—always supplying our every need. Look at the Essence Box and call out to me what God is like. God is sovereignty, righteousness, justice, love, eternal life, omniscience, omnipresence, omnipotence, immutability, and veracity. Now turn to Philippians 4:19. "And my God shall supply all your needs according to His riches in glory in Christ Jesus."

If we know these things, that is, what God is like and what He can do, we will never need to worry about a thing! Now, who in all the animal kingdom can teach us this lesson better than anyone? The birds! How do I know? Because the Lord Jesus pointed out these feathered teachers to His disciples and to us. Go to Luke 12, where we shall see what He said. While you find the place, I want to ask you a question. Are you a worrywart? Do you think what you will eat tomorrow and what you will wear are the most important things? Perhaps you do not worry about these things now, but the day may come when you are so tempted; then I want you to remember what you will learn today.

Perhaps the disciples were worrywarts, for the Lord told them one day, "Do not be anxious for *your* life, *as to* what you shall eat; nor for your body, *as to* what you shall put on. For life is more than food, and the body than clothing" (Luke 12:22–23). Then the Lord told His disciples to become birdwatchers! Does that surprise you? Sometimes people will say of someone who is forgetful, "He is a birdbrain." Oh, how mistaken they are! Birds are very wise indeed—certainly wiser than many believers who forget what God did for them in the past and can do for them now and in time to come. Let's let the birds teach us today.

Birds never sit around and mope and worry and bite their nails, worrying about where their next meal might come from. Nor do they wonder if their clothing is in style. They just know that God *will supply* their every need: new plumage in summer and winter, the right kind of food, a

place to stay whenever and wherever they need it. So they simply enjoy life moment by moment, and praise God's loving care in cheerful songs.

There are many kinds of birds. Possibly the Lord Jesus was thinking of how little any of us deserve God's loving care when He especially mentioned God's care of the ravens (Luke 12:24). The Jews did not like the ravens because they lived on dead and decaying foods, as well as on seeds. Maybe they thought that the ravens were not worthy of God's care! Yet, I wonder if they thought of God's grace to them. For you know, and they knew, that God gives sunshine and rain to believers and unbelievers alike, whether they thank and praise Him for it or not (Matt. 5:45).

To show them and us how tenderly God looks after all His creatures, the Lord Jesus said, "Consider the ravens, for they neither sow nor reap; and they have no storehouse nor barn; and *yet* God feeds them! . . . But your Father knows that you need these things [food and clothing]" (Luke 12:24, 30*b*). "Why, then, worry?" asked the Lord Jesus, "you are much more valuable than the birds."

Yes, God knows best what we need and when we need it. He is always faithful to supply our needs. That's why we can trust His promise of Philippians 4:19 and expect Him to take care of us. "And my God shall supply all your needs according to His riches in glory in Christ Jesus."

Meet the Ravens

What else does God's Word tell us about our teachers, the ravens? The raven is the first bird named in the Bible (Gen. 8:7). We learn that Noah sent him out to fly above the waters of the flood. The raven did not return to the ark; he found plenty of food—the dead bodies of birds and animals—floating on top of the waters. God feeds the ravens, then and now (Job 38:41; Ps. 147:9).

We also read that the Jews were not to eat ravens because they were "unclean" birds (Deut. 14:12, 14, 19), and that ravens like to live in lonely and deserted places (Isa. 34:11).

Elijah and the Ravens

We are told in 1 Kings 17:1–6 that God used the ravens to supply the needs of one of His faithful servants. At God's command, they fed the prophet Elijah. This is how it happened. During the time when King Ahab ruled over the Israelites, God's people turned away from the true God to worship Baal, the false god of wicked Queen Jezebel. Now God had promised His people blessings for as long as they served only Him, but He warned them not to make for themselves idols and bow down to them. Should they do so, God would command the clouds to hold back the rain (Isa. 5:6), and the heavens would become as bronze and the earth as iron to them (Lev. 26:1, 19). Now God's people had done this terrible thing: They had forsaken God. Would He make true His warning? He did!

In those days, God's faithful and brave servant Elijah came to King Ahab and said, "As the LORD the God of Israel lives, before whom I stand [whom I serve], surely there shall be neither dew nor rain these years, except by my word" (1 Kings 17:1). When he had said those words, he turned and left as quickly as he had come. Elijah was not really afraid of King Ahab; he only listened to God's special instructions to leave and go eastward. He was to hide himself by the brook Cherith (1 Kings 17:2–3). Surely, God knew why he must hide, and so, Elijah obeyed (Prov. 22:3*a*).

But where was he to go? To the little brook Cherith? Why, that was the place that dried up before all other rivers! Everyone knew that! Would that have worried you, to think that God would send you to a desert place instead of to a supermarket to stock up for the years ahead? It didn't worry Elijah in the least. He knew God looked after those who believed in Him. After all, God had promised, "in the days of famine they will have abundance [be satisfied]" (Ps. 37:19*b*). How God did that was up to Him.

I'll tell you why God sent Elijah to such a lonely, hopeless place—to show him and us that God is well able to supply all our needs (2 Chron. 16:9*a*). He had promised, "And it shall be that you shall drink of the brook, and I have commanded the ravens to provide for you there" (1 Kings 17:4), and He was going to do just that! Does that remind you of a promise God made you which you have learned? What was that promise, and where is it found? "And my God shall supply all your needs according to His riches in glory in Christ Jesus" (Phil 4:19).

Can God command the ravens? Of course He can. He made them, even as He made the heavens and the earth and all that is in them—including you. Does that tell you something? It should! God can and will command you, too. The question is, do you obey Him as readily as did the ravens, or do you drag your feet—if you obey Him at all!

God's promise was good enough for Elijah. We read that "he went and did according to the word of the LORD" (1 Kings 17:5*a*). Not long thereafter the earth showed the first signs of the drought. The grass turned brown, and the plants began to wither. The trees stood bare, and the birds flew off to find a new home. Eventually the ground turned hard and dry; great, ugly cracks appeared in it, ever widening. Even the big rivers dried up like mud puddles. Nothing would grow, and a dreadful famine came over all the land. Oh, how everyone wished it might rain once more, but there was to be no rain until the people were ready to return to the Lord God!

And what about Elijah? Elijah was well looked after in his secret hiding place. There was cool, fresh water for his thirst in the brook, and each morning and evening the ravens brought him bread and meat to eat (1 Kings 17:6). We are not told exactly what this food was, nor how great were the distances which the ravens had to travel to find it, but we can be sure that it was just the kind of food Elijah needed, for God supplied it. We do know that God owns every beast of the forest, all the birds, and "the cattle on a thousand hills" (Ps. 50:10–11). "According to His riches," He supplied Elijah's need, even as He supplies your need and mine! Don't you think that Elijah thanked the Lord over and over for His goodness and faithfulness to him every time he heard the flapping of those great, black wings overhead?

Next time you see a bird, will you remember what he can teach you? Will you look trustingly, expectantly, to the Giver of every good and perfect gift (James 1:17)? Will you remember to thank Him for His loving care of you?

What God Wants Me to Know

If you have never believed in the Lord Jesus, your greatest need is to do so now. God the Father knew that your greatest need is salvation. He did the most He can do for us—He gave His Son to die for our sins (John 3:16). Where would Elijah have been had he refused to accept God's provision? He would have died. If you refuse to accept God's provision of salvation, eternal punishment awaits you in the lake of fire.

No one ever need perish. As God sent the ravens to meet the need of Elijah, so He sent His Son to bring us eternal life. How can you have eternal life? By believing that He died to save you. Right now, while we all bow our heads, you may tell the Father that you are ready to receive His gift—eternal life through Jesus Christ, His Son.

Lesson Review

Guess who or what I am. I am the prophet God sent to a small brook. Elijah. I am the king of Israel whom Elijah came to see. Ahab. I am the false god the Israelites worshiped. Baal. I stopped coming down from heaven. Rain. I am the first brook to dry up. Cherith. I promised to supply Elijah's need. God. I brought food to Elijah twice every day. Raven. I look after every living thing. God. I am the way God treats you, though you do not deserve it. Grace. I should trust God's promise of Philippians 4:19. Believer. I can teach the lesson on God's loving care better than any of the animals. Bird.

Memory Verse

"And my God shall supply all your needs according to His riches in glory in Christ Jesus." (Phil 4:19)

Chapter Four

A Lesson in Contentment

A. Subject: A Lesson in Contentment—Exodus 16:1–20; Numbers 11:31–34; Psalm 78:24–35

B. Lesson Title: What the Worms and Quails Taught

C. Story Objective:

We should be content with such things as God thought good to give us and with those circumstances in which He has placed us (Phil. 1:12; 4:12) rather than desire what He has wisely withheld from us. This lesson comes down to us, not so much by direct communication from the animals involved, but rather by way of observation and application of the principles of covetousness and contentment as stated in the Word of God (1 Cor. 10:6). For ease of study, and for your convenience, these have been contrasted and grouped as *covetousness* and *contentment*.

D. Vocabulary and Doctrinal Concepts:
   1. Vocabulary: contentment, covet, covey, manna, migrate, pillar, quail
   2. Doctrinal Concepts:
      a. Covetousness (lust or inner desire):
         1) Is forbidden (Ex. 20:17; Rom. 7:7).
         2) Is hated by God (Ps. 10:3).
         3) Is called sin (Isa. 57:17; James 1:15).
         4) Is a product of the sin nature (Jer. 6:13; cf. Rom. 6:12; James 1:14).
         5) Is punished (Hab. 2:9; 2 Pet. 2:9–10).
         6) "Beware" of it (Luke 12:15).
         7) Is conquered through the filling of the Holy Spirit (Rom. 13:14; cf. Gal. 5:16).
         8) Is foolish and hurtful (1 Tim. 6:9).
         9) Leads to sorrow (1 Tim. 6:10).
         10) Hinders effective prayer (James 4:3).
         11) "Wage[s] war against the soul" (1 Pet. 2:11).
         12) Beguiles; entices (2 Pet. 2:18).
         13) Spells envy, materialism, and approbation lust (1 John 2:16).
         14) Is temporary (1 John 2:17).
      b. Contentment:
         1) In God's presence, eternally (Ps. 17:15)
         2) Found in the Lord (Ps. 36:7–9)
         3) In time of great pressure (Ps. 37:19)
         4) Through occupation with Christ (Ps. 63:5–6)
         5) In the Lord's blessings (Ps. 103:5; 132:15; Jer. 31:14*b*)
         6) For every living thing (Ps. 145:16)
         7) In the fear of the Lord (Prov. 19:23)
         8) Comes from within, through learning and suffering (Phil. 4:1)
         9) "Is a means of great gain" (1 Tim. 6:6)
         10) With necessities of life (Luke 3:14; 1 Tim. 6:8)

E. *Source Book* Keywords: grace (logistical), Israel, manna

F. Activities:
   1. Suggested Visuals: none
   2. Games, Songs, Worksheets
   3. Memory Verse: "Being content with what you have." (Heb. 13:5*b*)
   4. Opening and Closing Prayer

LESSON
WHAT THE WORMS AND QUAILS TAUGHT

Once we know that God will supply all our need, we should be perfectly content. But are we? Do you know what brought about the first sin among the angels and among mankind? Wanting something God thought best not to give (Isa. 57:17; James 1:15)! Remember, Lucifer, the super angel, wanted God's throne and God's power (Isa. 14:13–14); Adam and Eve wanted the fruit of the only tree of which God had forbidden them to eat (Gen. 3:6). And Balaam? Well, he wanted riches and honor. So, in his greed, he went to Moab against God's will (Jude 11). Did any of them find happiness when they got what they wanted? No!

How often have you said, "I want this or that"? And when you did not get what you wanted, you went off pouting; or else, when you did get it, you discovered it wasn't good for you—like eating too many candies! Where does everything we have come from? Straight from God (Deut. 8:17–18; 1 Cor. 4:7; James 1:17). We should be most thankful for His goodness to us and not wish for something else instead!

When God gave the Law to Moses, He said in one of His commandments, "You shall not covet" (Deut. 5:21). "To covet" is to want something for ourselves that God has given others. Do you ever wish you had your friend's toys and clothing, a finer home and a newer bicycle? Where does wanting things start? In our minds! Deep down, in our sin natures—that's where envy and jealousy begin. Instead, God wants us to have another thought—contentment. He tells us in His Word "being content with what you have"! Why? "For He Himself [the Lord] has said, 'I WILL NEVER DESERT YOU, NOR WILL I FORSAKE YOU'" (Heb. 13:5b). Let's remember that verse well!

You see, when we have the Lord, we have everything. How do I know? Because of Philippians 4:19. What does it say? "And my God shall supply all your needs according to His riches in glory in Christ Jesus." Right! God will supply all our needs! Our trouble is that sometimes we get our needs and our wants all mixed up! We would do well to learn from the animals; they never become disgruntled and discontent! I have never yet seen a bird that would rather make its nest under water, nor a worm that wanted to whistle like a bird.

The Israelites, Content and Complaining

Long ago, God's people, who had everything they needed to make them happy and content, had to learn a lesson on contentment instead. And who taught them? The worms and the birds!

One month and one day had passed since God brought the Israelites out of Egypt (Ex. 12:41). He had divided the Red Sea for them and had drowned their enemies in it (Ex. 14:28–29). By night, He guided the people in a pillar of fire, and by day in a pillar of cloud (Ex. 13:21). Now God had led the Israelites into the wilderness of Zin. Oh, how the Israelites had sung God's praises in those early days; how happy and content they had been (Ex. 15:1–19)!

But listen to them now: They have begun to change their 'tune.' They are whining and complaining because their food supply is running low. "Had we only stayed in Egypt," they grumbled; "there, at least we had plenty of food to satisfy our hunger. But out here, in this desert place, we shall surely starve" (Ex. 16:3, paraphrased).

Now I ask you, had God brought the Israelites out of Egypt to let them starve in the wilderness? Of course not! He had promised to take them to Canaan, a land all their own. Did God forget about Elijah's need when he was all alone in the desert? He did not! He had used the birds, the ravens, to look after His prophet. Yet, because God is all-powerful, He never needs to do something the same way twice. He has more ways than one to meet our every need. No, God had not forgotten to be gracious (Ps. 77:9); it was the Israelites who had forgotten what God is like! Now they needed to be reminded of it and to be taught a lesson.

Bread from Heaven

Open your Bible to Exodus 16:4–5. God said to Moses, "I will rain bread from heaven for you; and the people shall go out and gather a day's portion [amount] every day . . . on the sixth day . . . twice as much [for the seventh day was to be a day of rest]." That very same night, God gave them meat or quail to eat, and the following morning He gave them the promised bread or manna from heaven (Ex. 16:8). Would the Israelites be content now and do as God had instructed them—gather just enough for one day at a time, except on the sixth day? Let's see what the Word says.

A Lesson from the Worms

"And the sons of Israel did so, and some gathered much [more than enough for one day] and some little [less than enough for one day]" (Ex. 16:17).

One of the Israelites was very greedy and he said, "I'm gonna get me a great big tubful while I'm at it." Off he went, practically shoveling up God's gracious gift from heaven. But oh, what a surprise awaited him! He ended up with no more than he should have gathered, and those who had gathered less than they should still had enough (Ex. 16:18). "Let no man leave any of it until morning," Moses warned (Ex. 16:19). God wanted to test their faith; the next day there would be more where that came from. They should be content with what God had given them, but were they? We'll follow the greedy Israelite into his tent and watch what he does. Oh, oh, he's hiding some leftovers in a pot (Ex. 16:20).

Early the next morning, he lifted the lid. Phew! What a smell! And what was that wiggling about and crawling out of the pot? Worms and more worms! They seemed to be wagging their bodies before his face, just as someone would wag a finger, as they scolded without a word: "You should have been content; you should have been content!" I am sure he got the message and hung his head in shame. But would he and the others remember?

"We Want Meat!"

A year later, the Israelites had come past Mount Sinai, where God gave them the Law. They were on their way to Kadesh-barnea. But what's this we hear coming out of so many tents? Complaints and more complaints (Num. 11:10)! Moses heard them, too, and so did God: "We're getting tired of this manna; same old stuff every day; we want meat!" said those unthankful people. Well, God knew it was time to teach the lesson on contentment all over again. This time the quails would be the teachers.

How sad to think that any of God's people would turn up their noses at such things that God graciously gave to them! Reminds us of some boys and girls who make a face at leftovers. The Israelites needed not to till, or plant, or harvest any of their food. God gave as a free gift all their nourishment. Now, what was it we learned from Hebrews 13:5b? "Being content with what you have." Well, the Israelites certainly were not content with what they had (Num. 11:1–9). The Bible called manna "the bread of angels" (Ps. 78:25), but even angels' food was no longer good enough for them.

"You shall eat [meat], not one, nor two days . . . but a whole month, until it comes out of your nostrils," God said angrily (Num. 11:8–20). Even Moses was puzzled; how would God feed more than two million people with meat (Num. 11:21–22)? Had he, too, forgotten that God can do everything? I'll tell you how God did it: He commanded the east wind and the south wind to blow (Ps. 107:25a), and on these wind currents many coveys of quail were carried to the camp of the Israelites (Num. 11:31; Ps. 78:26–29).

You know that many birds migrate to other climates at certain times of the year. How do they know when and where to go? How do they find their way, and where do they get their strength? From the Lord (Jer. 8:7). People have marveled at the great distances these birds will travel—even crossing oceans. And what a record flight this was—a line of quails forty miles long, ten miles wide, and flying into the camp just one yard off the ground (Num. 11:31)! All the Israelites had to do was reach out and grab them!

For two days and a night they gathered quails (Num. 11:32). Oh, what 'pigs' they made of themselves! Many of the people became ill and died (Num. 11:33). Before the Is-

raelites could move on, they had to bury their dead. Do you know what Moses called that place? "Kibroth-hattaavah," pronounced "ke-broth-huttu-ahvuh," which meant the place of the graves of "the people who had been greedy" (Num. 11:34). I shouldn't wonder but that the Israelites were reminded of this second lesson every time they saw a quail fly by. Their sight, and the flutter of their wings, surely must have spelled out to them "being content with what you have"!

What God Wants Me to Know

Can you learn this lesson from the example of the discontented Israelites? Or will the Lord have to teach you the hard way? Next time you catch yourself thinking, "I want" whatever it may be, shake your head quickly, and think of Hebrews 13:5b instead. "Being content with what you have."

God wants every living thing to be content (Ps. 145:16). Yet, we can only be content when we want God's way for our lives. Real contentment starts when a person accepts God's plan of salvation. Do you want contentment now and for all eternity? Then listen. "He who did not spare His own Son, but delivered Him up for us all, how will He not also with Him freely give us all things?" (Rom. 8:32). God gave His Son to die on the cross for your sins. Will you receive Him as your Savior? Do it now; believe in Him, and such things as you never dreamed of shall be yours—here on earth, and in the presence of the Lord in heaven (1 Cor. 2:9).

Lesson Review

In what country were the Israelites slaves? Egypt. Who set them free? God. By God's power, the Israelites crossed what place? The Red Sea. How did they know their way? By a pillar of cloud and a pillar of fire. What was the name of the wilderness where the Israelites set up their tents and grumbled about food? Zin. What did God send that evening and the next morning? Quails and manna. What happened when the Israelites laid up manna overnight? It was full of worms the next morning. What happened at Mount Sinai? God gave them the Law. One of God's commandments is that the people should not covet, want things they do not have or want things that belong to others. Yet, a year later, when the Israelites were coming close to Kadesh-barnea, they wanted something. What was it? Meat. For how long would God give them meat? Thirty days. What kind of meat did God give them? Quails. What happened when the Israelites made pigs of themselves? They got sick and died. What lesson did the worms and the quails teach the Israelites and us? "Being content with what you have" (Heb. 13:5b).

Memory Verse
"Being content with what you have." (Heb. 13:5b)

Chapter Five

A Lesson on Being Lost and Found

OVERVIEW	

A. Subject: A Lesson on Being Lost and Found—Luke 15:3–7

B. Lesson Title: Lost Sheep Found

C. Story Objective:

The need of salvation and guidance can be stressed by showing the similarity of sheep and mankind (Ps. 119:176a) in characteristics and needs, and how these needs can be met (John 10:9–11).

D. Vocabulary and Doctrinal Concepts:
1. Vocabulary: rejoice, school of hard knocks, stray
2. Doctrinal Concepts:
   a. The character and needs of sheep, analogous to that of man:
      1) Both are apt to go astray (Ps. 58:3; Isa. 53:6).
      2) Cannot guide themselves, therefore need guidance (Ps. 119:133a; Prov. 20:24; Jer. 10:23). Our Shepherd guides us (Ps. 73:24; Isa. 58:11) through the Holy Spirit (John 16:13) and through His Word (Ps. 119:105; 1 Cor. 2:16).
      3) Cannot cleanse themselves (Ps. 19:12; 51:2; Jer. 2:22); rebound was provided (Ps. 119:9; 1 John 1:7, 9).
      4) Helpless when injured; provision—doctrine and promises (Ps. 46:1; Rom. 8:26; Heb. 2:18; 4:15).
      5) Defenseless; a wall of fire provided (Zech. 2:5).
      6) Cannot find water for themselves; water of life offered (John 4:10, 14; cf. Isa. 55:1) and led to pasture (Isa. 40:11).
      7) Easily frightened; the faith-rest technique given (Ps. 56:3; Isa. 41:10; Heb. 13:6).
      8) Do not belong to themselves; neither we nor the divine good we produce belongs to ourselves (Rom. 11:36; 1 Cor. 6:19–20; Gal. 5:22).
   b. The Shepherd:
      1) Ours by personal relationship (Ps. 23:1).
      2) Jesus Christ identified as the "good" (gracious) Shepherd; emphasis on salvation (John 10:11, 14; Rom. 5:8).
      3) One fold, one shepherd (John 10:16).
      4) That "great Shepherd"; emphasis on the Resurrection (Heb. 13:20).
      5) "Guardian of your souls"; emphasis on power to live the Christian way of life (1 Pet. 2:25).
      6) The "Chief Shepherd"; emphasis on rewards (1 Pet. 5:4).
   c. Lost and found:
      1) Lost, on the wrong way (Prov. 14:12; Isa. 53:6b).
      2) "Repent and live." The Lord has no pleasure in sinner's death (Ezek. 18:32).
      3) Christ came to "seek" and to save that which was "lost" (Ezek. 34:16; Luke 19:10).
      4) The lost are blind to the Gospel (2 Cor. 4:3).
      5) God is not willing that any be lost (2 Pet. 3:9).
      6) The Lord "may be found" (Isa. 55:6–7).
      7) "You will seek Me and find *Me*" (Jer. 29:13).
      8) "FIND REST FOR YOUR SOULS" (Matt. 11:29).
      9) Found through faith in Christ (Acts 4:12; Rom. 10:13).
      10) "Be found in Him" (Phil. 3:9).

E. *Source Book* Keywords: Christ (Good Shepherd), volition

F. Activities:
1. Suggested Visuals: shepherd with sheep

2. Games, Songs, Worksheets
3. Memory Verse: "For the Son of Man has come to save that which was lost." (Matt. 18:11)
4. Opening and Closing Prayer

LESSON
LOST SHEEP FOUND

All through their wilderness wanderings, for forty years, the Israelites never once got lost. They had no compass; they followed no map; they had a perfect guide—God Himself—who went before them in a pillar of cloud by day and in a pillar of fire by night (Ex. 13:21; Deut. 8:2*a*). Do you know *why* He led them? He led them because the Israelites were His people, "the sheep of His pasture" (Ps. 100:3); He was their Shepherd (Ps. 80:1). A shepherd must look after the well-being of his flock, for left to themselves they would surely get lost. I wonder how often the Israelites would have gotten lost, especially in the desert places, had God not led them.

It is terrible to be lost and not know one's way home! But it is even worse still to be lost in sin and never, ever find one's way to God and His heavenly home! We should all have been lost forever. But God was so concerned that this must not happen that He sent His Son, the Lord Jesus Christ, to earth to seek and to save us. Open your Bible to Matthew 18:11. "For the Son of Man has come to save that which was lost."

Here comes Professor Sheep. He has graduated from "The School of Hard Knocks" and will tell you from his own experience a lesson on being lost and found. Are you ready to learn from him?

Why the Sheep Was Lost

"Bah, baah-baah!" says the professor. What, you don't understand what he means? Well, then, since you do not speak 'sheepish,' let me do the talking for him.

"Ahem," says Professor Sheep, "the lesson I am about to teach you is one on being lost and found. So important is my lesson that God preserved it forever in His Book, the Bible (Matt. 18:11–14; Luke 15:3–7; 1 Pet. 1:23*b*).

"I once was one of the flock of a hundred sheep (Matt. 18:12). Perhaps I should tell you some things about the family of sheep to which I belong. Basically there are only two kinds of sheep—wild sheep and tame sheep. I belong to the tame sheep, of which there are several varieties. We sheep are highly useful animals. We supply man with both food and clothing. But in more ways than one, we are stupid, timid, and helpless, though I hate to admit this to you. What makes me feel a little better about this is that you are

very much the same as we are. You don't believe me? Well, I'll prove it to you, right from the Word of God. Turn to Isaiah 53:6: 'All of us like sheep have gone astray, Each of us has turned to his own way; But the LORD has caused the iniquity of us all To fall on Him.'

"Sheep stray very easily, and so do people. What makes you stray? Sin—the sin of wanting your own way rather than that of God? Your volition makes you stray. Another thing about us is that we cannot guide ourselves or find water to drink for ourselves. We need a shepherd. You are no different. Look up Jeremiah 10:23. 'I know, O LORD, that a man's way is not in himself; Nor is it in a man who walks to direct his steps.' See there? God has to direct your steps; He is the only one who can give you the water of life—salvation, and He it is who leads you to feed on His Word (Jer. 15:16).

"There is something else we have in common: We cannot cleanse ourselves. We sheep have to be dipped, and you must be cleansed: first, by accepting Christ's work on the cross, and after that by confessing your sins (1 John 1:7, 9). Well, back to my story. The kind shepherd, who owned us, looked after us well enough. Every morning he led us out to pasture, and under his watchful eyes, we—that is, most of us—grazed contentedly all day long. I believe you just had a lesson on contentment, or so I heard from my good friends, Professors Worm and Quail! I assure you, it's a mighty important lesson for you to learn!

"I should have been content, too, but I was not. One day I decided to wander away from my shepherd and from the rest of the flock. You see, the grass in the meadow beyond our own looked so much greener. All I wanted was a taste, just a little nibble here and there. So, off I went. At first it seemed like lots of fun. I chased a few butterflies and tried a tuft of grass here, a tuft of grass there, and moved farther and farther away from the rest of the flock."

The Knowledge of Being Lost

"Night was coming fast. Soon the wild animals would begin to prowl. Would they find me and tear me to pieces? As I thought of these dreadful things, I became more fearful by the minute. I turned this way and that—I was hopelessly lost. I dashed about in the dark and stumbled and fell right by the edge of a cliff. I was hurt and could no longer flee for my life. I cried pitifully. Oh, how I wished I had never left my shepherd! Believe me, it's a terrible feeling to be lost. Yet, it is only when you know that you're lost that you want to be found! I desperately wanted to be found! And found I was! This is how it happened."

The Seeking Shepherd

"Back home, the shepherd was counting his sheep. Had they all followed him back to the sheepfold? 'Ninety-seven, ninety-eight, ninety-nine!' There should have been one hundred sheep; it seemed that one was missing! Again he counted them. No, he had not made a mistake; one of his sheep was still out somewhere in the cold, dark, dangerous night—far, far away from the shepherd. The kind shepherd thought of his poor lost sheep. Was it hurt? He knew well that when sheep get hurt, they are helpless. He left all the other sheep in the safety of the shelter and went out into the night to seek and to save me!

"On and on he went, searching, calling, looking everywhere until he found me at last. Gently he picked me up and carried me home on his strong shoulders (Luke 15:5)."

The Found Sheep

"Can you imagine how glad I was to be found? Now I wondered how I ever could have wanted to stray from him! There was only one way I could show how thankful I was—I nuzzled his face gently and licked the hands that had saved me. Oh, what deep scratches were on them from pulling me out of the thorns along that sheer cliff! Once we got home, would you believe it—my shepherd invited all his friends and neighbors. 'Rejoice [be happy] with me,' he said, 'for I have found my sheep which was lost' (Luke 15:6)."

What God Wants Me to Know

"Wanting to have my own way made me get lost, same as it did all of you. 'All of us like sheep have gone astray [as I once did]; Each of us has turned to his own way' (Isa. 53:6a; Rom. 3:23). You, too, are helpless to save yourselves and would have been lost from God forever! But you can thank God for the Good Shepherd, the Lord Jesus Christ. He thought of you being lost in spiritual death and sin, far away from God. He did not want even one of you to perish, to be eternally lost (Matt. 18:14). He knew that you needed Him to come to find and to save you. Can you still say Matthew 18:11? 'For the Son of Man has come to save that which was lost.' The Lord Jesus wants to be your Shepherd. Will you believe that He came to save you, that He alone can take you to God's heavenly home (John 14:6)?

"As you know, most newspapers have a lost and found column. God, too, has one in His Book, the Bible. Let me show it to you: John 3:16–17. 'For God so loved the world, that He gave His only begotten Son, that whoever believes in Him should not perish, but have eternal life. For God did not send the Son into the world to judge the world, but that the world should be saved through Him.' Is your name in the lost column, or is it in the found column? You can make sure of that right now. When you believe in the Lord Jesus Christ, I assure you there will be joy in heaven (Luke 15:7). Why not believe in Him this very moment?

"If you are a found one, let me ask you this question: Will you ever stray again? Yes, I am afraid you will. When you choose to sin, you stray away from God and are out of fellowship. But remember, you can never again be lost (John 17:12a). No one, and nothing—not even the worst sin—can take you away from your Good Shepherd forever (John 10:28). But sin *must* be confessed before God can cleanse and forgive you and take you back into fellowship once more (1 John 1:9).

"Aren't you glad and thankful that you belong to Him? You are safe in His care and can be fed on His Word. You need not worry or fear any longer, because you are His. You, too, can be useful to Him. Do you want to know how? In our next lesson my friend, Professor Camel, will teach you a lesson on being useful. Thank you for listening, and bye now!"

Well, you heard all about being lost and found. Shall we bow our heads now and think about it and what it means to you and to me?

Lesson Review

In what ways are we like sheep? We stray. We cannot guide ourselves. We cannot find water. We need a shepherd. We need cleansing. And we are helpless when we are hurt. What did Professor Sheep teach us? A lesson on being lost and found. Who is said to be lost? Unbelievers. Can a believer ever get lost from God? No. Why not? Salvation is forever. How are we "found"? By faith in Christ. Who is our Good Shepherd? The Lord Jesus Christ. Why did He come into the world? To save the lost. What did He have to do to save us? He had to die for our sins on the cross.

Memory Verse

"For the Son of Man has come to save that which was lost." (Matt. 18:11)

Chapter Six

A Lesson on Being Useful

A. Subject: A Lesson on Being Useful—Ephesians 1:12

B. Lesson Title: Learning from the Useful Camel

C. Story Objective:

Every believer should be and can be useful and profitable to the Lord (Job 22:2; Rom. 14:7–8; Phil. 1:21). Indeed, God has foreordained that the believer live a fruitful and productive life (John 15:8; Eph. 2:10; Phil. 4:17b) and has made provision for that life through the power of the indwelling Holy Spirit (Zech. 4:6; Gal. 5:22–23). The believer's usefulness is directed first toward God, then to his fellow men.

D. Vocabulary and Doctrinal Concepts:
1. Vocabulary: caravan, desert, shod
2. Doctrinal Concepts:
   a. Description of the useful believer:
      1) He does God's will with readiness of mind (Eph. 6:6b).
      2) Christ is "exalted" in his body (Phil. 1:20).
      3) He has the divine viewpoint (Phil. 2:5).
      4) He is properly oriented to grace (1 Cor. 15:19; 2 Cor. 3:5).
      5) He makes efficient use of time (Ps. 90:12; Eph. 5:15–17).
      6) He is alert and eager for the doctrines of the Word (Job 23:12; Ps. 119:18; Matt. 11:15).
      7) He opens his mouth to "declare Thy praise" (Ps. 51:15).
      8) He controls his tongue (Eph. 4:29; James 3:2).
      9) He does not "withhold good . . . When it is in your power to do it" (Prov. 3:27).
      10) He cleanses his hands (James 4:8; 1 John 1:9) and lifts them up in effective prayer (2 Cor. 1:11; 1 Tim. 2:8).
      11) He recognizes divine authority (Ps. 95:6; Rom. 14:11; Col. 1:18b).
      12) He is quick to serve the Lord in witnessing (Eph. 6:15).
   b. Believer's responsibility to God:
      1) Love Him (Deut. 6:5; Matt. 22:37).
      2) Obedience, a proof of love (John 14:21).
      3) Live "for Him" (2 Cor. 5:15).
      4) Give self to the Lord (2 Cor. 8:5; cf. Rom. 12:1).
      5) Feet speak of service (Eph. 6:15).
      6) Attain the objective of the Christian way of life (Phil. 3:14).
      7) "Adorn the doctrine of God" (Titus 2:10).
      8) Maintain good works (Titus 3:8, 14).
   c. Believer's responsibility to other believers:
      1) Love one another (Lev. 19:18; Matt. 22:39; John 15:12).
      2) "Bear one another's burdens" (Gal. 6:2).
      3) "Do good" (Gal. 6:10).
      4) Treat others in grace (Eph. 4:31–32).
      5) Teamwork (Phil. 1:27).
   d. Believer's responsibility to the unsaved:
      1) Owes him the Gospel (Acts 1:8; Rom. 1:14–16).
      2) Honesty (Rom. 12:17).

3) Respect for country and authority (Rom. 13:1–9; 1 Pet. 2:13–15).
4) Prayer for their salvation (1 Tim. 2:1–4).

E. *Source Book* Keywords: divine good, God the Holy Spirit (filling of), witnessing

F. Activities:
   1. Suggested Visuals: camel
   2. Games, Songs, Worksheets
   3. Memory Verse: "We . . . should be to the praise of His glory." (Eph. 1:12*b*)
   4. Opening and Closing Prayer

LESSON
LEARNING FROM THE USEFUL CAMEL

*D*o you remember what Professor Sheep said your next lesson was going to be? A lesson on being useful. And who did he say would teach it? The camel. Let's get right into our lesson and see, first, what we can learn about the camel, and next, what we can learn from the camel.

Useful in Life

Have you ever seen a live camel? Where might you have seen one? Yes, most likely at the zoo. In the days of the Bible, and even today in the lands of the Bible, camels are quite a common sight. They are mentioned sixty-six times in the Word of God.

The camel is the second largest animal used by man, the largest being the elephant. Some camels have one hump on their backs; others have two humps. A grown camel is eight feet high or even higher; it lives to be forty or fifty years old and is one of the most useful animals—in life and after death. Do you wonder how camels are used?

Let's talk about the single-humped camel first. It is the faster of the two, for its legs are longer. It is used mostly for riding, racing, and for carrying messengers and mail (Esther 8:10, 14). It is also used in desert warfare. We read that once, when David fought the Philistines, he killed all their soldiers except four hundred who escaped on fast camels (1 Sam. 30:17). A camel is many times faster than a horse and can travel one hundred fifty miles in a day through hot deserts.

The two-humped camel is used for carrying heavy loads. It is never made to trot, but it walks some thirty to thirty-six miles a day with a load of up to five hundred pounds on its back. Remember, Joseph's brothers saw camels loaded with spices on their way to Egypt when they sold Joseph as a slave (Gen. 37:25).

Rich people today might own a big fancy car, or maybe even more than one; rich people of long ago owned camels. Those camels were treated with great care and were often decorated with chains of gold or silver and with costly ornaments (Judg. 8:21, 26). To have one's camels stolen meant to lose great riches (Job 1:17).

God made the camel to function in a most wonderful way. He gave this animal a clever mind, much patience, and strength. He planned for the camel to have very special feet—tough, broad, and spongy—which could walk across the hot desert sands without sinking or cracking. God also gave the camel four stomachs, a storage bag for water, and a storage bag for fat—the hump or humps—so that this animal can go for days on just a few dates and barley-meal cakes for food, and up to fifteen days without a drink of water! Camels have two special sets of muscles which they can use to bring up the food or the water they have stored away. They re-chew their food as cows do, and moisten it with water as they need it. God gave them a keen sense of smell. Camels can smell water a mile and a half away, long before their riders see it. They rush toward it quickly and never once miss finding it.

To make sure of their own safety from the dangers of the desert and from thieves, people who must travel across the desert always travel in large groups or caravans, with more camels than there are people. The Bible tells us that the great Queen of Sheba traveled this way when she came to visit wise King Solomon (1 Kings 10:1–2). And we think that the wise men from the East rode camels when they went to find the Baby Jesus, although the Bible does not say they did (Matt. 2:1).

Do you know how a camel is loaded, or how a rider gets on its back? The camel is made to kneel on the ground until it is commanded to rise once more to its full height. Then it begins the long journey. When night comes, the camel kneels down again to be unloaded. It may then graze on what few thorny and often bitter plants grow in the desert, and it seems that the camel much prefers these to green, juicy grass. Where water is found, the camel may store a fresh supply for many more days to come.

Other Uses of Camels

But there are still other ways in which the camel is useful to man. In summer its hair is clipped and made into cloth—rough cloth for the poor (John the Baptist wore camel's hair clothing, Matt. 3:4), coarse cloth for making tents, and the finest woolens for those who can pay for them. Camel's milk is used in Bible lands, much like we use cow's milk—for drinking, cooking, and making cheese. The Jews of long ago were forbidden to eat anything that came from the camel (Lev. 11:4), but the Arabs love camel meat and use it greatly. Would you believe it? Even the camel's dung is dried and used for making fires, instead of coal!

Useful after Death

Now let's find out how useful the camel is after it has died. The dead camel provides meat, and from its hide or skin, sandals and bags are made. Many desert travelers have survived until help could reach them by killing a camel and eating its flesh and drinking the still fresh water it contained! Don't you agree that the camel is indeed useful, both in life and in death?

The Ugly Side of the Camel

But sad to say, the camel also has an ugly side. It can become grumpy, and his feelings are easily hurt. If the camel gets angry at his rider or driver for either overloading or pushing him too hard, a camel will carry a grudge until the time comes to 'get even.' A camel will nip and bite and trample down the one who has offended it. So, to keep from getting hurt, camel drivers will often put down a bundle of clothes in front of the camel and get out of the way, but quick! Oh, how the camel goes to work on 'his enemy!' But later, when the camel is through showing its anger, it forgets the unfair treatment of its driver, and the driver can safely handle the camel again.

What God Wants Me to Know

"Oh, that was interesting," you say, "but where is the lesson I can learn from the camel? I cannot bear heavy burdens or run across the desert with a rider on my back. I cannot go more than three days without water, nor can I live on desert plants!" You are right! You cannot do any of these things; yet, as a child of God (Gal. 3:26), you can be useful to God and to those around you. In fact, you are to be useful! God made you, too, in a most wonderful way (Ps. 139:14). He intended that "we . . . should be to the praise of His glory" (Eph. 1:12*b*). That means that others can be made to see how wonderful the Lord is by the things we do.

We have just learned *about* the camel, so now let's see what we can learn *from* the camel. Just like the camel, we people come in different sizes and shapes. Some of us can run and work faster than others; some of us can do some things better than others. Once we have believed in the Lord Jesus, we all have the Holy Spirit indwelling us to help us to be useful to God. So it does not really matter what we can do, but what God can do through us (Zech. 4:6).

God can use our minds. He gave us sound minds, too (2 Tim. 1:7). He wants us to obey Him gladly, willingly, and to love Him with all our minds, with all our strength, and with all that we have. He tells us that we can show Him that we love Him by being "doers of the word" (John 14:21; James 1:22). How can we know what He wants us to do? By learning His Word. He is willing to give us patience and strength, not our own patience and strength of muscles, but the very strength and patience of God (Gal. 5:22; Eph. 6:10). We can have these when we have made sure that all our sins are confessed to God.

Instead of the ugly humps of the camel, we were given a storage place for the doctrines of the Word of God—our minds. There, we hide the spiritual water and food of the Word that we might remember and use it as we need (Ps. 119:11; Isa. 55:1; Matt. 4:4; 1 Pet. 2:2).

God gave us bodies that are just right to move about in and to serve Him in this world (1 Cor. 6:19–20). He wants us to let Him use our bodies as He thinks best. Many years ago, God needed someone to take His messages to the Jews. "Whom shall I send?" asked God, and a young man answered, "Here am I. Send me!" (Isa. 6:8). Do you know who this young man was? His name was Isaiah, and he became one of God's great prophets. One of the books in the Bible is named after him. God can use you, too, even now. Prove yourself useful to Him; begin by learning to obey at home and away from home; learn how to be a willing helper and to do what you should as unto the Lord.

Now, why do you think we were given hands and legs and feet? Just think how wonderfully well the Lord made our hands and feet. They serve us in so many ways every day. As soon as your hands receive a message from your brain, they go about doing what they are told. How useless they would be to you if they refused to obey your wishes. And your legs and feet? Well, they take you where your mind and body want to go. They never whine and complain, saying, "Must we?" or "But why?" like so many believing girls and boys will often do when they learn what God expects of them. Shall we look up two verses about hands and feet? "Withhold not good from them to whom it is due, when it is in the power of thine hand to do it" (Prov. 3:27, KJV), "having shod YOUR FEET WITH THE PREPARATION OF THE GOSPEL OF PEACE" (Eph. 6:15).

Willing, helpful hands are useful hands. Let yours be useful for the praise of the glory of the Lord! Feet that take us where we can tell others God's message of salvation are useful feet. Who knows, the Lord may want you to be a missionary in a faraway land someday. But you need not wait until then; you can start today by going to tell your friends about the Lord Jesus Christ (Acts 4:12). You can open your mouth and declare how wonderful God is (Ps. 51:15).

But like the camel, we, too, have an ugly side—our sin nature. It will make us get cross and want to get even when we should be kind and forgiving instead (Eph. 4:32). It will make our hands hit and push others rather than help them; it will make our mouths want to say bad, cruel things. How useful are we to the Lord when we let the sin nature be our 'camel driver'? Not one bit! Instead, we must let the Holy Spirit lead us to be useful to the Lord who owns us both in life and after death (Rom. 14:9). Then, if we have done well, we will be decorated and rewarded in heaven, not with chains but with gold, silver, precious stones, and crowns (1 Cor. 3:12a; Rev. 2:10b).

Being useful to the Lord is a great honor which brings much happiness. But you can only be useful when you have believed in the Lord Jesus Christ as your Savior, for only then can you receive the Holy Spirit. He will give you the powers to do the "good works" that are pleasing to God (Eph. 2:10). While we bow our heads, you may tell the Father in heaven that you now believe in His Son, and that you want to be useful to Him.

Lesson Review

What animal taught us that we, too, should be useful? The camel. How can you, believer, be useful to the Lord and to others? Be useful (Eph. 1:12a) through the Holy Spirit. Be willing to obey God, parents, and teachers; love God; confess all sins; learn the Word and do it; help others; and witness to the unbeliever.

Memory Verse

"We . . . should be to the praise of His glory." (Eph. 1:12b)

Chapter Seven

A Lesson about the Savior and Satan

OVERVIEW

A. Subject: A Lesson about the Savior and Satan—1 Peter 5:8; Revelation 5:5

B. Lesson Titles:
1. Lesson One: "The Lion That Is from the Tribe of Judah"
2. Lesson Two: The Devil, a Roaring Lion

C. Story Objective:

In the Bible, the lion is likened to the Lord Jesus Christ and to Satan. By contrasting the two, we will see how we must trust the Lord but beware of the devil.

Most references to the lion in Scripture are figurative, with only a few pertaining to the king of beasts himself. Only one reference ascribes the title "Lion that is from the tribe of Judah" to our Lord (Rev. 5:5), and only one reference compares the devil to a roaring, prowling lion (1 Pet. 5:8). Yet, from a study of the characteristics of the lion and their figurative uses, we gain great insight into the greatness and majesty of the Savior and the wiles and stealth of the devil.

D. Vocabulary and Doctrinal Concepts:
1. Vocabulary: adversary, deceiver, deception, deliver, discontent, prey, prowl, sober, tribe
2. Doctrinal Concepts:
   a. The nature of the lion:
      1) Strength (Judg. 14:18; 1 Sam. 17:37)
      2) Boldness, courage (2 Sam. 17:10)
      3) Rapacity (Job 28:8; 38:39)
      4) Ferocity (Ps. 7:2)
      5) Stealth (Ps. 10:9; Lam. 3:10)
      6) Cruelty (Ps. 17:12)
      7) Majesty (Micah 5:8)
   b. The lion's activities:
      1) Roars, growls (Job 4:10)
      2) Crouches in dens (Job 38:40)
      3) Prowls, lurks in secret places (Ps. 17:12)
      4) Yells (Jer. 2:15, KJV)
   c. Figurative uses of the lion:
      1) Courage (2 Sam. 17:10; 1 Chron. 12:8; Isa. 31:4)
      2) Strength (2 Sam. 23:20; Prov. 30:30)
      3) Confidence (Prov. 28:1)
      4) Judgment and divine discipline (1 Kings 13:24, 26; 2 Kings 17:25; Isa. 15:9; Jer. 2:30; Hosea 13:8)
      5) Earthly kingdoms and their rulers (Ezek. 32:2; Dan. 7:4)
   d. Lions, enemies of God's people:
      1) Tear the soul like a lion (Ps. 7:2)
      2) Lie in ambush (Ps. 10:9)
      3) Greedy for prey (Ps. 17:12)
      4) Ravening and roaring (Ps. 22:13)
      5) Enemy nations (Jer. 50:17)
      6) Have teeth like a lion (Joel 1:6)
      7) The devil (1 Pet. 5:8)
   e. Divine protection:
      1) Delivers "from the paw of the lion" (1 Sam. 17:37).
      2) Rescues from the mouth of the lion (Ps. 22:21; Dan. 6; 2 Tim. 4:17).
      3) "Tread upon the lion" (Ps. 91:13).
   f. Symbolic of the Lord:

1) Prophecy of the Second Advent (Gen. 49:8–10)
2) One of the four faces of the living creatures (Ezek. 1:10; 10:14); symbol of God's sovereignty (Rev. 4:7)
3) The Lord's voice in judgment (Hosea 11:10)
4) "The Lion that is from the tribe of Judah" (Rev. 5:5)

   g. Millennial passages (Isa. 11:6–8; 65:25)

E. *Source Book* Keywords: divine discipline, reign of Christ,

Satan (believer's defense, strategy against believer and unbeliever)

F. Activities:
  1. Suggested Visuals: none
  2. Games, Songs, Worksheets
  3. Memory Verse: "The Son of God appeared for this purpose, that He might destroy the works of the devil." (1 John 3:8*b*)
  4. Opening and Closing Prayer

LESSON ONE
"THE LION THAT IS FROM THE TRIBE OF JUDAH"

*D*o you wonder what animal is to be our next teacher? There is a riddle about him in the Bible. It goes like this: "Out of the eater came something to eat, And out of the strong came something sweet" (Judg. 14:12–14). Samson thought up this riddle and gave those who heard him tell it seven days to find the answer. Can you guess what animal Samson was thinking about? We find the answer in Judges 14:18. It was the lion.

This is how Samson made up the riddle. One day he met a roaring lion in his path. Samson had no weapons with him, yet by God's great power he tore the lion apart with his bare hands. Some days later he passed by the place and saw that all that was left of the lion were the bones and a few scraps of flesh. Wild bees had made their hive in the dead lion's skeleton and were storing up honey. Samson scooped up the honey and took it home to his parents. He had not told his parents about killing the lion; surely they would never guess where the honey came from—nor would anyone else. Yes, indeed, it would make a riddle!

Samson's lion is more than a good riddle, though; it reminds us of the two things we want to learn about—the great power of our sovereign God and the power and strength of the roaring lion, the devil.

The King of the Beasts

Of all the animals, surely there is none greater or more stately than the lion. The Bible says that lions "are stately when they walk" (Prov. 30:29–30). That means the lion is beautiful to look at in all that he does. To see him walk about the forest or jungle one would think he owned it all. And well he might, for no animal would dare challenge

him. After all, the lion is the strongest among the beasts (Micah 5:8).

Do you know how strong a lion is? With a single stroke of his paw, a lion can break the back of a horse! In only one leap, he knocks down his prey—dead! A sweep of his tail will throw a strong man to the ground; yet, remember, Samson, in the power of the Spirit, was stronger than the strongest lion!

Lions are the bravest of all the animals. I am sure they don't even know what the word "fear" means. Sometimes, when we want to describe how brave a person is, we might say he has "the heart of a lion" (2 Sam. 17:10). In Bible times, shepherds often banded together to hunt a lion or scare him away from their flocks. They would shout at the lion at the top of their voices, but he would only glare back at them with cold, glittering eyes. The lion would rather face death than turn his back and run!

In those long-ago days, there were many wild lions in Palestine. Remember reading how David killed a lion with a slingshot (1 Sam. 17:34–36)? Today, wild lions live only deep inside of Africa and India. A grown lion measures six to eight feet in length, not counting his tail, which is four feet long and ends in a tuft of blackish hair. Only the male lions have manes. They have beautiful but fierce-looking faces. If you saw a lion blocking your path, wouldn't you be frightened?

We are told that if we noticed the lion's mane to be smooth and lying close against his head and his tail hanging quietly between his legs, we'd have nothing to fear and could walk safely past him. But if his mane stood up and his tail twitched wildly, then look out! Now, I don't know about you, but as for me, I'd rather not try finding out if this is true or not. Compared to the king-like, mighty lion, how very weak and powerless we are!

The Fairness of the Lion

Because of their great strength and power, lions could be bullies. But really, they are quite fair. They will only attack people or animals openly when they have been provoked to anger, and they kill only to satisfy their hunger. They have been known to be gracious and forgiving. Just listen to what happened some years ago in London.

In the great and famous Tower of London, a lion was kept in a den. There the king of beasts was a prisoner, and food was thrown to him from time to time. One day, the keepers threw a little dog into the lion's den. That dog was to have been the lion's dinner, yet the lion did not hurt or touch him. Instead, the two lived together for many years and became close friends.

Every time the lion was fed, he saved some scraps for the dog. It wasn't long until the little dog was so used to the lion's kindness that he was no longer content to wait thankfully and patiently for his scraps. He began to growl at the lion, demanding his own share and choice first. You'd think the lion would surely punish the dog, or even gobble him up! But no; graciously, the lion stepped aside and let the dog eat first. He claimed his share only after the little dog was satisfied.

Isn't that just like you and me? God does so much for us every day that we soon forget to be thankful and satisfied with what He gives us. Instead, we want our own way, even if it means having to push God's better will for us out of the way! "Gimme, gimme, gimme," we demand, and what do we give God in return? All that we are and have, our time, our money, our service, our thanks? Of course not—just what's left over after we've had all we wanted! Shame on the little thankless dog, and shame, shame on us!

The Love of the Lion

How very much God must love us to put up with us! Lions have a very loving nature. They love and care for their own and will defend them to the death. When they must, the lion or the lioness will spank their own young cubs. They do it because they love them and never really hurt them. The great, sharp claws, which can tear like so many daggers, are pulled safely back among the soft pads, and the powerful teeth, which can crush the thickest bones, grip the fluffy bundles of fur without ever leaving a mark.

When the Lord spanks His own, He does so out of love (Heb. 12:6) and for our own good! Perhaps it hurts a lot; but it certainly won't harm us, and we'll be better off for it! I am sure that when the lion parents softly growl at their young, the young 'snap to' in a hurry. Oh, that we would pay attention to the Lord's voice as He speaks to us through His Word. He always speaks to us lovingly, warning us before He speaks to us in judgment. He spoke through His

Son, Jesus Christ, whom He sent to be our Savior. As you know, "The Son of God appeared for this purpose, that He might destroy the works of the devil" (1 John 3:8*b*). He was openly shown and could be seen. He came to die on the cross for our sins. If we accept God's offer of His Son, we will be accepted into the Father's family (Gal. 3:26; Eph. 1:6). We shall be loved forevermore!

"The Lion That Is from the Tribe of Judah"

But if we pay no attention to God's voice of love, we must hear His voice of judgment. Let me read to you what it says in Hosea 11:10: "The LORD, He will roar like a lion; Indeed He will roar, And *His* sons [people] will come trembling from the west." God's voice is more powerful and fearful than a lion's roar. Remember, He is not only perfect goodness, righteousness, and love; He is also just.

In the last book of the Bible, we read about "the Lion that is from the tribe of Judah" (Rev. 5:5). This is no real lion, but rather the Lord Jesus Christ. The word "lion" stands for ruler, or king, and even as the lion is the king of beasts, so the Lord Jesus Christ is the "KING OF KINGS, AND LORD OF LORDS" (Rev. 19:16). The word "tribe" means family, and the family of Judah is the very family from which our Lord came (Heb. 7:14).

Lions come and go; earthly kings come and go, but our King of kings is eternal. He is the same yesterday, today, and forever (1 Tim. 1:17; Heb. 13:8). No matter how powerful a lion may be, no matter how powerful earthly rulers may be, the Lord who owns them all is more powerful than they (Job 40:2*a*; Ps. 24:1; 50:10). He is what? Yes, omnipotent. Besides, He is omnipresent, in all places at the same time, which is something no one else can do. He is omniscient, He knows everything so He knows how best to help us and will most certainly keep His word.

At His word, lions came in among the settlers of Samaria, who did not worship the true God, and killed some of them (2 Kings 17:25). At His command the hungry lions shut their greedy mouths and became tame. Do you know when this happened, and to whom? Yes, to Daniel in the lions' den (Dan. 6).

Who is the "Lion that is from the tribe of Judah"? Yes, our Savior, the Lord Jesus Christ. When the "lion" comes to rule the earth, all animals will become tame as they were before Adam sinned. Then the lion, the lamb, the ox, and the calf will all lie down together and eat grass and straw, and a little child will be able to lead them (Isa. 11:6–7).

What God Wants Me to Know

"What a wonderful time that will be," you think. Yes, that is true, but you can have a wonderful time even now. Just knowing what God is like and trusting Him makes life great and wonderful for every believer! You have trusted Him for the most—to save you; can you trust Him to keep you safe? Of course you can! Just try it, will you?

Would you like to belong to the mightiest, the heavenly King, and someday rule with the King of kings? Then listen to His voice of love and warning: "Whoever believes in Him [the Lord Jesus] should not perish, but have eternal life" (John 3:16b). Will you do so right now?

Lesson Review

We saw in what ways the lion is like our Savior, the Lord Jesus Christ. The Bible even calls Him "the Lion that is from the tribe of Judah." Can you explain what this means? "Lion" means ruler or king. The word "tribe" means family, and the family of Judah is the very family from which our Lord came. Do you remember some of the ways the lion reminded us of the Lord? His sovereignty, omnipotence, love, fairness, grace.

Why did the Lord come to earth the first time? To save us. What will He do when He comes as the Lion of Judah? Reign on earth. What will He do for the animals then? Tame them all. But until then, wild animals will remain wild and often become dangerous to man. Why, even experienced hunters have to be very careful when they go after lions!

Memory Verse

"The Son of God appeared for this purpose, that He might destroy the works of the devil." (1 John 3:8b)

LESSON TWO
THE DEVIL, A ROARING LION

Now, you and I don't have to fear coming upon a lion suddenly and unexpectedly in this country; yet, did you know that we are cautioned in God's Word to *beware of the lion*? This lion is a very real danger to all who belong to God's family (Gal. 3:26). Are we still talking about the mighty Lion of Judah? No, for we are told to trust in Him and in His great power and love for us. Who, then, is this other lion? He is none other than Satan, the devil. If you will listen carefully to the last part of our memory verse, you will find out that God's Son had to come, not only to save us from sin, but also to destroy the works of the devil. "The Son of God appeared for this purpose, that He might destroy the works of the devil" (1 John 3:8b). Just what are the devil's works? Well, that's what you and I will discover today.

Lion, Beware!

Our great enemy, Satan, the devil, is as terrible as the mighty Lion of Judah, our Savior, is wonderful. In quite as many ways as the king of beasts reminds us of our Lord, the lion also reminds us of the devil. How do I know? Open your Bible to 1 Peter 5:8. "Be of sober *spirit*, be on the alert. Your adversary, the devil, prowls about like a roaring lion, seeking someone to devour." The part of the verse we want to look at right now is "your adversary, the devil, prowls about like a roaring lion."

Do you know what an "adversary" is? An adversary is an enemy. Who is your enemy, believing boy, believing girl? Look at this verse. Your enemy is the devil. He hates you because He hates God, and you belong to God! The harder you try to please the Lord, the more the devil dislikes it. The devil walks about *like* a roaring lion. He is *not a lion*, but *like one*! And, believe me, a roaring lion is a dangerous lion—one whose mane stands straight up, and whose tail lashes angrily from side to side. What would such a lion be up to?

Let's follow a real lion who is out walking about, shall we? He's not out for a nice stroll in the cool of the day; he is actually on the prowl, as it says in 1 Peter 5:8, "seeking someone to devour." He's out looking for a meal. He growls deep down in his throat, and his voice sounds like distant thunder. But the animals and birds who hear him know better. They scatter in fear as fast as their legs or wings will carry them. The lion's sharp eyes spot the least movement; his keen nose picks up every smell carried on the breeze. He cannot be bothered with small game—they are safe from him.

He treads softly, silently, when suddenly he spots a zebra, one of his very favorite dishes. Now he crouches down and aims; he leaps through the air like a shot and strikes with a terrible roar. Before the victim knows what happened, it's all over. Then the lion's sharp teeth dig in, and the claws tear the dead body to pieces. Greedily, he eats his fill to last him for two or three days, during which time he rests and waits for the next kill.

Satan, a Roaring Lion

Now you will understand better what Peter meant when he wrote that "the devil, prowls about like a roaring lion, seeking someone to devour" (1 Pet. 5:8). Satan is always on the lookout for believers who forget to be on guard against him! He doesn't literally eat us, tearing us limb from limb; what he is after is to keep us from serving, obeying, and honoring the Lord. He wants to make us useless to the Lord, and often he succeeds.

Peter knew what he was talking about. Once the devil had tried to "devour" him. The Lord Jesus had warned him that Satan wanted him badly and said, "But I have prayed for you, that your faith may not fail; and you, when once you have turned again [confessed your sin], strengthen your brothers [warn other believers]" (Luke 22:31–32). The time came when Satan indeed caught Peter in an unguarded moment. The Lord Jesus had just been led away a prisoner; soon He must die. Do you know what Peter did then? He was ashamed of having known the Lord Jesus and afraid to admit that he knew who Jesus was (Matt. 26:69–74). That must have been quite a 'meal' for Satan!

But Peter did not stay out of fellowship long, and he did exactly what the Lord had told him to do—he warned us of the roaring, prowling, lion-like devil, didn't he? He told us what to do, too. "Be of sober *spirit*," he said; "be on the alert [be watchful, alert in prayer, as God would always want you to think]" (1 Pet. 5:8a). Remember, to pray properly, you *must be in fellowship*! Be prepared for Satan's attack by having a mind crammed full of doctrine and Bible verses. Stand your ground! "Resist the devil!" (James 4:7). Don't run, but meet him head-on with the Word of God, just like the Lord Jesus did in the wilderness—remember Matthew 4? Do you know what will happen then? The devil will turn and run; he will flee from you (James 4:7). He won't be able to get away from you fast enough to suit him. But don't relax then, thinking you are rid of him for good; he'll be back again (Luke 4:13).

The Stratagem of the Lion and the Devil

Yes, the devil will be back again when you least expect him, just like the real lion! You see, lions do not usually hunt in daylight, out in the open where they can be seen. They prefer to lie in wait for their prey at night. Then they take their unsuspecting victims by surprise. They spring suddenly and have 'many tricks up their sleeve,' if we may say so. They use different ways to kill or cripple.

When a lion goes after big game, say a buffalo, he fastens his claws and paws on the buffalo's nostrils and mouth. He holds on tight until he has strangled or choked the animal to death. When he hunts zebra or horses, he will often strike with his paw to break their backs. Then, when the animal lies helpless before him, he may kill it quickly, or slowly and cruelly by ripping open its belly.

The devil, too, has many tricks by which he works (Eph. 6:11b). If scaring doesn't work on a believer, he'll try something else—deception, for instance. He makes right seem wrong, and wrong seem right. If that fails, he'll try to make us discontent, as he did Eve, wanting things we'd be better off without! But now that you know what he is up to, and what you can do about him, you don't have to let him get the better of you (2 Cor. 2:11).

What God Wants Me to Know

Will you just remember that no matter how powerful Satan may be—and he is powerful, make no mistake about that—our Savior is much more powerful than he. Satan may be the king and ruler over the bad angels and this world (2 Cor. 4:4a; Rev. 12:9), but he can only do what God allows (Job 1:12; 2:6). If you belong to the Lord, because you have put your belief in Jesus Christ, you are in His care (1 Pet. 5:7).

Remember Samson's lion? Remember David's lion? Remember what happened to Daniel in the lions' den? God gave them a great victory! Did Samson brag about what he had done? He did not! He knew that God's power had given him strength over the king of beasts! And listen to what David said after he killed the lion: "The LORD who delivered [rescued] me from the paw of the lion" (1 Sam. 17:37a). Listen to what Daniel said after he spent a night among the hungry lions: "My God sent His angel and shut the lions' mouths, and they have not harmed me" (Dan. 6:22).

As God protected them and helped them, so He will help you and protect you (Dan. 6:23b). Satan knows well enough that if he gets after you, he'll also have your Savior to deal with, for nothing and no one can ever separate you from the love of God (Rom. 8:35–39). It's true, you and I cannot kill Satan like we might kill a real lion, but we know that someday we shall be rid of him for good. The Lion that is from the tribe of Judah, our wonderful Lord, will have Satan, the roaring lion, thrown into the lake of fire (Matt. 25:41). Aren't you glad? Don't you feel like shouting, "But thanks be to God, who gives us the victory through our Lord Jesus Christ" (1 Cor. 15:57)?

Now, if you don't belong to the Lord, then this lesson was hardly for you. The tricky, roaring lion is not interested in you. You are hardly worth his attention until you begin to show an interest in the Lord Jesus Christ and His Word. Then he has one more trick to try out on you—he "has blinded the minds" (2 Cor. 4:4). He'll make you think that what you learn about Jesus Christ being the *only way* to heaven is not really so (John 14:6). "Pay no attention to that," he 'whispers' into your mind; "there are many other ways—trying hard and being good are just some of them; God will never turn *you* away!"

Don't you listen to that deceiver! Though his soft growl sounds more like a purr, it is not; his mane is up, and the lion's tail is twitching wildly. Listen to God's true Word instead! "For by grace you have been saved through faith; and that not of yourselves, *it is* the gift of God; not as a result of works, that no one should boast" (Eph. 2:8–9). Will you accept God's gift of salvation now? Will you move firmly to the side of your Savior and be His forever? "Believe in the Lord Jesus, and you shall be saved" (Acts 16:31).

Lesson Review

We have talked about three lions—the real lion, the Lion that is from the tribe of Judah, and the roaring lion. Listen to what I shall say, and tell me which lion I am thinking about. The king of beasts—the real lion. The Lion that is from the tribe of Judah—Jesus Christ. The roaring lion—the devil. The lion that wanted to have Peter—Satan.

The lion in whose body there was honey—the real lion. The lion who is King of kings—Jesus Christ. The lion who prowls about, looking for believers off guard—Satan. The lion from whose paw God delivered David—the real lion. The Lion who will tame all animals—Jesus Christ. The lion who is our enemy—Satan. The lion who uses many tricks—the real lion and Satan. The Lion who gives us the victory—Jesus Christ.

Memory Verse

"The Son of God appeared for this purpose, that He might destroy the works of the devil." (1 John 3:8*b*)

Chapter Eight

A Lesson in Wisdom

OVERVIEW

A. Subject: A Lesson in Wisdom—Proverbs 30:24–28

B. Lesson Titles:
1. Lesson One: Little but Wise: The Ants and the Rock Badgers
2. Lesson Two: The Locusts and the Lizard

C. Story Objective:

The believer's knowledge of Bible doctrine is most important, and his application of that knowledge to experience is essential for his spiritual growth (Prov. 8).

D. Vocabulary and Doctrinal Concepts:
1. Vocabulary: coyote, exceedingly, gecko, hibernate, locust, plague, ranks, rock badgers, shelter, sluggard, sustain, sword drill, thresh
2. Doctrinal Concepts:
   a. Knowledge:
      1) God, the source of knowledge and wisdom (Prov. 2:6; Rom. 11:33).
      2) Available to every believer (Prov. 2:7; 1 Cor. 2:7–13; 2 Cor. 4:6).
      3) Faith in Christ—the "beginning of wisdom" and knowledge (Prov. 9:10).
      4) "It is not good for a person to be without knowledge" (Prov. 19:2).
      5) Hear and apply knowledge (Prov. 22:17).
      6) Counsel and knowledge are excellent things (Prov. 22:20).
      7) Ignorance and indifference toward doctrine equals destruction (Hosea 4:6).
      8) Knowledge should not lead to pride (1 Cor. 8:1).
      9) The "surpassing value of knowing Christ Jesus" (Phil. 3:8).
      10) In Christ, "the treasures of wisdom and knowledge" (Col. 2:3).
      11) Add knowledge (2 Pet. 1:5–6).
      12) Grow in knowledge (2 Pet. 3:18).
   b. Wisdom:
      1) The fear of the Lord is wisdom (Job 28:28; Ps. 111:10).
      2) Wisdom is despised by fools (Prov. 1:7*b*).
      3) Listen to wisdom (Prov. 2:2).
      4) Application of doctrine brings happiness (Prov. 3:13; John 13:17; James 1:25).
      5) Get wisdom; do not forget it (Prov. 4:5).
      6) "The wisdom of this world is foolishness before God" (1 Cor. 3:19).
      7) "Teaching every man with all wisdom" (Col. 1:28).
      8) "Conduct yourself with wisdom" (Col. 4:5).
      9) Pray for wisdom (James 1:5).
   c. Literal rendition from the Hebrew of Proverbs 30:24–28:
      "Four things are small on the earth,
      But they are exceedingly wise:
      The ants are not a strong folk,
      But they prepare their food in the summer;
      The badgers are not mighty folk,
      Yet they make their houses in the rocks;
      The locusts have no king,
      Yet all of them go out in ranks;

The lizard you may grasp with the hands,
Yet it is in kings' palaces."

Note: These four helpless members of the animal kingdom are instructive to man, especially to the believer, in the following ways:

1) The ant: A highly social insect that has a well-ordered domestic economy. The ant pictures the industry and diligence that applies to the believer who takes in and stores doctrine in readiness for abnormal circumstances in life.

2) The rock badger (*Hyrax syriacus*—rock rabbit): Knowledgeable of its own vulnerability and inadequacy, sagacious; lives and seeks shelter in the clefts of the rocks; represents the believer who knows his safety lies in the Lord and in the doctrines of His Word.

3) The locust: Demonstrates harmony, coordination, and teamwork. Applies to the spiritually self-sustaining believer whose absolute standard and guide in life is the Word.

4) The lizard: Is small enough to be caught in one hand, yet is nimble and cunning enough to gain an entrance into palaces. Shows flexibility and confidence; applies to the believer's personal life, finding inner happiness, even in adverse circumstances, through living in the Word.

E. *Source Book* Keywords: Christ (the rock), Christian soldier, David, gnosis and epignosis, promises, Solomon

F. Activities:
1. Suggested Visuals: Christian soldier, Inner Happiness palace
2. Games, Songs, Worksheets
3. Memory Verse: "Let the word of Christ richly dwell within you, with all wisdom." (Col. 3:16*a*)
4. Opening and Closing Prayer

LESSON ONE
LITTLE BUT WISE: THE ANTS AND THE ROCK BADGERS

I wonder, if I gave you a test on what you learned from the animals in God's school, would you be able to pass it? Would you remember your lessons on faithfully obeying God's will; on trusting God to take care of all your needs; on being content with what He gave you; on being lost and found; on being useful; and on trusting the mighty Savior but being watchful against Satan? Would you still know what animals taught you those things, and what memory verses you had learned?

Do you know the difference between knowledge and wisdom? Knowledge is understanding what you have been taught; wisdom is using what you know. Let me give you an example: Many years ago there lived some wise men in the East. They had learned, perhaps from Daniel's teachings, that someday a King and Savior would be born to the Jews. This King would be the King of kings. Remember, we learned that He is sometimes called the "Lion that is from the tribe of Judah"? Well, He is also known as "the bright morning star" (Rev. 22:16) and a star "come forth from Jacob" (Num. 24:17). Night after night the wise men watched the sky for a special sign of His coming—a new and shining star. At last they saw it. "We saw His star," they called out. Now, that is *knowledge*, understanding what they had been taught (Matt. 2:2)! Did they let it go at that?

They did not. They set out to find the King and Savior of the world. And when they had found Him, they trusted in Him and worshiped Him (Matt. 2:1, 11). That is *wisdom*!

These men were great and wise men, indeed. Yet, not all great men are wise (Job 32:9*a*). It would be best if no one was great until he was first wise. The Word of God points out to us four little things on earth that are said to be exceedingly or remarkably wise. These four little wise things will be our teachers in this lesson and the next. Do you want to meet them? Then turn to Proverbs 30:24–28. "Four things are small on the earth, But they are exceedingly wise: The ants are not a strong folk, But they prepare their food in the summer; The rock badgers are not mighty folk, Yet they make their houses in the rocks; The locusts have no king, Yet all of them go out in ranks; The lizard you may grasp with the hands, Yet it is in kings' palaces."

Four Little Things, Exceedingly Wise

The first are the ants (Prov. 30:25); the second are the rock badgers (Prov. 30:26); the third are the locusts (Prov. 30:27); and the fourth is the lizard (Prov. 30:28).

Now, do you wonder what it is that makes these little things wiser than most creatures? Whatever could they teach us? Well, let's read on, and we shall soon find out. We'll take Teacher Ant and Teacher Badger in this lesson and invite Teachers Locust and Lizard to lecture us in the next lesson, shall we?

Go to the Ant!

Do you know what member of the animal kingdom goes to every picnic as an uninvited guest? Yes, the ant. Just watch: You have barely sat down and laid out your food, when the first one arrives. Before long, it is joined by many, many more. Throw them a crumb and watch how eagerly and busily they carry it away. Note their teamwork; they all pull together—not one of them insists on having his own way! Yes, ants are amazing little creatures—little but wise!

The wisest king who ever lived, King Solomon (1 Kings 3:12), wrote: "Go to the ant, O sluggard [lazybones], Observe her ways [learn from the ant] and be wise, Which, having no chief, Officer or ruler [ants have no guide, no one who 'cracks the whip' over them, seeing to it that the job gets done], Prepares her food in the summer, *And* gathers her provision in the harvest" (Prov. 6:6–8). Now let's go back to Proverbs 30:24–25. "Four things are small on the earth, But they are exceedingly wise: The ants are not a strong folk, But they prepare their food in the summer." Ants are very little. On their own they have no strength, but together they surely get things done!

Ants can be found all over the earth. There are said to be five thousand different kinds of ants, and like bees, they live in colonies. Surely you have seen their nests—ant hills. Ants make for themselves underground tunnels and rooms. The sand or earth they dig up is pushed to the surface and forms the little mounds which we call ant hills. Ants are wise in many ways. They divide their work among themselves. There are worker ants that do the heavy chores, soldier ants that guard the colony against outside enemies, nurse ants that look after the young and feed the helpless among them, and queen ants that lay many, many eggs. The ants we want to consider are the ants that are found in Palestine—those from whom King Solomon told us to learn.

Those ants are very active in summer but slow when the weather turns cold. They almost hibernate in winter. To be able to survive in the cold, they must work hard while the weather is warm. Like most of you, they have a favorite dish—grain—of which they lay up a great store in their underground pantries. Let me tell you just how wise they are! They find a place close to where people thresh and store their own grain—that is, wheat, barley, or corn. That way they are near their source of supply. Now they come, day after day, in search of food for the winter. At last their work is done. Let winter come; let the cold winds howl and the sleet fall. The ants are well prepared; they'll make it all right when hard times come their way! They can relax and live on the great treasures they have laid up for just such days ahead!

Learning from the Ant

Now, what did the ant teach you and me? That we should dig deep underground tunnels and rooms and store away foods? Hardly! Certainly it's wise to save for a 'rainy day,' but that was not our lesson. The ant is a reminder of the believer. A believer in himself and by himself is quite weak and helpless. True, there is strength in numbers, but even that is not enough. What you and I, as believers, need more than anything else is *knowledge* of God's Word and the many doctrines it contains.

Right now you are busy little ants gathering in spiritual food, here a little, there a little. The time in which we best learn is 'summer.' Not summer, like June, July, and August, but the time when we can learn, when all goes well and you can keep your mind on your lesson. Your safe place to store away knowledge is your mind. Then when 'winter' comes, you, too, will be well prepared. Winter in our lives stands for the difficult times that come to us when we are sick and suffer; when we are disappointed and sad; when everything seems to go wrong. When we draw from our store of doctrines and promises from God's Word, we are truly wise.

One of the bravest men who ever lived was David, King Solomon's father. But even he had times of fear. Did he sit down and cry then? Not David! He remembered what he knew about God and God's promises. "When I am afraid, I will put my trust in thee [God]," he said (Ps. 56:3). Trust he did, and his fears disappeared. He put his knowledge of God's Word to use, and so can you! Be wise as the ant is wise. Learn while you can, for God's Word is the only thing that will sustain you in troublesome times!

The Badger in the Rock

Our next teacher is the rock badger. Rock badgers live in the desert and are about the size of an ordinary rabbit but have very short ears and a short tail. They are weak and defenseless, for they cannot fight back. Their only protection is speed. The rock badgers know this. They have learned that their safety depends on how quickly they can run to the rocks where they have secret hiding places and shelter.

Mr. Badger is a bit out of breath from running, so let's give him time to slip through the crack of his rock. Now he's safe from his enemy, the coyote, for while the crack in the rock is just big enough to let the rock badger in, it is small enough to keep the coyote out. Mr. Badger has learned that the rock has never failed to protect him. He knows, and he applies. That's what makes him wise.

The Believer's Rock

Do you know that you, a believing boy or a believing girl, have just such a place of safety? Where is it found? Let's let David show us, shall we? Turn in your Bible to Psalm 31:1–3. David had been running from his enemies,

King Saul and his army. He knew just what to do. "O, Lord," he called, "be Thou to me a rock of strength, a stronghold to save me [to deliver me quickly!]." Where did David learn that the Lord was his secret hiding place and shelter? Perhaps he had learned it from the rock badgers (Ps. 104:18*b*). God did indeed deliver David from his enemies. Afterwards, David sang a song of praise to the Lord: "And David spoke the words of this song to the LORD in the day that the LORD delivered him from the hand of all his enemies and from the hand of Saul. And he said, 'The LORD is my rock and my fortress and my deliverer; My God, my rock, in whom I take refuge; My shield and the horn of my salvation, my stronghold and my refuge; My savior, Thou dost save me from violence. I call upon the LORD, who is worthy to be praised; And I am saved from my enemies'" (2 Sam. 22:1–4).

Be like the rock badgers; be like David, and know where your safety lies! Only the Lord can keep you safe, and the teaching of His Word shows you how you can find a place of peace and rest in time of danger and disaster. We are weak like the rock badgers, but the Lord is strong. So, when trouble heads your way—run! Run as quickly as you can to God's Word with all its promises. Be wise; believe God and His Word and rest relaxed in the "shelter of the Most High" (Ps. 91:1), where nothing and no one can touch you unless God so allows!

What God Wants Me to Know

Yes, the rocks are for the rock badgers, and the safe and sure promises of God's Word are for believers, and for believers only! Is there anything in God's Word for those who have not yet taken the Lord Jesus as their Savior? Of course there is! It's the wonderful good news that God sent His Son, the Lord Jesus, to save us from sin (1 John 4:14). God's Word can "give you the wisdom that leads to salvation" (2 Tim. 3:15). The starting place for getting wisdom is the cross (Prov. 9:10). That's where you begin to be wise! You must believe in the Lord Jesus Christ to be truly wise! Will you make this most important decision now?

Lesson Review

What were the first two of the four wise but little things from which we have learned? The ants and the rock badgers. In which way were they wise? Because of what they knew and did. See if you can think how we can learn from the ant. I will give you a clue: The ants find and store away their food during the summer so they will have it in winter. The believer should do what? Learn the Word and doctrine in good times so he can use it when troublesome times come. What did we learn from the rock badger? To know and believe God and His Word and to trust Him in times of disaster.

Memory Verse

"Let the word of Christ richly dwell within you, with all wisdom." (Col. 3:16*a*)

LESSON TWO
THE LOCUSTS AND THE LIZARD

*T*his lesson comes from the two "L's," Teachers Locust and Lizard, which are the third and fourth of the wise things mentioned in Proverbs 30:24–28.

The Locusts

Let's take a closer look at the locust. Perhaps you know him better by the name "grasshopper." We'll have a quick sword drill to see what the Bible has to say about him. Are you ready? Find the verses, read them aloud, and then we shall talk about them. Leviticus 11:22*a*: "These of them you may eat: the locust in its kinds." Locusts could be eaten. Matthew 3:4: "Now John himself had a garment of camel's hair, and a leather belt about his waist; and his food was locusts and wild honey." John the Baptist ate locusts and wild honey. Exodus 10:13: "So Moses stretched out his staff over the land of Egypt, and the LORD directed an east wind on the land all that day and all that night; and when it was morning, the east wind brought the locusts." Locusts fly in the direction of the wind. Jeremiah 46:23*b*: "Even though they are *now* more numerous than locusts And are without number." Locusts are countless in number. Exodus 10:15: "For they covered the surface of the whole land, so that the land was darkened; and they ate every plant of the land and all the fruit of the trees that the hail had left. Thus nothing green was left on tree or plant of the field through all the land of Egypt." Locusts blanket the sky and earth and eat every green thing leaving nothing in their wake.

Did you know that people of Bible lands call locusts "God's armies"? Do you know why they do? God has often used locusts to 'spank' nations. Can you think of a time when He did so? Way back in the days of Moses, when Pharaoh refused to let the Israelites leave Egypt, God sent ten plagues or judgments on the Egyptians. One of the plagues, the eighth, was the locusts. At God's command, they flew in on the east wind. They covered the land like a thick blanket; they hung in the air like a dense cloud; and they stripped the land of all growing things in the fields, gardens, and trees (Ex. 10:12–15).

But God also sent locusts to discipline His own people (1 Kings 9:9; 2 Chron. 7:13). The Bible says that God commands the locusts to eat up the land and at His command they go forth and strike like a well-trained army. They come, and nothing will stop them. Man has tried to dig deep ditches, hoping that the locusts will stop when they get to them. But the locusts fill the ditches and climb right on over each other. Man has tried to set fires, but the fires were snuffed out by the great number of locusts.

Do you wonder why such a destructive pest should be listed as one of the wisest of creatures and why we should take a lesson from him? Listen as I read to you what Proverbs 30:27 actually says: "The locusts have no king, Yet all of them go out in ranks."

Can you imagine a whole army of soldiers, marching purposefully and well-organized without a commanding officer? Whom would they obey, and from whom should they take orders? How would they know where to march and where to stop? No, we cannot imagine such a thing. And yet, locusts do just that. Like a mighty army, they march on and conquer. They have no leader whom we can see. The orders come straight from the Lord and are obeyed promptly (Ex. 10:4–6, 13–15). When God said "march," they marched; when God said "stop," not one locust remained behind (Ex. 10:19).

Learning from the Locusts

Every Christian is a soldier in the army of the heavenly King. Are you a good soldier of Jesus Christ (2 Tim. 2:3)?

Do you march together, work together, pray together for His cause? Did you ever watch soldiers marching on in unbroken ranks? Would it not look sloppy if every soldier

marched the way he wanted to, all out of step? Being out of fellowship with God puts us out of step. If you have sinned, be sure to confess your sin quickly and get back in step with the rest of the Lord's army.

God is the unseen ruler of your life, and He rules your life by the doctrines which are found only in His Word. Yes, Christian soldiers get their marching orders from the Word of God. Do you *know* what God expects of you? Then do it promptly, and be *wise*! Learn doctrine; know doctrine; apply doctrine!

The Lizard

Did you ever catch a lizard? It can be done, you know, but you have to be quick. Here's what Proverbs 30:28 says about teacher number four. "The lizard you may grasp with the hands, Yet it is in kings' palaces." Just what does the last part of the verse mean? Surely, you have no trouble understanding the first part of it, do you?

The lizard of Proverbs 30:28 is not the pretty little green lizard which we see in our backyards; it is the gecko or spotted lizard. It is quite common in Palestine and finds its way into the poor man's hut as well as into the king's palace. The gecko can do something our lizards here cannot do— scale smooth and slippery surfaces. Notice how the Lord designed the gecko's feet. On the underside of this kind of lizard's toes are adhesive disks. By means of these disks, the lizard clings with ease to any steep and smooth wall.

Up it goes, climbing slick marble pillars, polished metal surfaces, shiny walls right up to the very top. Quickly and easily it walks right into the palace, and no one stops it— not even the security guards! One of the reasons why nobody stops the gecko is that some people mistakenly think it is poisonous because of the spots on its back. But that is not so. The gecko is quite harmless—useful in fact—because, like all lizards, it eats small bugs and flies. And so the lizard has its choice: It may live in a hut or the king's palace. Which do you think it will choose?

Learning from the Lizard

Does this mean that because you are still 'little' that you, too, may slip into great palaces unnoticed? No, it means something far better, far greater to those who are the

children of God, the heavenly King (Gal. 3:26). Until we get to our palaces in heaven, we may live in simple or in splendid homes here on earth, that is true. But God has given us something wonderful with which we can cling to His promises—faith! When we trust God's Word and all that it teaches us, we'll live in a palace called Inner Happiness.

Watch what happens when you live there. All that God is and can do, all that He says and does so fills your palace that there can be no room for anything that is bad. If worries want to peep in the windows, the 'doctrine shutters' slam shut; if fears knock on the door, there is no answer. If troubles and sadness try to peek through the keyhole, God's promises block the way. And on the inside, you are completely, totally happy and content. Why, to think that there are believing boys and girls who would rather stay out of such a place is just hard to imagine! Follow the lesson of the lizard: Be wise and happy.

Summary

Now, before we let our teachers go, let's find out whether they have anything else to say to us. "Yes," says Teacher Ant, "Learn doctrine now, while you can. As I always say: 'He [or she] who gathers in the summer is a son [or daughter] who acts wisely'" (Prov. 10:5a). Teacher Badger? "I, too, want to remind you that God is your 'rock' (Ps. 71:3), and His Word is the only safe hiding place in times of trouble."

Teacher Locust, what have you to say to us? "Just this: Take your orders from God's Word; walk according to what He commands" (Gal. 6:16; Phil. 3:16). And finally, Teacher Lizard, what is it you want to leave with us? "Well," says Lizard, "I want to let you in on the secret to perfect wisdom and happiness: Just 'let the word of Christ

richly dwell within you, with all wisdom' and you cannot go wrong" (Col. 3:16).

What God Wants Me to Know

Do you know where all the treasures of wisdom and knowledge are hidden? In Christ (Col. 2:3). He alone can give us what we need—salvation, righteousness, and wisdom (1 Cor. 1:30). Would you like to have these things, and many more besides? They are yours "in Christ," if only you will accept Him as your Savior.

Lesson Review

What lesson did the wise things teach us? The ants gather their food in summer to use in wintertime; the believer takes in the Word now to apply it in time of need. The rock badgers are safe in the rocks where they have secret hiding places; the believer is safe in the Lord and His Word. Trust Him! The locusts take orders; believers take orders from God's Word. The lizard climbs up walls and lives in palaces. Believers should learn and apply doctrine and live in the palace called Inner Happiness.

Memory Verse

"Let the word of Christ richly dwell within you, with all wisdom." (Col. 3:16a)

Chapter Nine

Graduating from God's School

A. Subject: Graduating from God's School—Deuteronomy 32:11–12; Isaiah 40:31

B. Lesson Title: Learning to Soar like the Eagle

C. Story Objective:
Growth necessitates changes; therefore, God trains us to be spiritually self-sustaining.

D. Vocabulary and Doctrinal Concepts:
1. Vocabulary: molt, pinions, prey, refuge, talons
2. Doctrinal Concepts:
    a. Growth:
        1) Steps toward growth; learning and doing (Deut. 31:12).
        2) Faith leads to knowledge (Prov. 1:7a).
        3) Teach, and "he will increase *his* learning" (Prov. 9:9).
        4) Apply knowledge (Prov. 22:17; 23:12).
        5) Knowledge increases strength (Prov. 24:5).
        6) God's desire for us—knowledge of Him (Hosea 6:6).
        7) "Grow up in all *aspects* into Him" (Eph. 4:15).
        8) "Increasing in the knowledge of God" (Col. 1:10).
        9) "Your faith is greatly enlarged" (2 Thess. 1:3).
        10) "Continue in the things you have learned" (2 Tim. 3:14–15).
    b. Changes:
        1) Divinely appointed changes lead to growth (Ps. 55:19).
        2) "Conformed to the image of His Son" (Rom. 8:29).

3) We shall all be changed (1 Cor. 15:51–52; Phil. 3:21; 1 John 3:2).
        4) Changed "from glory to glory" (2 Cor. 3:18).
        5) God never leaves His work unfinished (Phil. 1:6).
        6) Reaching forth; pressing on (Phil. 3:13–14).
        7) Were dead, now made alive (Col. 2:13).
        8) "Discipline yourself for the purpose of godliness" (1 Tim. 4:7).
    c. The care of the divine Parent:
        1) Carried on eagle's wings (Ex. 19:4)
        2) Ever present (Deut. 31:6–8)
        3) Provides safety (Deut. 33:12)
        4) His everlasting arms (Deut. 33:27)
        5) Strengthens (Ps. 29:11; Isa. 40:31; Eph. 3:16)
        6) Protects (Ps. 91:4; 1 Pet. 3:12a)
        7) Encourages, helps, and upholds (Isa. 41:10)
        8) Teaches (1 Thess. 4:9; 1 Tim. 4:6b)
        9) Knows His own (2 Tim. 2:19)
        10) Trains the child (Heb. 12:6, 10)

E. *Source Book* Keywords: grow in grace, promises, spiritual life of the Church Age (suffering)

F. Activities:
1. Suggested Visuals: none
2. Games, Songs, Worksheets
3. Memory Verse: "But they that wait upon the LORD shall renew *their* strength; they shall mount up with wings as eagles; they shall run, and not be weary; *and* they shall walk, and not faint." (Isa. 40:31, KJV)
4. Opening and Closing Prayer

LESSON
LEARNING TO SOAR LIKE THE EAGLE

I am sure there isn't a girl or boy alive who hasn't wished he need not go to school! Why do you feel that way about school? You are tired of having to learn and study and do homework (Eccl. 12:12*b*). What you seem to forget is the importance of growing up. And learning is just a part of it at all! Wouldn't it be dreadful if you refused to grow physically? Why, you'd still be in your diapers and saying "Dada" and "goo-goo."

The things you learn now will make you the grownups you will be someday. Sure, you're impatient not to be told things and to be on your own. The day will come at last when you graduate from school, and you will leave home to do as you wish. Then you must put to use the things you have learned. You won't be able to run and ask your mother or teacher what you should do. You've left 'the nest' and must fly by yourself!

Just so, the Lord wants you to grow up spiritually that you might serve Him and please Him without being prompted and prodded. For the past few lessons we have attended God's school, where we were taught by animal teachers. Of course, there are many, many more animals in the Bible; all of them teach valuable lessons. But we cannot take time to visit all of their 'classrooms.' Instead, when you read the Word by yourself, see whether you can find out what these lessons are! For example, see whether you can figure out what lesson the fish taught Jonah (Jonah 1:1—2:10)! Today, we shall have a lesson from Mrs. Eagle on graduating from God's school.

"Get off your chairs, in your minds at least, and follow me to my classroom in the sky and to the high, rocky cliffs. There, I will teach you to soar higher and higher and higher until you reach the heights God intended for you to reach spiritually. How do you get there? Why, you *graduate*! Here, let me explain what I mean. There are many verses in the Bible about me. The one I like best is the one that describes my teaching methods—Deuteronomy 32:11. Let me read it to you. 'As an eagle stirreth up her nest, fluttereth over her young, spreadeth abroad her wings, taketh them, beareth them on her wings' (Deut. 32:11, KJV).

"Now here is how I teach my children to get ready to leave the nest: I stir up my nest! You look at me as if you don't know what I am talking about. No, I don't stir it with a spoon! Well, guess I'd better start at the beginning."

The Eagle's Nest

"We eagles might well be called the kings of the birds. We soar to greater heights than any other of the winged creatures. We fly toward heaven (Prov. 23:5*b*). We make our nests in the highest trees and in high rocky crevices that no one can reach (Job 39:27–28). From there we can sight our prey, the animals we eat, far away (Job 39:29). Our eyesight is keen; we miss nothing!

"One day I spotted the perfect place for the nest I intended to build. It was a high and lonely rock with steep and jagged sides. I laid the foundation for my nest—thorn branches, jagged rocks, and sticks. There was a special reason why I chose these, as you will find out before long. Unlike other birds, we eagles build a flat, not hollow, nest. I lined my nest with thick wool and with feathers, with furs of rabbits and lambs I had caught. It turned out to be a delightful nest, cozy and comfortable. The three little eaglets I hatched were snugly settled in the nest."

The Eaglets Nourished

"My eaglets needed constant care and looking after. You should have seen their wide open, hungry mouths; you should have heard them demand food. Small wonder the Bible says that an eagle "swoops on its prey" (Job 9:26*b*)! My eaglets also needed protection. Day after day and night after night I covered them with my feathers, and they were safe under my wings. Perhaps you don't know this, but the strength of the eagle lies in three areas—the beak, the talons, and the wings! One flap of a grown eagle's wings can kill a man!

"We have splendid feathers (Ezek. 17:3). From time to time we molt; we shed our feathers and then grow new ones. As a result we never ever look old, although we live long—a hundred years or more (Ps. 103:5*b*). Now back to my three eaglets. With all the tender care they received, they soon began to grow bigger and stronger. When they were fully feathered, I knew the time had come when they must be taught that they could not always depend on me."

The Eaglets Learn to Fly

"Yet my eaglets were too comfortable to move out. There was but one thing I could do; I had to stir up the nest. Do you wonder how I did it? Well, I tore away the soft, fluffy lining of our nest so that the sharp jagged rocks pricked the tender flesh of my eaglets, and they began to be quite miserable at home.

"Do you think I was a cruel mother? Not at all! I did it for their own good. Where would my eaglets be today if they had not learned to use the wings the Lord gave them? Where would they be if they did not know how to find their food? No, what I did, I did out of love for my children! They had to be made ready and willing for the first flying lesson. Home would soon be too small for them, even as your old clothing is outgrown before you know it!

"What did I do next? Turn to Deuteronomy again and see what God's Word said I did. 'As an eagle stirreth up her nest, fluttereth over her young, spreadeth abroad her wings, taketh them, beareth them on her wings' (Deut. 32:11, KJV). Yes, I fluttered over my young ones. When we eagles fly, we never flutter like other birds. Our long wings are strong and sure in flight; they are made to soar. The reason why I fluttered over the nest was to draw the attention of my eaglets away from themselves and from their complaining and whining over what had happened to their cozy little nest. I rose and shook my wings, spreading them wide, and they began to look up to me. Then they forgot their misery. Their little sharp eyes looked up in surprise, and could they talk they would have said, 'Mother, we didn't know you were so big! How we wish we could get out of this uncomfortable place and fly like you do!'

"That's the moment I was waiting for. What does it say I did next? I took them right out of the nest. Sometimes it only takes a sharp nudge of my beak to get an eaglet to move out of the nest. If that does not work, I grab him with my talons or claws and just throw him out. Now, don't go thinking that I am cruel, after all. Do you think I'd let my little eaglets crash to the ground? Did I feed them and look after them just so I could throw them to their death? Never! Instead of landing on the hard ground, my eaglets land on my soft wings. You'd know this if you had read the verse! I swooped right under my falling eaglets and caught them on my own strong wings. Then I gave them the thrill ride of their lives. I began to rise, a thousand, two thousand, yes, even up to six thousand feet above the ground. My little eaglets looked down to see their nest look smaller and smaller until it disappeared from sight. Now we circled into the clear blue sky.

"At first I could feel my eaglets clutch to my feathers tightly. Then they relaxed their hold. Suddenly I pulled aside sharply. My eaglets slipped, tumbled, and rolled off my wings. They stretched out their little wings and tried oh, so hard to fly. Of course, they were not nearly strong enough to stay up. I knew it and watched them carefully. When they were halfway to the earth, I shot under my little ones and caught them once more on my wings. Soon we repeated this lesson of flying, and the eaglets caught on to it until they learned to fly for themselves. Where are my children today? They are strong young eagles. They are on their own, perhaps even teaching their own little eaglets what they have learned from me. They mount up and soar into the sky, pointing to the Lord who gave them this great power and strength to rise above the things on earth."

As the Eagle, So the Lord

"Now why did I spend so much time telling you about my own eaglets' graduation? Because you, too, need to graduate. God does not intend for you to be a spiritual baby always. His care of you is very much the same as the care and teaching I gave my eaglets. See what I mean? Just look at the first three words of Deuteronomy 32:11 (KJV), and at the first three words of verse 12: 'As an eagle' and 'so the Lord.'"

The Israelites Made Ready to Leave Egypt

Once the Israelites had a cozy, snug 'nest' in Egypt (Ex. 1:7). The Egyptians had made them welcome. That was in Joseph's days. Surely this was a fine land in which to live, the Israelites must have thought. God had to make things rough for them before they were ready—in fact, more than ready—to leave 'the nest' (Ex. 1:13–14). God heard their cry (Ex. 3:7), and He began to 'flutter over the nest.' "I have come down to deliver them from the power of the Egyptians," God said (Ex. 3:8).

Now the Israelites began to see the greatness of God and the mighty miracles He worked (Ex. 7:3b). Under God's watchful care, the Israelites were led safely out of their hard 'nest.' God did not leave them to die in the wilderness. Turn to Exodus 19:4b. "I bore you on eagles' wings, and brought you to Myself." Like the mother eagle, God carried them on His 'wings'; He brought them to Himself. Often He had to teach them hard lessons, but He did it for their own good, and for ours (Rom. 15:4; 1 Cor. 10:11).

We Learn to Fly

Right now, you are still a boy or girl eaglet! You are in a softly feathered nest. You are cared for at home; you are taught the Word. Be like eaglets—hungry for the Word of God. That's the only way you can grow to be strong eagle Christians (1 Pet. 2:2). When God knows that you are ready to begin to unfold your wings to try to fly, He may well pull away some of your comforts. What might be a sharp rock in your nest? Perhaps a sickness or a disappointment, perhaps an ugly, hurtful word said by someone you love.

Should you begin to whine and complain then? Oh no! Look away from the hurt, from the sickness or disappointment. The Lord's still there! "He will cover you with His pinions [feathers], And under His wings you may seek refuge" (Ps. 91:4a). How big and powerful our God is! Will He let you down? Of course not! Just look at Deuteronomy 33:27. "Underneath [you] are the everlasting arms [God's]." Aren't you thankful to know this? When you've learned that you can safely trust the Lord and His Word all the time, you'll have learned to fly on your own! You'll mount up with wings of strength, just as eagles do. Graduate, will you? Grow up to soar to great spiritual heights to God's glory! Think you cannot do it? God gave you all you need—His Holy Spirit, His Word, His Son! The time will come, perhaps sooner than you think, when you must put to use what God gave you and what you have learned. In the meantime, wait, wait upon the Lord and grow stronger and stronger. "But they that wait upon the LORD shall renew *their* strength; they shall mount up with wings as eagles; they shall run, and not be weary; *and* they shall walk, and not faint" (Isa. 40:31, KJV).

What God Wants Me to Know

Are you God's young eaglet? You are, if you have believed in the Lord Jesus Christ (Gal. 3:26). If you haven't, you have the same possibility as has the eagle's egg—to be hatched! What I mean is that you can become God's eaglet. You have been born into your parent's family; now be born again—this time into God's family. "But as many as received Him, to them He gave the right to become children of God, *even* to those who believe in His name" (John 1:12). Do it now, and just see what God can do for you and with you!

Memory Verse

"But they that wait upon the LORD shall renew *their* strength; they shall mount up with wings as eagles; they shall run, and not be weary; *and* they shall walk, and not faint." (Isa. 40:31, KJV)

Chapter Ten

The Trinity

OVERVIEW

A. Subject: The Trinity—Genesis 1; Isaiah 6:1–3; Matthew 3

B. Lesson Titles:
1. Lesson One: Pictures of the Invisible God
2. Lesson Two: Two Pictures of the Trinity

C. Story Objective:

The doctrine of the Trinity declares God three in personality, one in essence. God the Father, God the Son, and God the Holy Spirit are not three Gods, but one God without blending or dividing of substance. They are presented with distinctions as three separate persons in the union of *one*. God's full title is a threefold name: God the Father, God the Son, and God the Holy Spirit (Matt. 28:19).

Each member of the Trinity is made up of the same divine characteristics, making each one equal to the other members (John 10:30; 16:15). God the Holy Spirit is as much God as God the Son; God the Son is as much God as God the Father.

The term "Trinity" is never once found in Scripture; nevertheless, it is a biblical truth. As seen in the Old Testament, the emphasis is on the oneness of God, His essence. However, a plurality of persons is in view in the meaning of *Elohim*, the Hebrew word for God (Deut. 6:4; Isa. 48:16).

In the New Testament, we find the emphasis placed on the individual persons of the Trinity and their individual responsibilities in the plan of redemption. Thus we learn that the Father planned our salvation (1 Cor. 8:6; Eph. 3:11), the Son executed it (John 4:34; 5:17; Heb. 10:7), and the Holy Spirit reveals it to unbelievers (John 16:8–11) and to believers (John 16:13–14; 1 Cor. 2:10).

In connection with redemption, the First Person of the Trinity can be seen as electing, loving, bestowing; the Second Person of the Trinity as suffering, redeeming, upholding; the Third Person of the Trinity as regenerating, energizing, sanctifying. These several factors of soteriology will be presented in future lessons in this series.

D. Vocabulary and Doctrinal Concepts:
1. Vocabulary: baptism, baptize, holy, hosts, Messiah, restore, Trinity
2. Doctrinal Concepts:
   a. The members of the Trinity introduced:
      1) God in essence, particularly the Second Person (Gen. 1:1; cf. John 1:3)
      2) The Holy Spirit (Gen. 1:2)
      3) The First Person (Gen. 1:3)
      4) The Trinity (Gen. 1:26)
   b. The Trinity in the New Testament:
      1) Present at the baptism of Jesus (Matt. 3:16–17).
      2) The same Spirit—Holy Spirit, the same Lord—Jesus Christ, the same God—the Father (1 Cor. 12:4–6).
      3) All have a part in the Christian way of life (2 Cor. 13:14).
   c. The doctrine of procession, in that order:
      1) The Father sent the Son (John 17:3; Gal. 4:4).
      2) The Father and Son sent the Holy Spirit (John 14:26).
      3) Christ sends "the Helper," the Holy Spirit (John 16:7).

E. *Source Book* Keywords: Christ (baptism), essence of God, John the Baptist, Trinity

F. Activities:
  1. Suggested Visuals: Essence Box, John the Baptist, Trinity
  2. Games, Songs, Worksheets

3. Memory Verse: "Holy, Holy, Holy, is the LORD of hosts, The whole earth is full of His glory." (Isa. 6:3*b*)
4. Opening and Closing Prayer

LESSON ONE
PICTURES OF THE INVISIBLE GOD

Y ou have seen this Essence Box so many times by now that you know the words inside it inside out, backwards and forwards—or do you? Let's see if you do! Let's name them: sovereignty, righteousness, justice, love, eternal life, omniscience, omnipresence, omnipotence, immutability, veracity.

Now, let's suppose that a stranger has just seen our Essence Box. He points to it and asks, "What's all this about?" You would immediately tell him, "This is what God is like." But now you would have to explain what these symbols mean to the stranger; what would you say about this crown, for example? Sovereignty. You would tell him that God is the mightiest King, the Supreme Ruler over all heaven and earth. How would you explain righteousness? Righteousness means that God is perfectly good. Justice—God is perfectly fair. Love—God is perfect love. Eternal life—God's life is forever life, a life which has no beginning and no ending. Omniscience—God knows all things. Omnipresence—God is in all places at the same time. Omnipotence—God is all-powerful. Immutability—God is unchangeable. Veracity—God is truth.

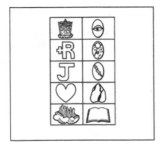

Until we get to be with God in heaven, we will never truly know how wonderful He is. But the more we know of His Word, the more we can know of Him. I think that by now you are ready to take a closer look at God as He is described in the Bible.

To begin with, we will learn a new word and its meaning. The word is "Trinity." Look as you might, you will not find the word Trinity in your Bibles, neither in the Old Testament nor in the New Testament. Why then do we use it, you wonder? Because it best explains what the Bible teaches about God. God is a Trinity. What do I mean by that? God is three persons—God the Father, God the Son, and God the Holy Spirit. Yet God is not three Gods. Rather, He is *one God*.

When the Bible says that God is one God (Deut. 6:4), it means that all three persons of the Trinity have one and the same essence. God the Father is sovereign; God the Son is sovereign; God the Holy Spirit is sovereign. God the Father is righteous; God the Son is righteous; God the Holy Spirit is righteous. God the Father is just; God the Son is just; God the Holy Spirit is just. God the Father is love; God the Son is love; God the Holy Spirit is love. God the Father is eternal life; God the Son is eternal life; God the Holy Spirit is eternal life. God the Father is omniscient; God the Son is omniscient; God the Holy Spirit is omniscient. God the Father is omnipresent; God the Son is omnipresent; God the Holy Spirit is omnipresent. God the Father is omnipotent; God the Son is omnipotent; God the Holy Spirit is omnipotent. God the Father is immutable; God the Son is immutable; God the Holy Spirit is immutable. God the Father is veracity; God the Son is veracity; God the Holy Spirit is veracity.

So, we see that the three persons in the Trinity are exactly alike; they are equally God. Sometimes the Bible calls them "the Godhead," as in Colossians 2:9 (KJV): "For in him dwelleth all the fulness of the Godhead bodily." Some people have twisted this to mean a three-headed God. That is a terrible thing to say. Our great God is one God, but is shown to us in *three distinct, separate persons*. He is a *Trinity*. What, then, does the word "Trinity" mean? Let's take it apart to find out. "Tri-" is the same prefix we see in triplets or trio and stands for *three*; "-nity" stands for unit or unity. The "u" has been dropped so that the word may be more easily pronounced, and so the word has become Trinity instead of Tri-unity. We might say that God is *one unit* made up of *three persons*. *Trinity*: tri and *unity* together mean one unit of three persons; in short—*Three-in-One*.

Think of it this way: Our United States is a country made up of many states. Each state is separate from the others, yet they form one country. Just so, each person in the Trinity is separate from the other, yet they form how many Gods? One God. That's why we often call God "the Great Three-in-One."

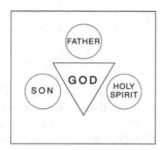

Did you know that there is also a "little three-in-one"? Who might that be? Every believer in the Lord Jesus Christ is a little trinity. He has a body, a soul, and a human spirit. That means there are three separate parts in one person. Do you understand that? Well, perhaps you do not, so I will use another example: an egg! You all know what an egg looks like. What does that egg look like when it is broken? It has three parts now, doesn't it? The egg has a yolk, a white, and a shell. The egg is made up of three separate parts, but it is still one egg.

It is easy to understand something when we can see it with our own eyes, but God cannot be seen. He is a spirit being (John 4:24). We cannot see with our eyes spiritual things like we can see the things around us—the chairs, the walls, or an egg. Does that mean God is not real? There is air all around you, but you cannot see it! God, too, is very, very real. In fact, your next breath depends on Him (Dan. 5:23*b*). We can know and see God through His Word. Shall we see what the Word teaches us about the Trinity?

The Invisible Godhead

The first picture of the invisible Trinity comes to us in the Book of Genesis. Open your Bibles to Genesis 1:26. We read, "Let Us make man in Our image." But, you say, I don't see a picture; I only see a few words here. Words are every bit as much a way to paint a picture as is a brush or pencil. Look again and put your minds to working. What does the word "Us" tell you? "Us" suggests more than one person. But how many persons does the word "Us" speak about?

The best way to study God's Word is to be curious. Ask, "What does the Word say?" Then ask, "What does it mean?" And last of all ask, "What does God want me to learn from this?"

Are you ready to ask the first question? "What does the Word say?" "Let Us make man in Our image." Who said it? When was it said? Where was it said and to whom? Long after God had created the heavens and earth and made the plants and the animals, God the Father said these words: "in Our image," meaning just like Us. To whom did He speak?

Turn to Genesis 1:2: "And the earth was formless and void, and darkness was over the surface of the deep; and the Spirit of God was moving over the surface of the waters." Which person of the Trinity was there with God the Father? The Holy Spirit. Who else? Let's go to Genesis 1:1: "In the beginning God created the heavens and the earth." God the Son was with the Father and He created all things (John 1:1, 3). Now look at Colossians 1:15–16: "And He [Jesus Christ] is the image of the invisible God, the first-born of all creation. For by Him [Jesus Christ] all things were created, *both* in the heavens and on earth, visible and invisible, whether thrones or dominions or rulers or authorities—all things have been created by Him and for Him." Now hold your place and find Isaiah 48:16: "Come near to Me, listen to this: From the first I have not spoken in secret, From the time it took place, I was there. And now the Lord GOD has sent Me, and His Spirit." God the Father was never without God the Son or without God the Holy Spirit. "I was there" refers to Jesus Christ who was with God the Father, "the Lord God," who also sent "His Spirit" or God the Holy Spirit from the beginning (John 1:1).

God the Great Three-in-One is eternal. Just as you have a full name, so God has a full name: God the Father, God the Son, and God the Holy Spirit. How many persons do we have here? Count them: "The Father"—one, "The Son"—two, "The Holy Spirit"—three. Three persons in one God.

So, God the Father had said, "Let Us make man" (Gen. 1:26*a*). To whom was God the Father speaking? That's right, to God the Son and God the Holy Spirit. Who is "Us"? God the Father, God the Son, and God the Holy Spirit. "In Our image" refers to whose image? God the Father, God the Son, and God the Holy Spirit. The Father *plans* all things. We have already said that the Son created all things, and the Holy Spirit restored or made over creation. Each one had His own special work to do. When it comes to our salvation, the Father planned it, the Son worked it out, and the Holy Spirit shows us our need to be saved and gives us new life when we are born again into God's family by believing in Jesus Christ.

What God Wants Me to Know

Perhaps this first lesson about the Trinity was hard to understand. We will not fully understand all about our wonderful God until we are with Him in heaven. But the important thing for you to remember is that when you think of God, always think of Him as a Trinity. God has shown Himself to us in this way in His Word so we may better learn about Him and about what He has done for us.

When the Father said, "Let Us make man," He even planned and knew what you would be like. He knew that there are many things we could never understand unless He would teach them to us. The real teaching of God's Word is done by the Holy Spirit (John 14:26), and the Holy Spirit is in us because of what the Lord Jesus Christ, God the Son, did for us on the cross. He wanted us to know these things about Himself so we in turn could love Him and serve Him better, so we could fully trust Him to take care of us day by day.

No one but a child of God can ever know all the things "God has prepared for those who love Him" (1 Cor. 2:9). Certainly, no unbeliever can even begin to understand the Trinity. But maybe the Holy Spirit, who is as much God as God the Father and God the Son, has awakened a thought in you. He cannot teach you what He teaches believers, but He shows you God's plan of salvation.

Have you ever prayed, "Dear God, show me how I can become a Christian"? God promised that if you or anyone else will seek Him, want to know Him with all your heart or mind, you will surely find Him (Jer. 29:13). Where is God? His home is said to be in heaven. Is there a way to God? Yes, Jesus says, "I am the way, and the truth, and the life; no one comes to the Father, but through Me" (John 14:6). Jesus is as much God as is God the Father and God the Holy Spirit. Only He can save you; "And there is salvation in no one else; for there is no other name under heaven that has been given among men, by which we must be saved" (Acts 4:12).

When you believe on the Lord Jesus Christ, some great things will happen to you. God the Father becomes your heavenly Father. He, God the Son, and God the Holy Spirit come to make their home inside of you (John 14:23). You are made spiritually alive; you now have a human spirit. You become a "little trinity" as you enter into a special, wonderful relationship to God the Great Three-in-One—the Trinity (Eph. 2:1, 5–6).

Lesson Review

What new word have we learned? Trinity. What does that word mean? Three-in-One. Who is Three-in-One? God. Can you name the Great Three-in-One? God the Father, God the Son, and God the Holy Spirit. Which one is the planner of all things? The Father. Which one made all things? The Son. Which one made all things new again? The Holy Spirit. What part did God the Father have in our own salvation? He planned it. The Son? He carried it out. The Holy Spirit? He shows it to the unbeliever and gives him a new birth. Can the Trinity be seen? No. Where, then, can we find out about God? From the Bible. Where was the first picture we saw of the Trinity found in God's Word? In Genesis. What two word pictures were our clues? "Us" and "Our."

Memory Verse

"Holy, Holy, Holy, is the LORD of hosts, The whole earth is full of His glory." (Isa. 6:3b)

LESSON TWO
TWO PICTURES OF THE TRINITY

We want to make two trips to see the next two pictures of the Trinity. Our first trip is to heaven; our second trip is to the river Jordan. Are you ready?

A Vision of the Trinity in Heaven

Many years ago, the prophet Isaiah had a vision; he saw something one does not usually see. He said, "I saw the Lord sitting on a throne, lofty and exalted, with the train of His robe filling the temple. Seraphim stood above Him, each having six wings; with two he covered his face, and with two he covered his feet, and with two he flew. And one called out to another and said, 'Holy, Holy, Holy, is the LORD of hosts, The whole earth is full of His glory.'" (Isa. 6:1–3).

Do you think Isaiah understood why the angels called "Holy, Holy, Holy" three times and why they did not say "Holy, Holy, Holy are the LORDS of hosts"? I think he did; do you? Right, Isaiah understood that God is Three-in-One. God the Father is holy, God the Son is holy, and God the Holy Spirit is holy. To be holy is to be set apart from all others.

Now, what does the word "hosts" mean? This is not the same word as hosts at a party, rather, "hosts" means "armies." God is the Sovereign Ruler of all armies, the angelic armies of heaven and the armies on earth. No armies ever move without His signal, even if they do not know this to be true. Here, in our verse (Isa. 6:3), hosts speak mainly of the heavenly armies. Do you know what "glory" means? It takes many words to describe the word glory. Such words as "honor, beauty, majesty" are used, but I wonder if any of them really fit. To me, "glory" means everything that God is, all wrapped up into one word. Let's all say Isaiah 6:3*b* together. "Holy, Holy, Holy, is the LORD of hosts, The whole earth is full of His glory."

After Isaiah described the Lord, the angels, and what they said, he seemed to be terrified. He had seen the Lord with his own eyes and was sure he now must die. But wait, didn't I say just a while ago that the Trinity cannot be seen? Yes, that's what I said, and now let me explain. Isaiah saw only one person of the Trinity; which one? The Lord Jesus Christ, God the Son, the second person of the Trinity. He is the only member of the Godhead who can be seen (John 1:18; 6:46), though not in our days. Isaiah saw Him as the Sovereign of all heaven and earth, seated on His throne. And so glorious was the sight and the beauty of the Lord's righteousness and justice, His holiness, that Isaiah felt his own unworthiness (Isa. 6:5). How could he—a sinner, though saved—stand before holy God and live to tell of it?

You know, when we see ourselves compared to what God is like, it *is* a miracle that God will let us come to Him in prayer, or serve Him, or finally come into His presence. Of course, to pray and serve God acceptably we must have all our sins confessed and put out of the way (Isa. 6:6–7; 1 John 1:9). And speaking of our own 'nothingness' in comparison to God's holiness and glory, we now see our second picture of the Trinity—this time on earth.

The Trinity at the Baptism of Jesus

There was one time in history when the Trinity was seen and heard on earth. Can you think when that great event took place? I will tell you. It was at the baptism of Jesus Christ. The wonderful story is told in Matthew 3. Turn to that book and chapter.

John the Baptist, the baptizer, was telling of the coming of the Lord Jesus. John the Baptist needed no synagogue or temple or pulpit; he spoke out in the open and his message was so powerful that soon the Temple stood empty. All had gone out to hear John.

The leaders of the Temple were puzzled. What did this John have to say that the people would rather go and hear him than come to the Temple? They decided to go and find out for themselves. They stood and watched and listened.

John was baptizing believers in the river Jordan (Matt. 3:6). And now John told them, "I baptize in water, *but* among you stands One whom you do not know" (John 1:26). "He who is coming after me is mightier than I, and I am not fit [not even worthy] to remove His sandals" (Matt. 3:11).

The people must have looked around curiously. Who could this mysterious Stranger be? Who among all that crowd might possibly be the promised Messiah? Had God at last kept His promise which He had made almost 500 years ago to Daniel (Dan. 9:25)? They had been waiting and looking so long for the Savior!

The very next day, John suddenly raised his head for coming closer and closer was Jesus, the perfect Son of God (Matt. 3:13; John 1:29). Jesus was now thirty years old. He was ready to do the Father's plan and had come to be baptized by John. John and Jesus were cousins, John being the older by six months. John had not seen the Lord Jesus in many years, perhaps not since they were small children, for John had lived in the wilderness for a long time (Luke 1:80). How would he know that this one would be the Son of God? Well, God had promised John a special sign. John was to keep right on baptizing until he saw that sign from heaven (John 1:31). Baptism in water represented identification with the Father's will. For believers it signified that they had accepted God's will for them in receiving Christ as Savior.

Now the Lord Jesus stood in front of John and asked John to baptize Him. John shook his head and tried to tell the Lord Jesus that he was not worthy of such an honor. "I have need to be baptized by You, and do You come to me?" (Matt. 3:14). But Jesus would not hear of John's refusal. He insisted that it be done; He must show openly that He had come to do the Father's will, to save us (Matt. 3:15). Jesus' baptism showed that He identified with the Father's plan for Him to go to the cross.

Gently John lowered Jesus into the waters of the Jordan until the waves covered Him. Then, as Jesus came up out of the water it happened—the promised sign of God! The heavens opened wide, and God the Holy Spirit came down in the form of a dove to rest upon Jesus' head. But this was not all; suddenly the voice of God the Father rang out loud and clear saying, "This is My beloved Son, in whom I am well-pleased" (Matt. 3:16–17). Now John, who may well have heard the miraculous stories of his own birth and those of Jesus, knew beyond the shadow of a doubt that Jesus was indeed the Son of God, the second person of the Trinity.

The Bible does not tell us if anyone else saw this wonderful sign. But does it really matter if anyone else saw the Holy Spirit like a dove or heard the voice of the Father that day? No. They did see Jesus, the Son of God! That is all that matters and what matters most to us is that God has spoken through John to us in His Word. We see this same scene in the pages of our Bible that God gave proof that He is Three-in-One. God the Son showed His readiness to do the Father's will in that He would die for our sins when He came to be baptized by John. God the Holy Spirit showed that He lived in Jesus to help and strengthen Him, and God the Father declared that He was well pleased.

It must have been a wonderful sight! What a picture of the holy Trinity! But let me ask you, how can God be in three separate places all at the same time? One person of the Trinity in heaven, the Father, one coming down through the air, the Holy Spirit, and one in the waves of Jordan, the Son. Right, God is omnipresent; His presence fills heaven and earth. And this same wonderful God is right here as we learn about Him being Three-in-One (Matt. 18:20).

What God Wants Me to Know

Let's pick another of God's characteristics out of the Essence Box—love. Whenever the Bible speaks of God, look to see if the verse or verses refer to one member of the Trinity or all three at once. Let's take the memory verse you learned on love, 1 John 4:19 (NKJV): "We love Him, because He first loved us." Who loves us? God? Yes, but which Person? Or all three?

God the Father loves us so much He sent His Son to die for our sins that we might be saved (John 3:16). God the Son loves us so much He died to save us (John 15:13). God the Holy Spirit loves us so much He gave us new life (Titus 3:5). God's love is three times love! Because His love for us is so great, we also love Him. The more we know of Him through His Word, the more we will love Him. It is God the Holy Spirit who makes real to us the things we learn about God (John 16:7). He helps us want to know all we can about each person of the Trinity. He puts God's love into our minds for others, especially for other believers who love the Lord Jesus. But He also helps us love those who do not yet know Jesus as their Savior.

Do you belong to God's family, to the family of the Great Three-in-One? You need not say so; God knows, and that is all that counts. You have heard of God's great love for you. He gave His Son so you might be made alive to live with Him forever. Love, eternal life, forgiveness, and a human spirit with which to love and understand the Trinity may be yours today. How? Accept God's love for you by believing in Jesus as your Savior.

Lesson Review

In the last two lessons we have learned about God the Great Three-in-One. What did we call the three persons of the Godhead? The Trinity. What were the other new words we had? Holy—set apart for God; hosts—armies; glory—all that God is. Where in the Bible is the word "Trinity" found? Nowhere. We saw two pictures of the Trinity, one in heaven and one on earth. What did Isaiah see? He saw the Lord Jesus Christ sitting on a throne in heaven. What did John the Baptist see? The heavens opened wide, and God the Holy Spirit came down in the form of a dove to rest on Jesus' head. Did John see the Father? No, he heard His voice.

Which of these is 'more' God than the others: God the Father, God the Son, or God the Holy Spirit? None; all are equal. When a Bible verse tells about God, we can generally find out about which person of the Godhead it speaks. Of whom does 1 John 4:19 (NKJV) speak? "We love Him, because He first loved us." Yes, the Trinity—all three persons. How did God the Father show us His love? By sending His Son. And God the Son? By dying for our sins. And God the Holy Spirit? By showing us our need to be saved and giving us a new birth when we believe on the Lord Jesus. Have you received God's three times love?

Memory Verse

"Holy, Holy, Holy, is the LORD of hosts, The whole earth is full of His glory." (Isa. 6:3*b*)

Chapter Eleven

God the Father: The Planner

A. Subject: God the Father: The Planner—Genesis 1:3–27; Luke 12:16–21

B. Lesson Titles:
1. Lesson One: The Planner of Creation
2. Lesson Two: The Planner of Salvation

C. Story Objective:

God the Father is the supreme, Sovereign Head of all things (1 Cor. 8:6). He is the one who planned and designed in eternity past all that was, and is, or ever shall be. He appointed the foundation of the earth (Prov. 8:29), prepared the elements (Job 28:26–27), and set the bounds for the seas (Job 38:11). He is who purposed to make man (Gen. 1:26) and to treat him in grace.

The divine plan eternally centers in the person of the Lord Jesus Christ (Eph. 3:11). It pleased the Father that in Him, Christ, the fullness of the Godhead should dwell (Col. 2:9), and that through Christ He would reveal Himself to mankind (John 1:18; 14:9b; 1 Cor. 2:16; Heb. 1:2).

The great principal point of the entire circle of the Father's purpose is found in the words of John 3:16. Through the grace plan of salvation, by one Son many sons are brought unto glory (Heb. 2:10). Since nothing but perfection can come from the hand of a perfect person, salvation is complete. Man can add nothing to improve the Father's plan, and man can take nothing from it (Eccl. 3:14; Eph. 2:8–9). The believer is both elected and accepted in Christ (Rom. 9:11; Eph. 1:5–6), and God's plan for his life continues in his best interest.

D. Vocabulary and Doctrinal Concepts:

1. Vocabulary: architect, essence, glorify, grace, perish, volition
2. Doctrinal Concepts:
   a. Planner of all things:
      1) "Whatever the LORD pleases, He does" (Ps. 135:6a).
      2) "Declaring . . . things which have not been done, Saying, 'My purpose will be established'" (Isa. 46:10a).
      3) Every purpose of the Lord shall be performed (Jer. 51:29; cf. Ps. 33:11).
      4) "HE HAS PUT ALL THINGS IN SUBJECTION UNDER HIS FEET" (1 Cor. 15:27a).
      5) His purpose is unchangeable (Heb. 6:17).
   b. Planner of creation:
      "Then God [the Father] said"; God plans creation (Gen. 1:3, 6, 9, 11, 14, 20, 24, 26).
   c. Planner of salvation:
      1) "My Father is working until now" (John 5:17).
      2) "He chose us [believers] in Him before the foundation of the world" (Eph. 1:4).
      3) "Works all things after the counsel of His will" (Eph. 1:11–12; cf. Dan. 4:35).
      4) Salvation through Christ from "before the foundation of the world" (1 Pet. 1:19–20).

E. *Source Book* Keywords: creation/restoration, eternity past, God the Father, salvation

F. Activities:
1. Suggested Visuals: none

2. Games, Songs, Worksheets
3. Memory Verse: "For God so loved the world, that He gave His only begotten Son, that whoever believes in Him should not perish, but have eternal life." (John 3:16)
4. Opening and Closing Prayer

LESSON ONE
THE PLANNER OF CREATION

Now, let's take John 3:16, a verse you already know and should have no problem to remember. Some think that this verse is the best loved verse in the New Testament. "For God so loved the world, that He gave His only begotten Son, that whoever believes in Him should not perish, but have eternal life" (John 3:16). What person of the Trinity does this verse speak of? God the Father. God the Father so loved us that He gave His beloved Son, the Lord Jesus, to save us from being separated from Him forever in the lake of fire.

Do you recall which person of the Trinity said in Genesis 1:26, "Let Us make man"? Yes, it was God the Father who spoke those words, for it is God the Father who planned all things that ever were, that are now, and that ever will be. He is the Great Planner.

Have you ever planned anything at all? Perhaps you have said, "Tomorrow I shall get up early and do all my chores so I will be free to play as soon as I get out of school. Then I will go to the ball game, and after that I'll spend the night at my friend's house." You would have planned all your activities; you would have been the planner.

Grown people have lots of plans also. Let's talk about Mr. Brown. He wants a new house. But before anyone builds a house, there must be plans. Since Mr. Brown wants a beautiful, well-planned house, he goes to see an architect. The architect designs the house and draws up plans on paper to show how each part of the house, each room, is to be built. Now the builder gets the plans and follows them exactly, from start to finish, and the house turns out to be very good. Mr. Brown is pleased.

What do you think would happen if a house is poorly planned? Well, there is no telling how it might turn out. The floors might not fit together, the walls may be lopsided, and the roof may not cover the entire house. The money would be wasted on such work. Do you see now how important a well-laid plan is?

Billions of years before man was put on earth, God the Father planned everything. We do not know how He did this, except that He always knew in His mind what He would do. There are many verses in our Bible which show us that the Father planned all things, that He designed our world and everything that is in it. Remember, that is why

Psalm 24:1a says "The earth is the LORD'S, and all it contains." Let us look up some of these verses about the Father, the Great Planner.

God's Plans for Creation and Restoration

Because God is sovereign He can do as He pleases. It pleased God the Father to plan all things. Let's look up Psalm 115:3: "But our God is in the heavens; He does whatever He pleases." The words "God" and "He" refer to God the Father.

Now turn in your Bible to Genesis chapter 1. As we read these verses, can you tell me what the Father planned? Genesis 1:3: "Then God said, 'Let there be light'; and there was light." Light. Genesis 1:6: "Then God said, 'Let there be an expanse in the midst of the waters, and let it separate the waters from the waters.'" The air we breathe. Genesis 1:9: "Then God said, 'Let the waters below the heavens be gathered into one place, and let the dry land appear'; and it was so." Land and sea. Genesis 1:11: "Then God said, 'Let the earth sprout vegetation, plants yielding seed, *and* fruit trees bearing fruit after their kind, with seed in them, on the earth'; and it was so." Plant life. Genesis 1:14: "Then God said, 'Let there be lights in the expanse of the heavens to separate the day from the night, and let them be for signs, and for seasons, and for days and years.'" The sun, moon, and stars. Genesis 1:20: "Then God said, 'Let the waters teem with swarms of living creatures, and let birds fly above the earth in the open expanse of the heavens.'" Sea creatures and birds. Genesis 1:24: "Then God said, 'Let the earth bring forth living creatures after their kind: cattle and creeping things and beasts of the earth after their kind'; and it was so." Animals. Genesis 1:26–27: "Then God said, 'Let Us make man in Our image, according to Our likeness; and let them rule over the fish of the sea and over the birds of the sky and over the cattle and over all the earth, and over every creeping thing that creeps on the earth.' And God created man in His own image, in the image of God He created him; male and female He created them." Man. Did you notice the same clue in each verse in Genesis 1? What was the clue? The words "Let Us make" or "Let there be." Those words show us that God the Father planned before the Lord

Jesus Christ created or carried out the plan, and before the Holy Spirit made things over.

Now turn to Psalm 135:6. "Whatever the LORD pleases, He does, In heaven and in earth, in the seas and in all deeps." Where was God the Father pleased to do the things He planned? In heaven, earth, the seas, and in all deep places. What do you think He planned to do in heaven? Well, there were the angels to be created, and in the lower heavens, there were the stars and planets. What did He plan in earth and sea? Before God ever could put anything on the earth He first had to plan to lay its foundation (Prov. 8:29). He had to tell exactly how far the waves of the sea might go (Job 38:11).

God's Plans Are Perfect

We can only read of how God planned, but we can see for ourselves how perfect God's plans are in every way. Look around you. Notice the plants; watch the big and little creatures on land, in water, and in the air.

Think of a plant coming up out of the ground. The tiny green shoot is so delicate you can cut it easily with your fingernail, yet in the Father's plan this plant received enough strength to force its way through hard earth and even rocky ground.

Think of the common dandelion. You have all seen the fluffy ball of fuzz clinging to the stem as the seeds ripen. I am sure you have picked one of them and blew the fluff apart. What happens then? When the seeds, for that is what the ball is made of, are fully ripe, they ride away on a puff of wind. Each seed has its own personal parachute. Off they go, carried by the breeze, and down they glide to their destination with never a tangled string, never a failure of mechanism. The chute always opens and works, for God's plan cannot fail.

Think of the turtle. It is slow and clumsy and would be completely helpless and at the mercy of its enemies, except for the Father's plan. And what is God the Father's plan for the turtle's safety? A tough, armor-plated shell into which the turtle can withdraw to be safe from its enemies.

Think of a fish. Notice how streamlined it is? That is God's plan for it to be able to move rapidly through the waters. Think of a bird. It flies effortlessly through the sky and lands or takes off just as easily. Man has merely copied the heavenly Father's plans when he designed ships and planes. But who showed God these things? "With whom did He consult and *who* gave Him understanding? And *who* taught Him in the path of justice and taught Him knowledge, And informed Him of the way of understanding?" (Isa. 40:14). No one! God is omniscient. His plans were perfect from start to finish, complete for everything that was to exist on and around this earth, in the world, where it should live, and what it should do—even to the tiniest little things—many of which we cannot even see.

Everything was done just exactly as God planned it. Nothing was too small or too big or too unimportant to escape God's attention. He is interested in all things, for He planned all things (1 Cor. 8:6a).

What God Wants Me to Know

God planned to make man in His own image—like Himself, and man was to be the ruler over all of God's creatures (Gen. 1:26–27). God the Father planned happiness and a heaven for those who would obey His will. He also planned sadness and punishment, spiritual death and eternal separation from God, for those who would not obey Him. He planned to let man decide for himself whether or not he wanted God's perfect plan. Who remembers what we called the ability to decide for ourselves? Yes, volition or free will.

Certainly you and I have said "yes" and "no" many times every day, and this same volition is used by you and by me when we hear the Word of God or His will for us. Imagine, if you will, that the turtle suddenly decides that God's perfect plan is not good enough for Him. So, He says, "Oh, shucks, I'm weary of dragging this old shell around. As far as I am concerned, it's just a big nuisance. I'll just pop out of my shell and fly through the air like a bird." How long do you think the turtle would survive? Would the turtle find the happiness he seeks in his own plans? Never!

Just so, believing boys and girls and men and women cannot ever hope to be happy outside of God's plan. Listen to God's Word carefully and learn from it what God's will is for you. Then decide whether you want God's way or your own way for your life.

God gives every one of us two choices. What two choices am I talking about? Well, if you remember your memory verse, John 3:16, you know one choice. Say it with me: "For God so loved the world, that He gave His only begotten Son, that whoever believes in Him should not perish, but have eternal life." Now turn to John 3:18b, and read what the other choice is: "He [or she] who does not believe has been judged already, because he has not believed in the name of the only begotten Son of God."

God never wants anyone to choose this way of punishment. The Bible tells us in 2 Peter 3:9 that God is "not wishing for any to perish [be lost or destroyed] but for all to come to repentance [or change of mind about Christ]." God's plan is that everyone who believes on God the Son shall have eternal life.

Today you can choose. If you accept God's plan for you, you have chosen the right way. You will become a child of God the heavenly Father (Gal. 3:26), and He will love you every bit as much as He loves His Son (Eph. 1:5–6). You will be made ready to live with God in heaven forever. Only you can decide. Which will it be for you?

Lesson Review

Before the world began, God the Father, the first member of the Trinity, God the Son, the second member of the

Trinity, and God the Holy Spirit, the third member of the Trinity, had a meeting and decided the work each one of them would do. Although their work was to be different, all have the same essence. All three members of the Godhead have exactly the same sovereignty, righteousness, justice, love, eternal life, omniscience, omnipresence, omnipotence, immutability, and veracity. What was the work of God the Father? He planned all things. God the Son was to work out the Father's plan, and God the Holy Spirit was to show God's plan to us. We have seen how perfect God's plan is for all of His creatures. It was part of God's perfect plan that each person have a mind of his own—volition with which to choose whether he will believe and obey God or not.

Memory Verse

"For God so loved the world, that He gave His only begotten Son, that whoever believes in Him should not perish, but have eternal life." (John 3:16)

LESSON TWO
THE PLANNER OF SALVATION

We all know that Adam and Eve used their free will to disobey God. As God had warned them, sadness and sickness, hardships and death came into the world (Gen. 3:14–19). It seemed as though Satan had ruined God's perfect plans altogether. But far from it. No one in heaven or on earth can ruin God's plans. God has the greatest plan of all! Can you think what that plan might be? The plan of salvation. Today we want to find out about this greatest of all plans and about the foolishness of those who think only of making their own plans and leave out God's plan altogether.

The Plan of Salvation

Just what is the salvation plan? Let me explain it to you this way: Suppose you were lost in the desert or forest with no hope of ever finding your way back home. Then someone trustworthy came along and said, "I'll take you back home; I know the way." Would you not be glad? Would you not accept the offer immediately? You would always think of that person as the one who saved you from certain death, your 'savior.'

Salvation is the plan which God worked out to save from eternal death all who are lost in sin. Salvation is God's plan for saving sinners. You may not be lost in a desert or forest, but you are lost or may once have been lost in sin. We are all born lost sinners. How did we get that way?

Lost in Sin

There was once a time when a man and a woman enjoyed unbroken relationship with God in the Garden of Eden. Then, through their own disobedience they broke that relationship with God and became lost in sin (Gen. 3). Hidden among the trees in the Garden, they were as far away from God as if they had actually been lost, hopelessly lost, in the desert. Worse than that, they knew there was no way they could find their way back to God by themselves.

Sought by the Savior

That was when God's perfect plan began to be worked out. The Son of God, the second person of the Trinity, came to seek and save the first sinners (Gen. 3:9). He offered to bring them back once more to the heavenly Father (Gen. 3:15). Although the words of Genesis 3:15 sound different from the words of John 3:16, they spell out one and the same thing—God's plan of salvation, the greatest of all plans. Adam and Eve believed God and accepted His offer. They were still sinners, that is true; but they were now saved sinners. Once again they had a relationship with God, but this time it was a permanent relationship. They were no longer lost, but they still had their sinful natures and these were passed down to each person born into the world (Rom. 3:23; 5:12). So, we are all born sinners. The only difference between us is that some of us are still lost while others are already saved.

How God's Plan of Salvation Works

God the Father made His plan of salvation in eternity past before the world began. God knew that the man whom He planned to make, Adam, would turn against Him. You and I would wonder if it would be worthwhile making man in the first place. It was worthwhile to God. Why? "God so loved the world" (John 3:16a), even a world of lost sinners.

God is a perfect person. From His perfect person came a perfect plan and a perfect Savior. Let's look at God's plan step by step, shall we? (1) A way back to God for sinful man. (2) A Savior. (3) A way by which man can enter into God's plan.

The way back to God would be open if a sinless person paid the penalty, spiritual death, for man's sin. God the Son offered Himself to be our Savior. Would the Father agree to give up His beloved perfect Son? "For God so loved the world, that He gave His only begotten Son, that whoever believes in Him should not perish, but have eternal life" (John 3:16). Yes indeed! God the Father agreed, "You are My Son; today I caused You to be born" (simplification of Psalm 2:7, the doctrine of divine decree). Long before the Son came into the world, the plan of salvation was in the mind of God and was as good as done. This is why, even long before the cross occurred, people were saved simply by believing that God would send the promised Savior, the Messiah. But how would man be able to have God's great salvation? Would man have to prove himself good enough? Would he have to earn his salvation? Could he buy it? No! God's plan of salvation is a grace plan.

No one deserves salvation; no one can earn it or buy it. It is a gift, free for the taking! That is what grace means. "For by grace you have been saved through faith; and that not of yourselves, *it is* the gift of God; not as a result of works, that no one should boast" (Eph. 2:8–9). Salvation is free simply by believing! "That whoever believes in Him should not perish, but have eternal life" (John 3:16*b*). What could be simpler than that? Simple for you and for me, that is, but not for God. Salvation cost God immeasurably, but it costs us nothing! God the eternal Son left heaven and came down to earth in the body of a man to die for our sins, to save us from the punishment which was to be ours. God the Holy Spirit shows us the plan; all we need to do is decide if we will accept it or refuse it. We only have a simple little decision to make. Have you considered God's plan, or are you ignoring it and putting it off for another time? Then listen to this story that the Lord Jesus once told about a man who left God out of his plans.

The Rich Fool, Luke 12:16–21

Once there was a very rich farmer. He owned lots of good, productive land. Because God graciously sent rain and sunshine to make things grow, the farmer received many a rich harvest of food. Soon his barns and sheds overflowed and he had more than he knew what to do with. Can you imagine that?

"What shall I do, since I have no place to store my crops?" he thought (Luke 12:17). So he began to make his plans and he said, "This is what I will do: I will tear down my barns and build larger ones, and there I will store all my grain and my goods. And I will say to my soul, 'Soul, you have many goods laid up for many years *to come*; take your ease, eat, drink *and* be merry'" (Luke 12:18–19).

Yes, that is what he thought he would do; his plans were to tear down the old storage places and build bigger and better ones. Now he would not have to work for the rest of his life and could enjoy himself and live it up! How selfish of him! Never once did he think what God might want him

to do with the great wealth He had given him. Never once did he think of helping others who may have less than he. Never once did he think of his eternal future—only of living right now. Notice, he said "I" and "my" eleven times.

What did God think of that? God called him a fool. "You fool!" God said. "This *very* night your soul is required of you [this very night you will die]; and *now* who will own what you have prepared [what will happen to the things you are planning for]?" (Luke 12:20). Others may inherit this man's riches, but what good will that do him? Salvation is not for sale, so he cannot buy his way into heaven. He had brought nothing with him into the world, and he certainly could not take his riches with him (1 Tim. 6:7).

What God Wants Me to Know

How different things could have been had the rich fool paid attention to God's plan of salvation. "For God so loved the world, that He gave His only begotten Son, that whoever believes in Him should not perish, but have eternal life" (John 3:16). His way to heaven would have been made certain had he only trusted the Lord Jesus Christ instead of trusting in his riches. Riches are fine for what they can afford you here on earth in this life, but God has planned far greater riches for all who accept His salvation plan, riches that will last us for now and for all eternity. God's Word, with its many, many promises, is infinitely more valuable than riches of gold. All that God owns may be yours in Christ.

Think about the rich fool. He thought he had more than enough and a whole lifetime ahead of himself to enjoy his riches. Now think about yourself. Do you know how much longer you will live? No, nor do I. That's why God's salvation plan is a *"now"* plan. Don't wait a second longer, or else it may be too late. If you will make the right decision in a moment of time, eternity with God is yours forever. What about it? Will you be fools, or will you be wise? "Believe in the Lord Jesus, and you shall be saved" (Acts 16:31).

God not only has a plan for our salvation, but He has a plan for the rest of our lives. We who know Jesus as our Savior are to "glorify God." To glorify God, we honor, worship, and make Him great, not ourselves or other people, only God. Ephesians 1:11–12 tells us why we are here: That we "should be to the praise of His glory." It took only faith in the Lord Jesus Christ to save us, for salvation is a gift from God (Eph. 2:8–9), but God's plan for us after we are saved is that we should walk in "good works" (Eph. 2:10). Check yourself often: Am I living according to God's plan for me? Remember, you can know God's plan from God's Word! Am I trusting that God's plan is best for me? Am I acting as God would have me act? Obedience to God's plan will always make you happy and satisfied.

However, our salvation is no guarantee that we will have only happiness. What if someday everything seems to be going wrong for us? Need we be upset? Has God the

Father suddenly slipped up? Has He made a mistake in His plans for us? No, He has not! Let's listen to three different men in the Bible who trusted God's better judgment, no matter what.

First, we will hear what Job has to say. "For He [God] performs [does] what is appointed [planned] for me" (Job 23:14*a*). Next, the prophet Isaiah. He says, "This also comes from the LORD of hosts, *Who* has made *His* counsel [plan] wonderful and *His* wisdom great" (Isa. 28:29). And last, the Apostle Paul. "And we know that God causes all things to work together for good to those who love God, to those who are called according to *His* purpose" (Rom. 8:28). Have you ever heard that verse? Sure, many times. But there is a big difference between hearing, or even knowing, a verse by heart and knowing with certainty that it is true. Paul was sure that all things, no matter how terrible they seemed, were part of God's perfect plan. Are you sure? God may put you to the test before very long. Then remember that God never makes mistakes. He is the perfect planner. Are you not glad you have accepted His plan for time and eternity?

Lesson Review

God the Father planned the earth and everything in it. Can you tell me what the greatest plan of all is? Yes, God's plan of salvation that was the work of Jesus Christ on the cross. Since the time of Adam and Eve's sin, we all have been lost in sin. That's why we need to be saved. Not all people think that they need God's salvation plan for them selves. Some hope to make it to heaven on their own good works; others think only of the here and now. Do you remember the story of the rich fool that the Lord Jesus told when He was on earth? That's right. There once was a very rich farmer who was very selfish and left God out of his plans. God called him a fool.

God does not want any of us to be foolish enough to leave Him out of our plans. Just remember, it is not what you or I can do or will do, but what God has already done for us. Salvation is a gift of God's grace, and accepting Jesus Christ as your Savior is the most important decision you can make.

Does God's plan for us stop after we become His children? Not at all. Actually, His plan for us has just begun. He wants us to be made more and more like our Lord Jesus Christ (Rom. 8:28–29). I know that you will agree with me that we have a long, long way to go. But someday, we will be exactly like Him and enjoy eternal life in the presence of the Great Planner of all things.

Memory Verse

"For God so loved the world, that He gave His only begotten Son, that whoever believes in Him should not perish, but have eternal life." (John 3:16)

Chapter Twelve

God the Father: The Father of Our Lord Jesus Christ

OVERVIEW

A. Subject: God the Father: The Father of Our Lord Jesus Christ—Genesis 22:1–18

B. Lesson Titles:
1. Lesson One: A Father and His Son
2. Lesson Two: God the Father and His Son

C. Story Objective:

In the words of Psalm 2:7, "I will surely tell of the decree of the LORD: He said to Me, 'Thou art My Son, Today I have begotten Thee,'" God the Father acknowledges His eternal and unchangeable relationship to God the Son, our Lord Jesus Christ. This relationship is twofold (2 Cor. 1:3). In His divine nature, the Son is coequal and coeternal with the Father (John 1:1, 18; Phil. 2:6; Heb. 1:2). In His human nature, the second person of the Trinity is the "only begotten Son" (John 3:16), the first person being both the Father and the God of Jesus Christ (Matt. 27:46; 2 Cor. 11:31a), and the Son having humbled Himself to become true humanity and subordinate to the Father, obedient even unto death (Phil. 2:8; Heb. 9:14) that our salvation might be accomplished.

The term "only begotten Son" should be rendered "the only born Son" or "uniquely born Son," and is to be understood in the sense of (1) the uniqueness of the second member of the Trinity as eternal God, yet proceeding from the Father to be manifest in the flesh (John 1:14, 18); and (2) the uniqueness of the only one born into the world without a sin nature through divine conception, i.e., the virgin birth (Luke 1:35; Acts 13:33; cf. Ps. 2:7).

To accommodate our finite understanding, the Holy Spirit inspired the writers of Scripture to use the terms "Father" and "Son" because they best express that intimate relationship which has always existed between these infinite persons of the Trinity. Although "The Father loves the Son, and has given all things into His hand" (John 3:35), "He . . . did not spare His own Son, but delivered Him up for us all" (Rom. 8:32a). Thus God provided Himself with a "burnt offering" to take away the "sin of the world" (Gen. 22; cf. John 1:29—the Bible story used to illustrate this doctrine).

D. Vocabulary and Doctrinal Concepts:
1. Vocabulary: burnt offering, Calvary, confess, crucify, fear (respect), "only begotten," sacrifice, sin offering, slope, true humanity
2. Doctrinal Concepts:
   a. The Father-Son relationship (John 14:11).
   b. God the Son, Revealer of the Father (Matt. 11:27; John 1:18).
   c. The Father recognizes His Son (Matt. 17:5).
   d. Coequal in glory (John 1:14).
   e. His "only begotten [only born]" Son (John 3:16, 18).
   f. Coequal in power (John 5:17–31).
   g. The Son "proceeded forth" from the Father (John 8:42; Rom. 8:3).
   h. Coeternal (John 10:30; Col. 2:9).
   i. The Father of our Lord Jesus Christ (Rom. 1:3–4).
   j. The Son subordinate to the Father in His humanity (1 Cor. 15:28).

E. *Source Book* Keywords: Abraham and Isaac, Christ, God the Father

F. Activities:
  1. Suggested Visuals: Abraham and Isaac, Abraham with Isaac on altar
  2. Games, Songs, Worksheets

3. Memory Verse: "Blessed *be* the God and Father of our Lord Jesus Christ, the Father of mercies and God of all comfort." (2 Cor. 1:3)
4. Opening and Closing Prayer

LESSON ONE
A FATHER AND HIS SON

A very definite part of God's plan is that we learn as much about Him as we possibly can. You see, we cannot possibly love God until we get to know Him! But how can we get to know Him since we cannot see Him, and since we have never met Him personally?

Let me put it this way: I have never met Johnny's father, so I know nothing about him. I do not know what he looks like, where he works, or even what kind of work he does. But I surely would like to find out about him. Who best can describe Johnny's father to me? His son Johnny, of course.

Now, who do you think can tell us about the heavenly Father better than anyone in all the world? Open your Bible to John 1:18: "No man has seen God at any time; the only begotten God, who is in the bosom of the Father, He has explained *Him*." Right; God the Son. He has seen the Father in heaven from all eternity, and so He can tell us best what God is like (John 1:1). While He was on earth, He told people in person; now, He tells us about God through His Word (1 Cor. 2:16). God's Word is truth, and the information He has for us is accurate. God the Father always knew how important were the words of Jesus Christ, His Son. That is why God the Father said, "This is My beloved Son, with whom I am well-pleased; listen to Him!" (Matt. 17:5*b*).

Are you ready to listen when God speaks to you through the words of your Bible, through your pastor or Bible class teachers? I hope you are because "faith *comes* from hearing, and hearing by the word of Christ" (Rom. 10:17). Our next two lessons will be about two fathers and their sons—God the Father who is the father of our Lord Jesus Christ, and Abraham who is the father of Isaac. Listen well and see if you can discover in what way our stories will be the same and in what way they will be different.

Abraham and Isaac, a Father and His Son, Genesis 22:1–18

Had you lived in the days of Abraham, you could have met one of the greatest believers of all time. Let's pretend we can meet him now. This is Abraham and his name means "father of a multitude of nations," as we learn from Genesis 17:5. Yet, strangely enough, Abraham had no children to call his own, but he had God's promise that someday he would be the father of a great number of nations. Suppose we could ask Abraham, "Sir, if God allowed you only one wish, what would you ask Him for?" I am sure that he would answer that more than anything in the world, he would like a son of his own (Gen. 15:1–2).

Many years passed, and at last God fulfilled His promise. A son was born to Abraham and his wife Sarah. God had told the happy parents to name their son Isaac (Gen. 17:17, 19; 18:12) because Sarah had first laughed in disbelief at the thought of having a baby in her old age. The Hebrew name "Isaac" means "laughter," and, indeed, with his birth laughter and joy had come to the home of Abraham and Sarah.

Abraham's Love for Isaac

Oh, how Abraham loved his son Isaac, and what a fine boy he was! They watched him grow year by year, and loved him more and more. Isaac was the most precious thing in Abraham's eyes. Perhaps Abraham loved Isaac more than he should have loved him. We do not know for certain, but we do know that God was going to test Abraham to see whom Abraham loved more—God, the giver of the gift, or Isaac, the gift of God.

Abraham's Love Tested

One day God called Abraham and said, "Take now your son, your only son, whom you love, Isaac, and go to the land of Moriah; and offer him there as a burnt offering on one of the mountains of which I will tell you" (Gen. 22:1–2).

Just what was it God had asked of Abraham? That he would first kill and then burn as a sacrifice, an offering to God, his only beloved son, Isaac, for whom he had waited for so many years. And when was he to do it? In a year from now, or two, or ten? No, look at verse 2—"now"! Can you imagine how Abraham must have felt when he heard those words? How would you have felt? What would you have done?

Did Abraham argue with God and say, "Oh no, Lord, surely you could not mean my son! How can you expect me to do such a thing? Why, Lord, I love that boy more than my own life. I don't want to hurt him!" Not Abraham; he did not complain or argue. Instead, he rose early the next morning and cut the wood for the fire. Then, he saddled his donkey, took two of his servants and his son, Isaac, and went to the place God had told him about.

Abraham's Thoughts

They had traveled some time in silence, and surely Abraham had done a lot of thinking. What might his thoughts have been? Perhaps they went something like this: "God promised me a son. He kept His promise. He also promised to make me a father of many nations. Surely He will keep that promise also. If God asked me to offer up Isaac for a burnt offering, He must have a reason for me to do this. Could God want to see whom I love more—God or Isaac? God can do all things: He can give me a son and He can take him from me. He can make him come back to life by raising him from the dead." And so it was that Abraham was ready to follow God's perfect plan for his life. He was willing to give the son whom he loved to the God whom he loved even more.

Abraham's Faith

"On the third day Abraham raised his eyes and saw the place from a distance. And Abraham said to his servants, 'Stay here with the donkey, and I and the lad will go yonder; and we will worship and return to you'" (Gen. 22:4–5). Calmly, Abraham took the wood for the burnt offering and put it on Isaac's shoulders for him to carry; Abraham carried the coals and the knife, and the two went off together (Gen. 22:6).

After they had walked awhile, Isaac said, "My father!" "Here I am, son," Abraham answered. "Behold, the fire and the wood, but where is the lamb for the burnt offering?" Abraham must have looked lovingly at his son. With perfect peace in his mind, he told Isaac, "God will provide for Himself the lamb for the burnt offering, my son" (Gen. 22:7–8).

By now they had come to that place of which God had told Abraham. There Isaac's father built the altar and laid the wood in order upon it. It was only then that Isaac found out that he would be the lamb for the sacrifice, for his father bound him and laid him on the altar (Gen. 22:9).

Isaac's Obedience

Isaac had grown to be a strong young fellow. He could have fought his father; he could have jumped down from the pile of wood and run away quickly, but he did nothing of the sort. He knew that his father loved him, even now that he held the knife in his hand, ready to cut his throat. He would obey his father, though it might mean his death.

"And Abraham stretched out his hand, and took the knife to slay his son" (Gen. 22:10). Did he no longer love his son? No, he may well have loved Isaac more than ever now that he knew how much Isaac showed his love for him through his complete obedience. Slowly, Abraham raised his hand when suddenly, the Lord called to him out of heaven, "Abraham, Abraham!" The Lord said, "Do not stretch out your hand against the lad, and do nothing to him; for now I know that you fear [you are trusting] God, since you have not withheld your son, your only son, from Me" (Gen. 22:11–12).

The Substitute Burnt Offering

God had spared Isaac's life. Just as Abraham looked up, he saw a ram caught by his horns in the nearby shrubs. God had indeed provided Himself with an offering! Abraham went quickly and took the ram to offer it in Isaac's place (Gen. 22:13). I am sure that both the father and the son praised and thanked God over and over again. "And Abraham called the name of that place [that mountaintop] The LORD Will Provide, as it is said to this day, 'In the mount of the LORD it will be provided'" (Gen. 22:14).

What God Wants Me to Know

The Lord greatly blessed Abraham because he had been willing to give up his only son whom he loved so much just to please the Lord (Gen. 22:15–18). No wonder God called Abraham "My friend" (Isa. 41:8)!

You may already belong to God's family (John 1:12). Do you love your heavenly Father more than anyone or anything? God the Father gave Abraham a wonderful gift, his son Isaac. Now did Abraham love the gift better than the Giver? No, he loved the Giver better and obeyed and trusted Him, no matter what. When God tested Abraham's love to see whether he loved God enough to do anything God asked of him, Abraham made a perfect score on his test. In school, your teacher gives you tests to see how well you have learned your lessons. In the Christian way of life, God tests us to see how well we have learned to trust Him. We, too, like Abraham, must believe God's promises to pass God's tests.

Our memory verse, 2 Corinthians 1:3, tells us that God the Father of our Lord Jesus Christ is the God of mercy and comfort. "Blessed *be* the God and Father of our Lord Jesus Christ, the Father of mercies and God of all comfort" (2 Cor. 1:3). When the tests come into our lives, He will help us to bear them by His grace and by His strength. He comforts us through these tests so that we will not get upset or worry. When we pass God's tests by faith, He will richly bless us as He blessed Abraham.

While Isaac lay bound and helpless on the altar waiting to die, God showed Abraham a burnt offering to take his place, a ram caught by his horns in the bushes. We, too, are condemned to die because we are all sinners (Rom. 5:12), but God loved us and planned a way out for us. He provided a sin-offering to die in our place. Who was it? Yes, God's own Son, our Lord Jesus Christ. He died that you and I might live. Was that not a wonderful way to prove His great love for us?

God the Son obeyed His Father; Isaac obeyed Abraham, and Abraham obeyed God. Would you like to obey God also? His greatest commandment is that you believe on His Son (1 John 3:23). Will you do this now while we bow our heads and close our eyes? You can say, "Father, I now believe that your Son is my Savior who died in my place." When you do, God the Father will accept you as His son or daughter not because you deserve it, but because He loves His Son in whom you have now trusted. God the Father will accept you "in the Beloved" (Eph. 1:6).

Lesson Review

We found out five important things about a father and his son. Their story is found in Genesis 22:1–18. What were the things which made Abraham and Isaac outstanding believers in their day? (1) Abraham was willing to give his only son to God. (2) Isaac was willing to die in obedience. (3) Abraham the father prepared the wood for the burnt offering, and Isaac himself carried it up the mountain. (4) God the Father saw that Abraham truly loved God and provided a ram to die in Isaac's place. (5) Isaac was saved.

Memory Verse
"Blessed *be* the God and Father of our Lord Jesus Christ, the Father of mercies and God of all comfort." (2 Cor. 1:3)

LESSON TWO
GOD THE FATHER AND HIS SON

*N*ow let us look at the other Father and His Son. Who did I say they were? God the Father and God the Son. If you listened well to our last lesson you should have no trouble comparing the two stories step by step. We will see how much alike they are and yet, how very different. And will you please remember that these stories are not just so many words on a sheet of paper; they are real happenings about real people who once lived and loved each other. They tell us about our real God and His amazing love for us who do not deserve His love and grace in the least.

This story is not found in just one chapter of the Bible. Rather, it is the great love story which God tells us little by little from the Book of Genesis to the Book of Revelation, but it could well be summed up in the words of John 3:16.

Can you say that verse with me? "For God so loved the world, that He gave His only begotten Son, that whoever believes in Him should not perish, but have eternal life."

Just what do those words "His only begotten Son" mean? Do they puzzle you? God is the Father of our Lord Jesus Christ from all eternity. Both have the same essence, but when the Lord Jesus Christ, God the Son, came down from heaven to be our Savior, God the Father became His God and Father in a different way—in much the same way as God is our God and Father. Still, the Lord Jesus was different from all of us in that He was the only person born without a sin nature. He had no human father like you and I have; God was His Father. That is why the Bible says that Jesus is God's "only begotten" or "uniquely born" Son, and it means that He was the only one born without sin. Jesus

Christ became true humanity and eternal God in one person. It is about God the Father and His Son we want to hear today.

God the Father Loves His Son

No one could have loved God the Son more than God the Father did. You and I cannot even begin to understand God's love. He loves because He *is* love. When we love someone, we try to do nice things for them, don't we? Well, in His great love, God the Father gave the Son "all things" (John 3:35): The world and all in it, the heavens with all their countless stars, the angels, man, the animals—all things were put in His Son's hand to do with as He pleased.

What joy there was when God the Father sent His Son into the world! No doubt there must have been much gladness in Abraham's family when Isaac was born, and perhaps Abraham's close friends were delighted as well. But when God's uniquely born Son came, there was even greater joy. The angels in heaven rejoiced and sang, "Glory to God in the highest," and they brought the good news of His birth "for all the people" (Luke 2:10, 14). So glad were the shepherds when they heard the angels that they left their sheep and ran to see the Baby in the manger.

The Boy Jesus was much loved, not only by Mary and Joseph and all those who knew Him, but also by His heavenly Father. How pleased God the Father must have been to watch His perfect Son grow in size and become strong in His spirit. How wise He was and how full of grace (Luke 2:40, 52), always pleasing, always obedient! One just could not help loving Him!

Yes, in this way and up to this point our two stories are much the same, but now watch and see if you can tell the difference.

The Proof of the Father's and the Son's Love

Neither Abraham nor Isaac had any idea that someday they would have to face such a great test as God would put in their way. In fact, Isaac did not know that he was to be offered up until he lay bound on the altar. Now, where does the difference in our stories come in? Right. Both God the Father and God the Son knew from all eternity what would happen. Both are omniscient. Both knew the plan of salvation. God the Son had offered Himself to the Father. When He lay there as a tiny baby in the manger, He knew why He had come (Heb. 10:5–7). He had come to die for the sins of the world.

What about God the Father? Had anyone told Him to give His only Beloved Son that sinful man might be saved? No! No one did. He did it of His own free will because He "so loved the world." Shall we look at points one and two in our two stories? (1) Abraham was willing to give his son Isaac, but God the Father actually gave His only Son; and (2) Isaac was willing to die, and so was the Lord Jesus Christ.

The Son's Obedience

The Lord Jesus is the only person who could ever say, "I always do the things that are pleasing to Him [the Father]" (John 8:29), but His perfect life did not and could not save us. He must be obedient unto death, even the death of the cross (Phil. 2:8). And so the day came when God the Son allowed wicked men to lead Him up the hill of Calvary. "Calvary" is the name of a mountaintop in the same range of mountains to which God had sent Abraham and Isaac. In fact, it is quite possible that it is the very same mountain of which Abraham had said, "The LORD Will Provide," for on that mountaintop the Lord *did* provide our so-great salvation.

Now, to point three: Isaac carried the wood up the mountain, did he not? Of what was the cross made on which the Lord Jesus was crucified? Yes, wood. Who carried it up the slope of Calvary? Jesus did (John 19:16–17). Do you remember what Isaac had asked his father along the way? Where is the lamb? But Jesus need not ask. As omniscient God, He always knew that He would be "the Lamb of God who takes away the sin of the world" (John 1:29). How horrible the thought of sin and death must have been to eternal God. Yet in His humanity, Jesus went to His death without a word of complaint (Isa. 53:7).

Like Isaac, He let Himself be bound without a struggle; like Isaac, He could have snapped the ropes easily and walked away. Remember: He is God Almighty. "All authority has been given to Me in heaven and on earth" (Matt. 28:18*b*). He could have walked away, but He did not, for He had come to do and finish the work the Father had given Him (John 17:4).

As we get to point four, we see a big difference. While God showed Abraham a ram to sacrifice in Isaac's place, we are told that God "did not spare [save] His own Son, but delivered Him up for us all" (Rom. 8:32). He watched as the Lord Jesus was nailed to the cross, the innocent—free from sin, for the guilty—you and I. Why did He not stop His Son's suffering? Why did He not send His angels and strike dead those who hurt His Son? Did God no longer love Him? Far from it. God proved His love for us by letting Jesus Christ die for our sins (Rom. 5:8).

ABRAHAM AND ISAAC (Gen. 22:1–18)	GOD THE FATHER AND SON (John 3:16)
(1) Willing to give his only son	(1) Gave His only begotten Son
(2) Son willing to die	(2) Son willing to die
(3) Isaac carried wood	(3) Jesus carried cross
(4) Ram died for Isaac	(4) Jesus died for us
(5) Isaac was saved	(5) Believer is saved

Our Sins Judged in God's Son

Many people miss this point completely. They say, "God is love," and they are right. He is! But they forget that God is also righteous and just. He cannot overlook sin and make believe it is not as bad as all that. Sin is sin and sin must be punished, or else God is not just. Now think of it! If the Father did not even spare His perfect, beloved Son when He was made sin for us, why should the Father not punish anyone who refuses or does not want the salvation Christ has provided on that mountaintop? You and I deserved to be judged for our sins, but God put all our sins on Christ instead. That's why we read in God's Word that "Salvation belongs to the LORD," from start to finish (Ps. 3:8; cf. Ps. 2:7). God accepted His Son as an offering in our place. What happened in Isaac's case happens to us as well; Isaac was saved and so is everyone who believes on the Lord Jesus Christ.

God's Thoughts

What did God the Father and God the Son think during those long, painful hours? Well, I can tell you exactly what they thought. They thought of you and me. God the Father thought of how very much He loves us and wants to save us to live as His dear children now and forever (John 3:16; 1 John 4:9). God the Son thought of us. Through the pain, through bearing our sins and being judged for them, He thought of us as His joy! He stayed on the cross for us (Heb. 12:2b). He did not walk away from that cross free. Instead, He made us free from sin and spiritual death. Then, at last He cried out, "It is finished!" Yes, God's plan of salvation had been worked out for us. All that is left for you to do now is to do some serious thinking yourself!

What God Wants Me to Know

Think back to the cross, to all that God did for you there. The Father gave His Son for you. The Son gave Himself to save you from eternal punishment in the lake of fire (John 3:36b). He died that you might live forevermore. Then God the Father raised His Son from the dead. He also gave "Him the name which is above every name, that at the name of Jesus EVERY KNEE SHOULD BOW, of those who are in heaven, and on earth, and under the earth, and that every tongue should confess [admit, name] that Jesus Christ is Lord, to the glory of God the Father" (Phil. 2:9–11). Only the Lord Jesus can save you (Acts 4:12). Are you ready to let Him do it right now?

Lesson Review

Let's make a game of our review, shall we? I will give you the four answers to my questions. These are the answers: "God the Father, the Lord Jesus Christ, Abraham, and Isaac."

Who wanted a son of his own more than anything? Abraham. What did he call this son? Isaac. What is the name of the only begotten Son of the Father? Jesus Christ. Who is the Father of the Lord Jesus Christ? God the Father. Who is the only one born without a sin nature? Jesus Christ.

The next two questions have more than one answer. Watch them closely. Who loved His/his only Son/son dearly? God the Father and Abraham. Who asked whom to offer up whom? God the Father asked Abraham to offer up Isaac. Who obeyed His Father in all things? Jesus Christ. Who was the Lamb offered up for the world? Jesus Christ. Who carried the wood up the mountain? Isaac. Who carried the fire and the knife? Abraham.

Who am I thinking about? Nobody asked Him to offer up His Son? God the Father. Who did not know and who did know that He/he was to be the sacrifice? Isaac did not know; Jesus Christ knew. Who provided a ram to die in whose place? God the Father provided a ram to die in Isaac's place. Who never struggled when he was tied to the altar? Isaac. Who said, "In the mount of the LORD it will be provided"? Abraham. Who would have given his son willingly, but did not have to? Abraham. God saved this one's life but not that One's? Isaac's, not Jesus Christ's. Who provided someone to take our place on Calvary's mountain? God the Father. Who were the two fathers in our last lesson? God the Father and Abraham. Which person of the Godhead must we trust for our salvation? Jesus Christ.

Memory Verse
"Blessed be the God and Father of our Lord Jesus Christ, the Father of mercies and God of all comfort." (2 Cor. 1:3)

Chapter Thirteen

God the Father: The Father of All Believers

<table>
<tr><td colspan="2" align="center">OVERVIEW</td></tr>
</table>

A. Subject: God the Father: The Father of All Believers—Luke 15:11–32

B. Lesson Titles:
1. Lesson One: The Prodigal Son
2. Lesson Two: Once a Son, Always a Son

C. Story Objective:

God the Father of our Lord Jesus Christ is also the God and Father of all who have personally believed in His Son (John 1:12; 20:17b). The fatherhood of God does not extend over the entire human race (John 8:42, 44, 47), but is conditioned upon a simple act of faith on the part of any individual (Gal. 3:26).

The power to transform a member of the human race into a child of God belongs to God alone, God the Holy Spirit being the agent of regeneration (John 3:5–8; Titus 3:5b). When someone believes on the Lord Jesus Christ, he is entered into a personal relationship with God—a child in God's family—and as such he can address God as "Father" (Rom. 8:15). His position in God's family is secure forever (Rom. 8:38–39).

The Holy Spirit testifies that through faith in Christ "we are the children of God" and "fellow heirs with Christ" (Rom. 8:16–17). Like all loving fathers, God the heavenly Father provides what is best for His children (Matt. 7:11). "The estate that falls" to us (Luke 15:12) is stated to be "an inheritance *which is* imperishable and undefiled and will not fade away, reserved in heaven for you" (1 Pet. 1:4). Like all children, we will fail and lose fellowship with God; like all children, we will have to be disciplined for our own good (Heb. 12:5–11). But our heavenly Father is ever ready to receive His children back into fellowship as soon as they return to Him by way of confession (1 John 1:9).

D. Vocabulary and Doctrinal Concepts:
1. Vocabulary: drought, famine
2. Doctrinal Concepts:
   a. General Scripture: God the Father of all believers (2 Cor. 6:18; Gal. 4:6; Eph. 1:5; 2:19; 3:14–15; 4:6; 1 John 3:1–2, 10)
   b. Birth into God's family (John 1:12–13; 3:3–6; Titus 3:4–7; 1 Pet. 1:3–4)
   c. Love of the Father (Prov. 3:12; John 14:21, 23; 16:27; Heb. 12:6)
   d. Provision of the Father (Matt 4:4; 7:7–8; cf. James 4:2; John 14:16, 26; 16:23; Phil. 4:19; Col. 1:12–14; James 1:17)
   e. Discipline, a prerogative and duty of the Father, to encourage restoration to fellowship (Job 5:17; Prov. 3:11; Rev. 3:19)
   f. Eternal security (Eccl. 3:14; John 10:28–29; 1 Pet. 1:5)

E. *Source Book* Keywords: God the Father, parables (prodigal son)

F. Activities:
1. Suggested Visuals: prodigal son and father
2. Games, Songs, Worksheets
3. Memory Verse: "For you are all sons of God through faith in Christ Jesus." (Gal. 3:26)
4. Opening and Closing Prayer

LESSON ONE
THE PRODIGAL SON

What was the relationship of Abraham and Isaac? A father and son relationship. In speaking to Abraham, Isaac would call him "my father," and Abraham would call Isaac "my son." How did Isaac become Abraham's son? By birth. Isaac was born into Abraham's family. When you were born into this world, you were born into a family. At the head of each family is the father. You call the head of your family "father," don't you? Ever since you could think and speak he has been "father" or "dad" to you, and that is as it should be. I am sure you have never thought of calling him "Mr. Smith." Of course not; you are closely related to him. He is your father. But is he my father also?

Suppose I saw your father coming down the road and ran after him, shouting, "Daddy, Daddy!" He would pay no attention to me because he is not my daddy. But if I called him by his name, he would turn around to see what I wanted. No, your father is certainly not my father, nor is my father your father.

There are only two ways of belonging to a family: by birth or by adoption. Once you are in a family you cannot get out of it. Even if you should move away, or marry and change your name as women do, you are still a member of that family. No matter how bad you are, or what shame you may bring to your parents, they cannot say, "He is not my son; she is not my daughter," for you are, and that is a fact. No matter how you feel about them, the fact remains that they are your parents.

Do you know what I am leading up to? I want to show you that God is not the Father of all the people in the world, as some would like to think. He is the Father of all those and only those who have trusted in the Lord Jesus Christ (John 1:12; Gal. 3:26). Once a person is born into God's family, he is a child of God forever. God has become his heavenly Father, and nothing can change that fact! God loves His children whether they are good or bad; whether they love Him and honor Him, or whether they are a shame to Him.

That is something for us to think about, is it not? God the Father, who is the Father of our Lord Jesus Christ eternally, is also the Father of all of us who have believed in God the Son. We call Him "Father" just as easily as we call our human father "Daddy" or "Father." That's what we want to learn about in this lesson and the next.

Our Lord gave us a beautiful illustration of how very much God the Father loves all of His children. Open your Bible to Luke 15:11–26.

The Parable of the Prodigal Son

"A certain man had two sons; and the younger of them said to his father, 'Father, give me the share of the estate that falls to me.' The father divided his wealth between them. And not many days later, the younger son gathered everything together and went on a journey into a distant country, and there he squandered his estate with loose living. Now when he had spent everything, a severe famine occurred in that country, and he began to be in need. And he went and attached himself to one of the citizens of that country, and he sent him into his fields to feed swine. And he was longing to fill his stomach with the pods that the swine were eating, and no one was giving *anything* to him. But when he came to his senses, he said, 'How many of my father's hired men have more than enough bread, but I am dying here with hunger! I will get up and go to my father, and will say to him, "Father, I have sinned against heaven, and in your sight; I am no longer worthy to be called your son; make me as one of your hired men."' And he got up and came to his father. But while he was still a long way off, his father saw him, and felt compassion *for him*, and ran and embraced him, and kissed him. And the son said to him, 'Father, I have sinned against heaven and in your sight; I am no longer worthy to be called your son.' But the father said to his slaves, 'Quickly bring out the best robe and put it on him, and put a ring on his hand and sandals on his feet; and bring the fattened calf, kill it, and let us eat and be merry; for this son of mine was dead, and has come to life again; he was lost, and has been found.' And they began to be merry" (Luke 15:11–24).

Pictures in a Family Album

Now I want you to think of this page in your Bible as a page out of a family photograph album. The first snapshot shows us the father and his two sons. Can't you just see them standing there and smiling? The father in the middle, the younger son on his left, the older son on his right side.

Next we turn to the second picture page. Something seems to have gone wrong with the younger son. His smile is gone; in fact, he has a sour look on his face. He seems sulky and unhappy. He has been doing a lot of thinking. Possibly you, too, have had thoughts like his running through your mind. "Father constantly keeps after me," he thinks, "always telling me what to do and what not to do, how to do it and how not to do it, how to behave and how not to behave. I'm just plain sick and tired of it all." Not very nice thoughts, are they? But that's not all; he also thinks, "If I just had the money father is going to give me someday, I'd run off and have my own way."

Do you know what has happened to the younger son? He is still home physically as far as his body is concerned, but he is already miles away from his home and father in his own mind. What has separated him? His own selfishness and greed, his own bad way of thinking.

Let's turn to the next picture. Here we see the younger son smartly dressed with all his belongings neatly wrapped, starting out on a journey. He waves goodbye to his father and is happy to be on his own at last.

But from now on we find seven blank pages where other happy pictures could have been had the son stayed home. We know what happened to our young friend because we have just read about him. What would the Lord Jesus have us learn from His story so far?

What God Wants Me to Know

If you looked really hard at the pictures, you would have recognized the father in our story as God the Father. Now can you guess who the two sons might be? Believers in the Lord Jesus Christ. How did we become God's children? By believing in His Son. Our memory verse, Galatians 3:26, is a very important verse to learn and to remember. "For you are all sons of God through faith in Christ Jesus." We are God's children now and for all time. We do not deserve it; yet God accepts us "in the Beloved," His Son (Eph. 1:6). First John 3:1*a* says, "See how great a love the Father has bestowed upon us, that we should be called children of God." Once we are in the family or top circle, we cannot get out. There is nothing we can do, no sin or failure, that will ever remove us from being a child of God. Does God want His children to return His great love? How can we best do it? The Bible tells us how. It says "that we should be holy and blameless before Him . . . In love" (Eph. 1:4*b*). The Lord Jesus tells us in John 14:15, "If you love Me, you will keep My commandments." As long as we obey our heavenly Father, we are blameless before Him. When we

want our own way instead and disobey God, we are like the younger son who left home. Does that mean we are no longer God's children? Not at all. Once a son, always a son! Confess, that is, name your disobedience to your Father in heaven. Then you can ask Him to help you to be a son or daughter He can be proud of!

But what about those who have never accepted for themselves God's plan of salvation through God's Son? What is their relationship to God the Father? They are not related to Him as we, believers, are. Theirs is a relationship of the creature to the Creator.

God had created Adam in the "likeness of God" (Gen. 5:1*b*). But as you know, Adam became a sinner. Since then, Adam's children, that means all of us, were born sinful humanity (Gen. 5:3; Rom. 5:12). To gain entrance into the human family, you must be born of human parents. To get into the family of God, "you must be born again" (John 3:7). You did nothing to receive your first birth; you do nothing for your second birth. Simply believe in the Lord Jesus Christ and you will become a child of God. Then God could look down into our room and say, "you are all sons of God" (Gal. 3:26).

Lesson Review

If we know the Word of God, it is easy for us to tell who does and who does not belong in God's family. God the Father is the Father of some people, but not of others. What verse tells us that only one group of people are God's children, and who are they? Galatians 3:26, believers in the Lord Jesus Christ.

Memory Verse
"For you are all sons of God through faith in Christ Jesus." (Gal. 3:26)

LESSON TWO
ONCE A SON, ALWAYS A SON

Most fathers love their children. How might your father show his love for you other than by telling you so? He provides for your needs and cares for you daily. God's love for His children is even greater than that

of a human father. He not only gives us what we need, but often what we want. The Lord Jesus told us about the heavenly Father's love and care. He said, "Your Father who is in heaven give[s] what is good to those who ask

Him!" (Matt. 7:11*b*). That was what the father in our story did; he gave money to the younger son when he asked him for it, didn't he?

Proof of a Father's Love

There is another way in which your fathers can show you how much you mean to them—by correcting and disciplining you when you have it coming. Your father does not discipline you to be cruel and hateful, but to show you he cares about how you grow up. He does exactly what God expects of him. So don't moan and groan and complain and sulk. Instead, be glad, for even God corrects and disciplines those whom He loves (Heb. 12:6*a*). He cares so much that He wants us to be like His own perfect Son (Rom. 8:29). Remember: That is part of the Father's plan for His own. If God did not discipline us, we would not know how often we fail Him (Ps. 119:71). Let's see today what had to happen before the younger son realized how he had failed his father and how stupid he had been.

The Younger Son in a Far Country

When we left off last time, we talked about all those empty pages in the family album, seven of them. The younger son had left home and had gone on a journey to a far country. He hoped to have a lot of fun and do as he pleased. Carelessly, he spent his money on foolish things and good-time friends until soon it was all gone. Now he was poor and lonesome, without a real friend (Luke 15:13–16).

Just about that time there came a terrible drought. It had not rained for so long that nothing would grow and a mighty famine arose in the land. Would the younger son remember his father and the 'good old days'? Would he run home for help? No, the younger son is like so many of us; we will try everything else first. Then, when all fails, we will go to our heavenly Father.

And so the younger son looked around for help among the citizens of the land. Finally, he found one man who would let him feed his pigs. What a terrible job for someone who had been used to being waited on hand and foot, who once had everything he could possibly want! As he threw the garbage to the pigs and watched them eat, he grew hungrier and hungrier by the minute. How he wished he could eat along with them, but no one let him eat even so much as the pig slop. Do you see now how God dealt with this boy?

At last, when the younger son was most unhappy and half starved, he remembered his father's home. Why, how stupid he had been! He had never had it so good! Oh, how he had failed and disappointed his good and kind father. Then he thought about his father's servants and how they always had more food than they could eat. That was when the younger son made up his mind to go back home. He knew that what he had done was sinful. So bad did he feel about having brought shame and hurt to his kind father that he wondered if his father would want him back as a son.

Once a Son, Always a Son

Just because the younger son lives in the pigpen, does that make him a pig? No! Just because he has wronged his kind father, does that make him an outsider to his family? No! Once a son, always a son. Would his father know this and recognize him as a son, or would he indeed make him a servant in his own home? Let's see.

The father had often thought about his runaway son. He missed him so much and wished daily that his younger son would come back home. Can't you just see the next picture in the photo album of the Bible family? The father stands at the door of his house. He shades his eyes from the glare of the sun and looks down the road which his son had traveled so cheerfully some time ago.

He sees someone coming down that road. Why, it was his son—his boy; he was really coming home! Oh, but just look at him! He is weary, dirty, ragged, and so thin! The bag of money which was once bursting full is hanging down empty. But dirty and ragged or not, he was still his father's son. So the father runs quickly to meet him. He hugs and kisses him, for he loves his son as much as ever.

Welcome Home!

Do you recall what the son told his father? How he had wronged him and sinned against God, and how he hoped the father would accept him as a servant? His telling the father that he had done wrong was fine, but the rest about being a servant was all nonsense. It was just as unnecessary as is feeling sorry for sin in order to be forgiven.

The father welcomed his son home gladly. He sent for the very best clothes, shoes, and a ring; he ordered a big meal prepared for his younger son and invited friends to share his happiness over the son's return. I think the next picture could well show a happy group of people, and it would make a lovely ending to our story. But is this the end of the story?

The Jealousy of the Older Son

There was only one who was not glad that the younger son had returned. Who was it? The older son. He thought that the younger brother certainly did not deserve being made so welcome. He was downright jealous. Jealousy is a sin. It makes an ugly picture of the older son, does it not?

Perhaps we ought to leave it out of our album just like we left out the younger son's pictures while he was away from home. What did the father tell his older son? That he loved him as much as he loved his younger son, and that all he had belonged to his older son as well (Luke 15:25–32). For as long as the older son refused to come into the house, he was every bit as far away from home as the younger son had once been. I do hope he changed his mind soon and did not miss out on all the fun!

What God Wants Me to Know

That finishes our story, but we would do wrong to close our picture album and go home right now. Instead, let's do what we did last time—look beyond the pictures to ourselves. Where we had a story from the Bible, we will now have the story of our own lives.

Ask yourself, "Is my own picture in God's family album?" The answer is "no" if you have not believed that the Lord Jesus is your Savior. The only way to belong to God's family is "through faith in Christ Jesus" (Gal. 3:26b). But that does not mean that God does not love you. He does. He loves you so much "that He gave His only begotten Son, that whoever believes in Him should not perish, but have eternal life" (John 3:16). Accept the Father's love right now; believe in His Son and listen to a very important lesson which every child of God must know.

God the Father has many children. How did they become His children? By faith in His Son. God's children may differ from each other in looks, in obedience, in faithfulness, in service, and in their love for their heavenly Father. Their sins may be as different as were the sins of the younger son and older son. Still, God loves all of His children with the same amount of love. If you are a child of God, put yourself in the place of the two sons of our story.

They will always be sons whether they are at home, that means in fellowship, or away from home, that means out of fellowship. They belong to God's family eternally; that means eternal relationship with God. There is nothing you or I can do to change that!

Perhaps you are like the younger son, dissatisfied with everything. Should you be? Just what are the riches your heavenly Father has given you? Do you really know? Salvation, eternal life, the Bible with its many promises for now and all eternity, and many, many things besides. "But," you might say, "I am not like the younger son. I have not left home." Oh yes, you have—perhaps not this very minute, but any time you sin. Remember that the son "who left home" as well as the son "who did not want to come inside the house" is an illustration of every believer who sins.

Sin puts us out of fellowship with God. But thank God, there is a way back home to our heavenly Father. It is an easy road—easy for us, but it was hard for the Lord Jesus Christ who died so that we might be forgiven over and over and over again (1 John 1:7, 9). We can come 'home,' back into the bottom or fellowship circle, if we will just confess or name our sins to the Father (1 John 1:9). Say, "Father, I have sinned against You, I have lied to my parents"; or "I have been jealous"; or "I was proud, and I know these things are sinful." That's all! "If we confess our sins, He is faithful and righteous to forgive us our sins and to cleanse us from all unrighteousness" (1 John 1:9).

Our heavenly Father is so ready to forgive us and take us back that He not only forgives the sins we have confessed to Him, but He also cleanses us from sins we do not even know we have done! The son in our story waited a long time before he came home. God had to teach him a hard lesson. Don't be like him. Don't wait even until nighttime. Don't walk back; run and confess your sins as soon as you realize you have done something wrong, in thought or deed! Will God the Father give a party every time you confess? Well, in a way He will. First of all, your sins are forgiven and you are restored to fellowship. Last of all, the angels in heaven rejoice over every sinner who finds his way back to God (Luke 15:7). What kind of a picture do you make today?

Lesson Review

I am going to ask you six questions and you will tell me whether the answer is "in or out of the top or family circle" or "in or out of the bottom or fellowship circle." All right? (1) Where are all who have believed in the Lord Jesus Christ, in or out of the top or bottom circles? Watch this one, it's tricky! All are in the top circle, but only those who are in fellowship at the time are in the bottom circle. (2) Where was the younger son when he fed the pigs? In the top but out of the bottom circle. (3) Confession is the way back into what circle? Bottom. (4) When we have done the worst sins possible, are we in or out of the top circle? We can never get out of the top circle. (5) Was the older son in or out of the bottom circle when he found out why there was gladness at his father's house? Out. (6) When we are thinking sinful thoughts, are we in or out of what circle? Out of the bottom circle.

Memory Verse
"For you are all sons of God through faith in Christ Jesus." (Gal. 3:26)

Chapter Fourteen

God the Son: The God-Man

OVERVIEW

A. Subject: God the Son: The God-Man—John 1:14

B. Lesson Titles:
1. Lesson One: God's 'Show and Tell' to the World
2. Lesson Two: The God-Man-Savior

C. Story Objective:

The doctrines of the incarnation of the Son of God and the hypostatic union are the very foundation of Christianity and undergird all other doctrines in the Church Age concerning the person of Jesus Christ. They span eternity past and future and cover thirty-three momentous years of time—"the days of His flesh" (Heb. 5:7).

In order to cancel out the penalty for our sin and provide our salvation, the eternal Son of God had to become the Son of Man, a true member of the human race, for as God He is not subject to death. It was a stupendous undertaking for the Creator to lower Himself to our sphere that He might lift us up to His own. Conceived by the Holy Spirit and born of a virgin (Luke 1:31–35; Gal. 4:4), God "was revealed in the flesh" (1 Tim. 3:16b) and "dwelt among us" (John 1:14a).

In this unique Person of the universe are inseparably united two natures forever: undiminished deity and true humanity (Luke 1:31–35; John 1:1–2). Through Him, who is the exact representation of the essence of God, the Father reveals Himself to mankind (Heb. 1:1–3).

The incarnation of the Son of God terminated with His ascension, but Christ continues in His hypostatic union forever. His incarnation accomplished our redemption; His hypostatic union is the basis of His priesthood and mediatorship (Eph. 2:15; Col. 1:21–22; 1 Tim. 2:5–6; Heb. 4:15; 10:20).

D. Vocabulary and Doctrinal Concepts:
1. Vocabulary: ages, disciples, dwell, eternity future, eternity past, flesh, gods, idols
2. Doctrinal Concepts:
   a. Jesus Christ is the unique person of the universe.
   b. As God, Jesus Christ has neither beginning nor end (John 8:58; 17:5; 1 John 5:11–12), is eternally related to the other two members of the Trinity (Isa. 48:16; Matt. 16:16; Heb. 5:5), and never changes (Heb. 13:8).
   c. As man, Jesus Christ is born (Matt. 1:25); experiences a normal growth pattern (Luke 2:40, 52); knows fatigue (John 4:6), hunger (Matt. 4:2), thirst (John 19:28), testing (Heb. 4:15), suffering (Heb. 2:18), and death (Phil. 2:8; Heb. 2:9; 12:2; 1 Pet. 3:18).
   d. As the Son of God, He is the exact representation of the Father (Heb. 1:3).
   e. As the Son of Man, He took on the likeness of man (Rom. 8:3; Phil. 2:7; Heb. 2:14) and was said to be the "seed" of the woman (Gen. 3:15), the promised "seed of Abraham" (Heb. 2:16, KJV), and the "seed of David" (Rom. 1:3, KJV).
   f. The Incarnation is confirmed by the Lord Jesus Himself (John 8:23; 17:8; Heb. 10:5–9), by the Father and the Holy Spirit (Matt. 3:16–17; John 5:32, 36; 8:18), by the Apostle John (John 1:11, 14; 1 John 1:1–3; 4:2), by Luke (Luke 1:31–32, 35; 2:7; cf. Luke 1:1–3), by the Apostle Paul (2 Cor. 5:16), and by the writer of Hebrews (Heb. 1:1–4).
   g. The boundaries of the Incarnation are given in John 6:62 and 8:14b, and the purpose of His coming as

well as His hypostatic union are stated in Hebrews 2:17; 9:15 and 1 John 3:8; 4:14.

E. *Source Book* Keywords: Christ, hypostatic union, the Incarnation

F. Activities:
1. Suggested Visuals: none

2. Games, Songs, Worksheets
3. Memory Verse: "And the Word became flesh, and dwelt among us, and we beheld His glory, glory as of the only begotten from the Father, full of grace and truth." (John 1:14)
4. Opening and Closing Prayer

LESSON ONE
GOD'S 'SHOW AND TELL' TO THE WORLD

Have you ever thought how important words are? Not just the few new words you have learned in our last few lessons, but any words! It takes words to carry on a conversation; it takes words to fill a letter or a book. It takes words to think and to make your thoughts known to others; it takes words to teach this lesson, and it takes words to pray (Hosea 14:2).

Words and speech are a marvelous gift from God to man. No other creature has this ability to clearly think and express thoughts. Why do you suppose God gave this gift to mankind? To let us know His plan and His thoughts, His will and His purpose for our lives. Best of all, to show Himself to us that we might know and love Him. Even so, it is hard for us to come to know God in a real way and as a real person, for He is invisible to our eyes. Perhaps if He spoke to mankind in a voice, we might understand Him.

God did that long, long ago. Think back to a lesson you had about God giving the Law to Moses. That day, when all the Israelites had gathered at the foot of Mount Sinai, God spoke to them in person. How did God's people react when they heard His voice? They were scared to death and begged Moses to pass along God's words to them for fear they might die (Ex. 19:16; 20:18–19). Instead of understanding God, most people feared Him, or else did not care and paid no attention to His Word.

Dr. Paul White served the Lord in Africa as a missionary doctor. He tells this story of his African helper "Daudi," the African version of "David," and his pet dog. Daudi had dug row upon row of neat little trenches in his small garden patch. Now he was walking up and down the rows, dropping green peas, one by one, into the prepared soil. Soon he hoped to have a fine harvest. Daudi's dog followed close to his heels. But as soon as Daudi had finished planting the peas and turned his back on the dog, guess what happened? The dog dug out the seeds faster than Daudi had planted them. Then he ran to Daudi, his tail wagging happily.

Daudi was sad. What should he do? He loved the dog and did not want to punish him. So he talked to him softly, explaining why he had planted the peas and why his pet should leave them alone. The dog wagged his tail, but as soon as Daudi had turned his back on him, the dog went back to his digging. Time after time, Daudi patiently replanted the peas. He gave the dog a bone to keep him away from the garden, but it was no use. He spoke sharply and even whipped the dog, but it did no good. The dog just did not seem to understand. Daudi shook his head. There was but one way he could make himself understood—he would have to become a dog himself. But, of course, that was impossible!

What is impossible for man is not impossible for God (Luke 1:37). God can make Himself into anything He wishes, and so that we might understand Him, He made Himself into a human being. He became man, yet stayed God in one person forever. Starting today, we are going to study the most wonderful, the most interesting person who ever lived on the earth—Jesus Christ, the God-man.

Open your Bible to John 1:14: "And the Word became flesh, and dwelt among us, and we beheld His glory, glory as of the only begotten from the Father, full of grace and truth." Usually, when we speak of "the Word" we think of our Bibles. How do we know that this verse does not speak of our Bibles? That's easy, is it not? The Bible is God's written Word. It did not become flesh and blood, did it? Who, then, is this verse talking about? Perhaps God the Father? No, we are told in John 4:24*a* that God the Father is a spirit, and we are told in John 1:18 that no one has ever seen Him. Well, could "the Word" possibly be God the Holy Spirit? No, as His title says, the third person of the Trinity is a Spirit; that is, He, too, is invisible. That leaves the second person of the Trinity—God the Son. Let's be sure the verse really means Him. "In the beginning was the Word, and the Word was with God, and the Word was God. He was in the beginning with God. All things came into being by Him, and apart from Him nothing came into being that has come into being" (John 1:1–3).

The Word Became Flesh

Yes, Jesus Christ is the Word of God—not the written Word, but the living Word! So that we might come to know God in a personal way, God the Father sent His Son to be His own 'show and tell' to the world.

The Christmas story, which we all love so well, tells us how God the Son "became flesh." It starts with Mary, the angel Gabriel, and the shepherds on the night of His birth and ends two years later with the wise men coming to see God's only begotten Son. But wait, is this where this most beautiful of all true stories begins? Is this where it ends? Not at all! Instead, we must travel all the way back into eternity past, before time began. Then, we will look at the thirty-three most exciting years of history. Finally, we will travel into eternity future. What a lot of ground to cover in so little time!

Charting the Lesson

God has no beginning. He was there from all eternity past, long before the beginning of time. "In the beginning was the Word, and the Word was with God, and the Word was God" (John 1:1). All right, who are we talking about? God the Son. When was He with God the Father and with God the Holy Spirit? Always. And He will be with them for all eternity future. To make sure you understand, eternity past is the time before time began; eternity future is the time yet to come after time on earth is completed.

The Meeting in Eternity Past

You already know that the Trinity met in eternity past to set up the plan for our salvation. You also know that God the Son offered to become our Savior. However, there was a problem God had to solve first. The second person of the Trinity is eternal life, as are the other two Persons. He could not die! He is God and therefore immutable; He cannot change (Heb. 13:8). He is holy and can have nothing to do with sin. Almighty God can solve every problem, no matter how big it might seem. Where do you think God began in the working out of His great plan?

The Invention of Time

God invented time; "In these last days has spoken to us in *His* Son, whom He appointed heir of all things, through whom also He made the world" (Heb. 1:2). "World" here should read "ages" which is a period of time expressing God's plan for man. Carefully, God prepared all things for the coming of His only begotten Son into the world. Time went on, day by day, year by year. Little by little God made plain where His Son should be born, what His name would be, and what He would come to do. More than three thou-

sand years had gone by in time on earth, but God does not count time as we do (2 Pet. 3:8).

The God-Man Enters the World

The right time had come. The special little body God the Holy Spirit had prepared for the Son of God was all ready. All the Son of God had to do now was to put it on. Did He leave heaven? God does not have to leave one place to be in another at the same time (Jer. 23:24). God is omnipresent! So it was that while the tiny helpless baby lay in the manger, He held up the whole world and carried on a conversation with God the Father (Col. 1:17; Heb. 10:5–9). He knew why He had come, do you?

His Full Name and Title

Who was this amazing Baby? We know Him best by His full name and title, "The Lord Jesus Christ." Look at that name! It is the most important name in the world. Do you know what it means? "Lord" means that this person is God—God the Son, the second person of the Trinity. "Jesus" is a name for a human being, a man. Finally, "Christ" means "the Anointed One," the one whom God had specially marked out to be our Savior. Jesus Christ is the "God-man-Savior." We will learn more about Him in our next lesson.

What God Wants Me to Know

Think about how much the Lord Jesus Christ did for you. God solved your biggest problem, your sin problem. Will you trust Him to solve your little problems day by day?

Perhaps you have not let God handle your sin problem yet. Do you know what Jesus Christ, God's own 'show and tell,' came to show and tell? That God so loved you that He gave His Son to die on the cross and that you may have eternal life through believing on Him (John 3:16). Because of what the Lord Jesus Christ did, God says that every knee should bow to His Son (Phil. 2:9–11). Notice, *should*, not *must*. God gives you a choice. He wants you to receive His love gift of salvation through His Son, the God-man-Savior. Will you do it now?

Lesson Review

Which member of the Trinity could once be seen on earth? God the Son. We know Him best by what name? The Lord Jesus Christ. Can anyone give us a three-word explanation of what that name means? God-man-Savior. What other name is He given in John 1:14? The Word. As the living Word of God, He came to be God's own 'show and tell' to the world. What was He going to 'show'? What God is like. What was He going to 'tell'? How much God loves us. What does this part of our memory verse mean: "The Word became flesh"? That God the Son put on a human body and was born as a man.

In eternity past, God invented time so we would understand His perfect plan better. At the right time, He sent the God-man-Savior into the world. John 1:14 says that the Word "dwelt [lived] among us." For how long? Thirty-three years.

LESSON TWO
THE GOD-MAN-SAVIOR

*I*n which ways is Jesus different from you and from me? Who is the Father of Jesus Christ? God the Father. He had no human father, do you? Of course, you do. That's one way in which He is different. Our human fathers are sinful (Rom. 5:12) and we inherited their sin nature along with Adam's sin. God is sinless. Since Jesus had no human father, was He sinful or sinless? Sinless (1 John 3:5). You are a true human being, but Jesus was more than that; He was and still is God. Jesus Christ is true God and true man in one person forever, the God-man. Be sure you understand that He is not half-God and half-man, but *all* God and *all* man in one person. The unbelieving ancient peoples had idols that were half-god and half-man. Their fish-god, Dagon, had the tail of a fish and the top half of a man. But this is not like the Lord Jesus at all.

There is still another way in which Jesus Christ is different—the most important way of all. I'll give you our side; you tell me His side—all right? We all must be saved, and only He can do what? Save us. These are the greatest ways in which our Lord is different from us. But now, let's see in which way He is the same, shall we?

Do you know the first way in which Jesus was like us? Right, He had a human mother and so do we. What else did He have that we have also? A body. He got tired, hungry, and thirsty, just like we do. He could feel pain and sorrow; He had enemies and friends as we do. His body died and was buried and rose again, as ours will someday. Yes, He had to be like us so we can understand God, and yet He had to be different so He could help us. No one else could have shown us what God is like; no one else could have saved us from sin (Acts 4:12). No one ever spoke like He did or did what He could do (John 7:46). Shall we follow Him around as did the people of His day?

The Days of His Flesh, Hebrews 5:7

Of all the years of history and of all the things that have happened so far, I think the most exciting years must have been the thirty-three years when the God-man lived on earth. First of all, there was His miracle birth. Then followed the happy years when Mary and Joseph, his step-father, were allowed to bring up the Son of God in their own home. What a joy it must have been to watch a perfect Son grow year after year! Jesus had birthdays just like we have, and at last He had grown to be a strong man. He was now thirty years old.

Is it not strange that up till now only a few people had even heard of Him? Why, here was God the Son right among them, and they did not seem to know or even care to know. You and I can hardly imagine such a thing! But there were some who did know and did care; John the Baptist was one of them. Everywhere he went, John announced that God's promised Son had come, that in fact He was already among them and they did not know Him (John 1:18, 26). Did John know who the Son of God was? Yes, for God had shown Him to John at His baptism, remember (John 1:31–34)?

The day right after Jesus was baptized He began to call His disciples or helpers. I wonder what made them follow Him? He did not promise them money. He told them He owned nothing, not even a place where He might lay His head (Matt. 8:20). That might have frightened some people off, but not His disciples. He warned them that they would be hated because He was hated (John 15:18–21); He even offered to let them leave Him (John 6:67). Why did they follow Him, and why did they not go away then?

We Saw His Glory!

I'll tell you why in their own words. Shall we ask John, the beloved disciple of the Lord Jesus, first? It seems that John spoke for the others as well as for himself. Listen and tell me where he said this: "And we beheld His glory, glory as of the only begotten from the Father, full of grace and truth." This is part of your memory verse, John 1:14. Now, find 1 John 4:14 in your Bible to see what else John said: "And we have beheld and bear witness that the Father has sent the Son *to be* the Savior of the world."

Now let's hear what Peter has to say. He, too, spoke for the others. Of course, they did not know that Judas would turn against the Lord Jesus when Peter said, "And we have believed and have come to know that You are the Holy One of God" (John 6:69).

Do you know what I think it must have been like to look at the Lord Jesus while He lived on earth? I am going to have to give you an example so you will understand what I mean. When you look into the mirror, whose reflection do you see? Why, your own, of course! If I could not see you from where I stood, but I could see your reflection in the mirror, I would know that I am looking at you.

The Exact Image of God's Essence

We are told in Hebrews 1:3 that Jesus Christ, the God-man, is the "exact representation," the reflection of God's essence, the exact image of Him whom we cannot see from where we are. That is why the Lord Jesus Christ could say, "He who has seen Me has seen the Father" (John 14:9); "I and the Father are one" (John 10:30). That was what those whose eyes were really open could see then and what we can see now—"the glory of God [everything God is and does] in the face of Christ" (2 Cor. 4:6b).

What He Came to Show and Tell

What a show and tell that must have been! Jesus performed miracle after miracle, so many in fact that John wrote: "And there are also many other things which Jesus did, which if they were written in detail, I suppose that even the world itself would not contain [would be too small to hold] the books which were written" (John 21:25). Yet Jesus did not come to show God's power; rather, He came to show God to man and to tell of God's great love.

However, just telling of God's love would have never saved us. He came to prove God's love for us by dying on the cross (1 John 3:16). More than that, He came also to defeat or win a victory over the devil. Now the devil and sin need not have power over God's children, and we need not fear him any longer.

After His work on earth was finished, the God-man-Savior rose again from the dead and showed Himself to His friends. Then He returned to heaven from where He had come (John 20:17b). You will learn more about the work our Lord did on earth. You will also learn of His death and what happened after that.

God and Man in One Person Forever

The Lord Jesus Christ is seated at the right hand of the Father (Heb. 1:13). He is as much man now as when He was on the earth; He is as much God as He has been from all eternity; He is our own God-man.

What God Wants Me to Know

What is the God-man doing in heaven? We will have a whole lesson about that someday soon, but I can let you in on it now. He is helping those who have trusted Him in many wonderful ways. He prays to the Father for us (Heb. 7:25). He defends us when we sin (1 John 2:1) because His work on the cross allows God to cleanse us from all sins as soon as we confess them to the Father (1 John 1:7, 9).

It will take all eternity to thank and praise our God-man-Savior for all He has done for us, won't it? But we can begin now while we are still on earth. As He once reflected or showed forth the glory of His Father, every believer can reflect the glory of the God-man-Savior. How? You and I can become God's 'show and tell' to the world. When we are in fellowship, we can "proclaim the excellencies of Him" (1 Pet. 2:9b) and we can "go home to your people [our people] and report to them what great things the Lord has done for you [us]" (Mark 5:19b)! We can because we and the Lord are one (John 17:21–23).

What the Lord Jesus Christ has done for us He is ready to do for anyone who will believe on Him. Listen to what the written Word says about the living Word: "He is able to save forever those who draw near to God through Him" (Heb. 7:25). Hear the words of the Lord Jesus Christ Himself: "I am the way, and the truth, and the life; no one comes to the Father, but through Me" (John 14:6). Will you come now, in your mind, believing that the Father sent His Son to be the Savior of the world—your own God-man-Savior?

Lesson Review

In what way was the Lord Jesus Christ the most unusual person ever to be born into the world? He was both God and man in one person. Was He both God and man in eternity past as well? No. Is He still God-man? Yes. How long will He be the God-man? Forever. What does the name "the Lord Jesus Christ" mean? The God-man-Savior.

In what other way was the Lord Jesus different from all others? He was the only begotten Son of our heavenly Father; He was the only one born without a sin nature. He was perfect. How was that possible, since we are all born with a sin nature and Adam's sin? God was His Father. We mentioned that the Lord Jesus Christ was God's 'show and tell' to the world, and today we will discover why He is the very best Friend we have ever had.

Memory Verse

"And the Word became flesh, and dwelt among us, and we beheld His glory, glory as of the only begotten from the Father, full of grace and truth." (John 1:14)

Chapter Fifteen

God the Son: The Mediator

A. Subject: God the Son: The Mediator—1 Timothy 2:5–6*a*

B. Lesson Titles:
1. Lesson One: The Man-in-the-Middle
2. Lesson Two: Bridging the Sin-Gap

C. Story Objective:

God and man were at enmity with one another because of man's position in Adam (Isa. 59:2; Rom. 5:12). In order to bring mankind back into a relationship with God there had to be a mediator who was equal to both parties. Jesus Christ, the eternal Son of God, became a man to be equal with mankind; at the same time He remained deity (Phil. 2:6–8). He was therefore qualified to propitiate God (1 John 2:2) and reconcile man to Him (Col. 1:22).

By dying on the cross, Christ removed the sin problem (Heb. 9:15) and thus became the Mediator between God and man. Where once stood the barrier of sin now stands Christ, the Reconciler and Mediator, as the only means of access to God (John 14:6).

D. Vocabulary and Doctrinal Concepts:
1. Vocabulary: to bridge, chasten, enmity, inherit, iniquity, mediator, quarrel, ransom, scourge, transgression, trespasses
2. Doctrinal Concepts:
   a. The necessity for a mediator: Sin produced spiritual death which separated man from God.
      1) Sin comes between God and man (Gen. 3:8).
      2) God and man must be brought into harmony through a mediator; laying hands upon both demands equality with both parties (Job 9:32–33).
      3) Our sins caused us to be separated from God (Isa. 59:2).
      4) Death through sin (Rom. 5:12; 6:23*a*).
      5) The promise of a mediator (Gal. 3:19–20).
   b. The qualification of a mediator: A mediator must represent both parties in the mediation.
      1) "The Word was God"; "the Word became flesh" (John 1:1, 14; Heb. 2:14).
      2) Jesus Christ—the God-man (Rom. 1:3–4).
      3) "God sent forth His Son, born of a woman" (Gal. 4:4–5).
   c. The work of the Mediator: Jesus Christ removed the cause of the enmity.
      1) "Abolishing in His flesh the enmity . . . that he might reconcile" (Eph. 2:15–16).
      2) Ransomed mankind; declared to be the only mediator between God and man (1 Tim. 2:5).
      3) Became the Mediator of the new covenant to the Church (Heb. 8:6).
      4) Suffered for sins to bring us to God (1 Pet. 3:18).

E. *Source Book* Keywords: Christ (Mediator), Job

F. Activities:
1. Suggested Visuals: none
2. Games, Songs, Worksheets
3. Memory Verse: "For there is one God, *and* one mediator also between God and men, *the* man Christ Jesus, who gave Himself as a ransom for all." (1 Tim. 2:5–6*a*)
4. Opening and Closing Prayer

LESSON ONE
THE MAN-IN-THE-MIDDLE

Have you ever had two good friends, both of whom you loved very much, who became mad at each other? Maybe one hit the other or said something mean about him, so they quit speaking to each other. You found yourself right in the middle. You were just as good a friend to the one as to the other, and you hated to see the good times you all had together spoiled. What would you do? Why, you would try to patch up the quarrel. You would be glad to do anything to get them together again. You would go between them, equally loving to both. Perhaps you would suffer a little yourself by their quarrel, but wouldn't you be happy to see them make up? If you did this for your friends, you would have been the mediator between your quarreling buddies.

The word "mediator" may be new to you. But this little saying may help you to remember this new word and its meaning. Here we go: "The man-in-the-middle is the mediator." Did you know that the God-man was the go-between for all mankind? Our Lord Jesus is our mediator who goes between man and who else? Yes, God.

Sin Comes between God and Man

Once, in the long ago, God and man enjoyed wonderful relationship and fellowship with each other. When was that? In the days when Adam and Eve lived in the Garden of Eden. Do you remember learning that God the Son came down every evening to walk and talk with the first couple in the Garden? What good times they had together! But when Adam and Eve sinned, all that was changed. Ashamed of their sinfulness and afraid, Adam and Eve hid from the presence of the Lord.

What Adam and Eve did not understand was that they need not look for a place to hide, for their "iniquities have made a separation between you and your God" (Isa. 59:2). As sinners, the penalty of death was already upon them and their sin stood in the way—as high as a wall reaching right up to heaven, as deep and wide as any gap can be—and there seemed to be no way for Adam and Eve to come to God.

God can have nothing to do with sin, for He is holy, righteous and just. Man cannot rid himself of sin any more than a dead man can bring himself back to life, for remember Adam and Eve were now dead in "trespasses and sins" (Eph. 2:1b). Both sides needed a go-between. What do *we* call such a person? Yes, a mediator. "The man-in-the-middle is the mediator!"

The Need of a Mediator

For the moment Adam and Eve did not think they needed a mediator. Like so many people today, they tried to do something for their salvation. What was that? Right, they made themselves coverings of fig leaves (Gen. 3:7b).

But let us suppose Adam and Eve sewed enough fig leaves together to build a bridge across the sin-gap. Do you know what those fig leaves stand for? Open your Bible to Titus 3:5 and see if you can tell me! "He saved us, not on the basis of deeds which we have done in righteousness, but according to His mercy, by the washing of regeneration and renewing by the Holy Spirit." The fig leaves stand for our own good works! Right! Now what do you think would happen if Adam and Eve tried to walk across this kind of a bridge? They'd never make it. No, Adam and Eve had to learn they could do nothing to save themselves. What they needed was a mediator between themselves and God. But where could such a mediator be found? As you know, Adam and Eve were the only people then alive!

Could an angel possibly do anything for them? No, we do not read that God sent an angel to tell them how they might have a relationship with Him again. Instead, we read that God Himself came to seek out the sinners. He came because He loved them, even as many years later "the Son of Man" came down to earth in the body of flesh and blood "to seek and to save that which was lost [in sin]" (Luke 19:10).

How "Lost" is Man?

Just how "lost" are we from God? Let's see. Again we must begin with the first man, Adam. God had created him in His own image (Gen. 1:26a; 5:1). Then the first man and woman became sinners. They were still in the likeness of God, but now by their own negative volition they had a sin nature. When their children came along, they took after their parents; they were sinners just like them. Why? Because they inherited Adam's sinful nature, his sin, and were born spiritually dead (Gen. 5:3; Rom. 5:12).

Adam's sin was passed down to us and will be passed down to our own children and grandchildren for as long as there will be people upon the earth. The Bible lumps all of us together when it says, "all have sinned and fall short of the glory of God" (Rom. 3:23). We are all lost from God; we are on Adam's side, and that is the wrong side of the big sin-gap. We are on one side, and God is on the other. Between us is an impassable gap of *sin*.

Find Isaiah 59:2 in your Bible: "But your iniquities have made a separation between you and your God, And your sins have hidden *His* face from you, so that He does not hear." There you have it, our iniquities, our wrong ways, our sin natures have separated us from God! Read Isaiah 64:6. "For all of us have become like one who is unclean, And all our righteous deeds are like a filthy garment; And all of us wither like a leaf, And our iniquities, like the wind, take us away." Here it is again: We are "all" as an unclean thing to God and our sins have taken us away from Him. That's how lost we are—completely and helplessly lost in sin, spiritually dead, and lost from God. That is bad news, is it not? But wait, this is only part of it; there is good news to come. Although neither Adam nor Eve, nor any of us can patch up this 'quarrel' between God and all mankind, God did it all for us. He sent His own Mediator!

The last verses we will look up are found in 1 Timothy 2:5–6a. We will read it together. "For there is one God, *and* one mediator also between God and men, *the* man Christ Jesus, who gave Himself as a ransom for all." I want you to say it over to yourself every day! Think about it and what it means to you! Then you will get much more out of our next lesson, all right?

What God Wants Me to Know

Just as God did everything for us in bridging the gap of sin, so He keeps on doing things for us who have believed in the Lord Jesus. How wonderful it is to know that we will never, ever be separated from God for all eternity as we once were before we believed in Jesus Christ!

Still, it is possible for us to be separated from God in time. The same thing which kept us from coming to God in the first place—sin—now breaks our fellowship with God on earth. Have you wondered lately why good things do not happen to you? Could it be that sin has come between you and God (Jer. 5:25)? Well, what are you waiting for? Confess your sin to the Father. Our Great Mediator is at His right hand. He took care of all sins at the cross, and there is nothing left for you to do but name them to Him. No need to "feel sorry for sin"; no need to "ask forgiveness." These emotions are every bit as useless as Adam's fig leaves were in the Garden! Just name your sins and be glad that on the cross the salvation work of Jesus Christ, God's Son and your Mediator, keeps on cleansing from *all* sin (1 John 1:7). Right away your fellowship with God is restored and you can go on having a good time serving and pleasing Him.

We have not come far enough along in our lesson to see just *how* the Lord Jesus Christ bridged the gap between God and man. But for now it is enough that you know He did! He made the bridge, and all that is left for you to do is to walk across it. "How?" you wonder. Well, how do you cross any bridge, for that matter? By faith, that's how! Suppose you were to cross a bridge over a river. Would you first try to find out who designed and who built the bridge? Would you see if it was strong enough to hold your weight, or long enough to span the river? You would not! You would trust that the bridge would support your weight. Well, if you can trust the work of imperfect men, how much more can you trust the work of perfect God! He not only designed the bridge of our salvation, He built it! And if that was not enough, He gave us His plan and all the information we could possibly ask for in writing.

Aren't you glad He does not insist that you understand every part of it before you can cross over to His side? All He asks of you is that you believe! "Believe in the Lord Jesus, and you shall be saved" (Acts 16:31).

Lesson Review

Now why in the world do we need a mediator? Because God can have nothing to do with sin. Why? Because He is holy, righteous and just. Couldn't God pretend that sin was not really there? Could He not say that some sins are not as bad as others? Why not? It would not be fair or just. God has to carry out the penalty He pronounced on sin. What was the penalty? Death (Gen. 2:17). Do you think a dead person can have a relationship with a living one? Of course not! Much less can a spiritually dead person have a relationship with eternal God. Since man was helpless to do anything about the sin-gap, God had to do it. He had to send the Mediator.

Memory Verse

"For there is one God, *and* one mediator also between God and men, *the* man Christ Jesus, who gave Himself as a ransom for all." (1 Tim. 2:5–6a)

LESSON TWO
BRIDGING THE SIN-GAP

*D*id you ever walk in the mountains and suddenly come to a deep ravine between two cliffs hundreds of feet apart? To jump would mean certain death. If only someone would build a bridge to span the two cliffs, you could get across! Maybe God allowed these cliffs and ravines in nature so He can teach us how helpless we are to come to Him in our own strength! If you had thought about your memory verse last week, you may have guessed what kind of a bridge God built across the gap of sin. Listen to our lesson and see if you were right!

One God

The first part of our memory verse, 1 Timothy 2:5–6*a*, is, "for there is one God." We have already learned that God is one God in three persons. What did we call the Great Three-in-One? The Trinity. In what way are the Three one? In essence. Which two of these characteristics tell us that God is holy? Righteousness and justice. Right! God's holiness keeps Him from having a relationship with lost, spiritually dead sinners. They can only come over to God's side if someone puts a bridge across the sin-gap.

One Mediator

"For there is one God, *and* one mediator also between God and men." Now where must the Mediator be? In the middle. Who is this Mediator? Could it possibly be *sin*? Sin stands between men and God! Why couldn't it be sin? Sin separates, while a mediator does what? Brings two sides together again. Who then is the Mediator? Let's hear what the next part of our verse says, for it gives us the answer: "*The* man Christ Jesus."

The Man, Christ Jesus

Can you tell me why it says here "*the* man Christ Jesus" and not "God the Son"? Well, let me tell you. Remember, God is eternal life. God cannot die. The Son of God had to become a man before He could die for our sins. He is true God and true man in one person—not half-God and half-man—but all God and all man, the God-man-Savior!

To be a mediator, a person has to be equal, the same, and on good terms with both sides. Let's pretend we are patching up a quarrel between two boys. Let's give the boys names, shall we? To our left is Tom, to our right, Jim. In the middle is Larry. Would Larry make a good mediator if he were a stranger to the other two fellows? No! More than likely Tom and Jim would tell him to mind his own business and that they did not ask him for help. But if Larry is every bit as good a friend of Tom's as he is of Jim's, he can make a wonderful go-between.

Long, long ago there lived a man whose name was Job. He once was the richest man in the East. God had blessed him with a large family and had given him great herds of cattle, sheep, and camels. Everyone thought that Job had it made! But then disaster struck. Job lost his children, all his property, and most of his servants. Then, he even lost his health. "What had happened?" wondered Job's friends, "Surely God must have a big quarrel with Job. Maybe Job had done some terrible sin." Even Job got confused in the end. He cried out, "For *He is* not a man as I am that I may answer Him, That we may go to court together. There is no umpire [mediator] between us, Who may lay his hand upon us both" (Job 9:32–33).

What Job meant was that he wished he could talk to God as he might to one of his friends and find out what it was all about. Why would God treat him as He had done? Was there at least one person who might go back and forth between God and Job to make things right between them? Of course, what Job did not know was that God was not having a quarrel with him because Job had believed in the Lord. God was having a quarrel with Satan.

God also has a quarrel with us because our spiritual death has made us His enemies. We, too, need a mediator in the worst kind of way. Why could "*the* man Christ Jesus" be the perfect Mediator between God and men? As God, our Lord has the same essence as the Father and the Holy Spirit; as man, He was flesh and blood like we are. As God, He is sinless; as man, He must remain sinless to be able to die for our sin.

A Ransom for All

As far back as Genesis 3:15, God had promised that someday there would be a go-between, a mediator, to make things right between God and us: "And I will put enmity Between you and the woman, And between your seed and her seed; He shall bruise you on the head, And you shall bruise him on the heel." How was He going to do that? Let's read the last part of our memory verse: "who gave Himself as a ransom for all."

A "ransom" is the price of a prisoner's freedom. God had said the penalty for sin must be paid. Was it a million dollars? Two million, or more? Much, much more! Look at what our verse says: "who [He] gave Himself"! The penalty was spiritual death. Our freedom from the punishment of sin was paid for when the perfect Son of God took our sins and died on the cross in our place. Was that not a terribly high price to pay for stinkers like us (1 Pet. 1:18)?

We are on earth, and God is on His throne in heaven. Between heaven and earth hung the God-man-Savior one day. "He was pierced through [hurt] for our transgressions [sin], He was crushed for our iniquities; The chastening for our well-being *fell* upon Him [He suffered for us], And by His scourging [bruising] we are healed [drawn together]" (Isa. 53:5). Yes, the cross of our Lord Jesus Christ became the bridge over the sin-gap, and His work for our salvation was finished.

But then our Great Mediator rose from the dead and went back to His Father in heaven. We have a living Savior, a living Mediator at the right hand of the Father. He is ever ready to help you. Isn't that wonderful to know?

What God Wants Me to Know

Do you know what happened at the very moment you believed in the Son of God? We will use a chain to show you how Jesus Christ became your Mediator. One link of our chain will stand for you, and another link stands for God the Father. God is perfect righteousness (+R), and nothing less than perfect righteousness can please Him. Man is "minus" righteousness (−R), not good enough to please God. Man cannot come to God as he is. That is why the Lord Jesus came to pay for our sinfulness when He hung on the cross (2 Cor. 5:21). When we believe in Christ Jesus, we receive His perfect righteousness and are now pleasing to God.

Jesus Christ is the missing link between God and man, the middle link. Remember: "The man-in-the-middle is the mediator." Jesus is linked to God by His essence, for He is God (Heb. 1:3). How are we linked to Him? Yes, by faith. When we believed that the Lord Jesus Christ died for us to pay the penalty for our sins, we were put "in Christ" and can never, ever be lost again (Eph. 2:6).

After the Lord Jesus rose from the dead, He went back to the Father. Although we are still here on earth, in a way He took us back to the Father with Him (Eph. 2:6—positional truth). Do you see how safe we are "in Christ?" We are safe because we are one with Him. Christ is in God, one with the Father, and we are in Christ. Who did this for us? The one and only Mediator, our Lord Jesus Christ, the God-*man*-Savior.

Without Him, you and I can do nothing at all (John 15:5). Jesus Christ is in us to fellowship with us (1 John 1:3*b*) so that we can fellowship with God the Father. We pray in Jesus' name and know the Father will do what we ask (John 15:16; 16:23). Have you ever thanked God for your wonderful Mediator?

"For there is one God, *and* one mediator also between God and men, *the* man Christ Jesus, who gave Himself as a ransom for all." He died for *all* so that *all* may be brought back to the Father. The "all" includes you too! There is only one way to God. Jesus Christ is that way. He said that no one can come to the Father any other way but through Him (John 14:6).

Sin no longer keeps you from coming to God. The sin-gap is bridged by the cross of the Lord Jesus Christ. That is why Acts 4:12 says, "there is salvation in no one else; for there is no other name under heaven that has been given among men, by which we must be saved." Notice it says "must be saved," not could be saved, or might possibly be saved—no! We *must* be saved by believing in God's Son, Jesus Christ. This very second, God is waiting for you to make your decision. The Mediator is ready to bring you to the Father forever. Will you believe in Him right now?

Memory Verse

"For there is one God, *and* one mediator also between God and men, *the* man Christ Jesus, who gave Himself as a ransom for all." (1 Tim. 2:5–6*a*)

Chapter Sixteen

God the Son: His Mission

A. Subject: God the Son: His Mission—Matthew 11:5–6

B. Lesson Title: Why God the Son Came into the World

C. Story Objective:

During His incarnation, the Lord Jesus Christ, undiminished deity and true humanity, lived among men as one who served (Luke 22:27). Although He is ever the Sovereign of the universe, He had not come "to be served, but to serve" (Matt. 20:28). His mission required that He veil His glory (John 17:5) and instead take on the "form of a bondservant" (Phil. 2:7).

His ministry, however, was characterized by the performance of miracles. These miracles were to establish His credentials to prove that He truly was the promised Messiah and to gain a hearing for His message (Ps. 77:14; John 10:36–38; 14:11). God the Father verified His Son's claim by word and miracles (Matt. 3:17; Acts 2:22), while the Holy Spirit sustained Him all during His mission (Luke 4:1).

Jesus Christ had come to offer Himself as the Savior of mankind (Luke 19:10; 1 Tim. 1:15). He had come "to His own," but for the most part, the people were not ready or willing to receive Him as their Savior from sin and its penalty of spiritual death (John 1:11). They rejected His message and claim; yet they clamored for His miracles. But to those who recognized Him as the Christ, the Son of the living God, He was precious, for He had the "words of eternal life" (John 6:68–69; 1 Pet. 2:7).

In order that His mission might be fulfilled according to God's plan, His trail of fame led Him to the cross (1 Pet. 1:19–20; cf. Luke 4:37). This chapter presents the Lord's credentials; the next chapter presents the final phase of His ministry on earth.

D. Vocabulary and Doctrinal Concepts:
1. Vocabulary: dumb, identification tag, leper, leprosy, miracle, mission, passport, serve, signs, wonders
2. Doctrinal Concepts:
   a. The beginning of Christ's ministry (Matt. 4:17)
   b. Various aspects of His ministry (Matt. 9)
   c. His credentials, in His own words (Matt. 11:5–6)
   d. His rejection (Matt. 13:54–58)
   e. Recognition and faith (Matt. 14:33; 16:13)
   f. Why He came: to save sinners (1 Tim. 1:15)
   g. Proof of who He is from the Father and the Holy Spirit (Matt. 3:16–17)
   h. Proof of who He is from His miracles:
      1) The blind see (Matt. 9:27–30).
      2) The lame walk (Matt. 15:30–31).
      3) The deaf hear, the dumb speak (Mark 7:37).
      4) The lepers are cleansed (Luke 5:12–15).
      5) The dead are raised up (Luke 8:41–42, 49–56).

E. *Source Book* Keywords: Christ (birth, teaching ministry), hypostatic union, John the Baptist, miracles

F. Activities:
1. Suggested Visuals: none
2. Games, Songs, Worksheets
3. Memory Verse: "Christ Jesus came into the world to save sinners." (1 Tim. 1:15*b*)
4. Opening and Closing Prayer

LESSON
WHY GOD THE SON CAME INTO THE WORLD

*S*uppose the Lord had sent me to teach in some foreign land, perhaps as a missionary; I would need more than an introduction to show others who I am and what I have come to do. I would need a passport. That passport would have my picture and a lot of information about me. It would tell where and when I was born, what my name is, what I do for a living, where I am going, and to what country I belong.

When a soldier goes to war, he is given a small metal identification tag or I.D. tag. The soldiers call it a "dog tag." Maybe some of you have such a tag with your name and address on it. It would tell others who you are in case of an accident, especially when you are far away from home where no one knows you by sight.

When the Lord Jesus Christ came down from heaven, He certainly came from a far, far away place. Did you know that He, too, had something to show to prove who He was? Was it a passport? Or an I.D. tag? Well, you might say it was both; yet it was not something He carried or wore, but what He *did* that proved who He was and what He had come to do.

God with Us

God the Son had left His beautiful heavenly home to come live among men. How glad the whole world should have been! What a welcome He should have been given! Every man, woman, and child should have knelt down willing to serve and worship Him (Phil. 2:10–11). But only a few did: some poor shepherds who heard of His coming from the angels; some wise men who had seen His star in the East; old Simeon and Anna who had eagerly waited for Him; but that was all. How sad to read, "He came to His own, and those who were His own did not receive Him" (John 1:11).

Just think of it, here was God the Son, who had created the heavens and the earth and all that is in them for His own glory, who owns all and rules over all (Ps. 24:1)! But, He had not come as God and King; He came as the God-man-Savior, as God's 'show and tell' to the world. He had made Himself lower than the angels and had become a man.

As "Son of the Most High" (Luke 1:32), God the Son could have been born in a palace and had riches and been waited on hand and foot. But no! Just like you and me, when we were born, He "brought nothing into the world" (1 Tim. 6:7a). He had not come to be served by us, but to serve us instead (Matt. 20:28). The Bible puts it this way: "For you know the grace of our Lord Jesus Christ, that though He was rich, yet for your sake He became poor, that you through His poverty might become rich" (2 Cor. 8:9).

As He Who Serves

What have we ever done that God should lower Himself to serve us? Not a thing! It was by His grace that He came and that He said, "I am among you as the one who serves" (Luke 22:27b). What kind of work, what kind of a service had He come to do? Open your Bible to 1 Timothy 1:15b: "Christ Jesus came into the world to save sinners." He came to save us, and His work was to carry out the Father's plan to go to the cross and to die for our sins. But how was one to know if Jesus really was the promised Savior, the Son of God? After all, other people had come along before His time and had claimed to be the Christ of God (Acts 5:36–37). Even John the Baptist had wondered how he might know Him.

Approved of God

Jesus was now about thirty years old (Luke 3:23). It was time for Him to begin His work on earth, for already John was announcing that the Savior was among them. According to God's plan, John had gone before Him and had prepared the way for Him (Luke 1:76–78; John 1:1–34). John was baptizing people daily, for God had told him "He upon whom you see the Spirit descending and remaining upon Him, this is the one" (John 1:33). John was just waiting to be shown who this One would be.

We learned about the baptism of the Lord Jesus in our lesson about the Trinity. It was then that our Lord showed His first identification or sign. Let's pretend we can see it for ourselves. Do you know what it was? The sign was God the Father's voice: "This is My beloved Son, in whom I am well-pleased" (Matt. 3:16–17), and the dove, God the Holy Spirit, showing John that He had come down to help Jesus in His mission on earth (John 1:32).

But it was not enough for John to know and to tell others about the Lord Jesus. The Lord Jesus had to prove that He really was who He claimed to be.

Miracles, Wonders, Signs

We are told that after His baptism "Jesus returned to Galilee [where He had grown up] in the power of the Spirit; and news about Him spread through all the surrounding district" (Luke 4:14). What do you think made Him so well-known in so short a time? The people had heard some wonderful things about Him, and they wondered if what they had heard was true. Many of them followed the Lord Jesus from place to place. Shall we go with them, in our minds, and hear what they heard and see what they saw? Let yourself think of what it must have been like in those days; make believe that you are in that great crowd. Look that crowd over! What a strange sight it is—the sick, the lame, the crippled, and the blind are there as well as those who are well in body. They are all following Him; they are hoping to see Him do some wonders and miracles.

The Blind Receive Their Sight

Did you ever hear such a noise? Why, these people are trying to outshout one another. What are they saying? The two men nearest to us keep calling out, "Have mercy on us, Son of David!" What is the matter with those two? That is easy to see, isn't it? They are blind. They heard about Jesus; they believe that He is God's promised Savior who can do as much as God can do, for He is God! If only He would make them see!

Now the crowd has stopped. The Lord Jesus has gone into a house. Only the two blind men still push their way through the crowd. They are going right after Him into the house, and they are still crying out for Him to be gracious to them. And we are standing and watching Him who is "full of grace and truth" (John 1:14b). What will He do? He asks, "Do you believe that I am able to do this?" The blind men nod their heads. "Yes, Lord," they say. Now the Lord Jesus reaches out and touches their eyes! Look, the two blind men have received their sight! They can see! How marvelous! They can hardly wait to tell everyone about it. But no, listen to what Jesus tells them: "See *here*, let no one know *about this*!" (Matt. 9:28–30). Why, He had commanded them not to tell a living soul! Why not? Remember: He Himself must show who He is. He Himself must tell what He had come to do. Making people well in their bodies was His way of showing them who He was and that He had come to save sinners.

The Lame Walk; the Deaf Hear; the Dumb Speak

The long line of sick folks keeps right on coming, day after day, after day. Will it ever stop? Had the Lord Jesus come to heal everyone in the world? It almost would seem like that. How exciting to see the lame throw away their crutches and to hear the dumb, those unable to speak a word, shout for joy! How wonderful it must have been for the deaf to hear His voice and the voices of their loved ones!

Listen to the crowd! They are amazed at all Jesus is doing, and they exclaim, "He has done all things well" (Mark 7:37). Now I ask you, could this be anyone but God Himself?

The Lepers Are Cleansed

Now stand aside for this man. He has leprosy! See, everyone is making room for him; no one would want to touch him for fear they would get the sickness as well. It seems the leper has eyes only for the Lord Jesus. He knows

Jesus is God, and he says, "Lord, if You are willing, You can make me clean" (Matt. 8:2). He knows that Jesus is sovereign and omnipotent. He is trusting that the Lord Jesus will do what He thinks is best for him. And wonder of wonders, Jesus touches this man and says, "I am willing; be cleansed" (Matt. 8:3). Right away the man is well. What miracles, what wonders!

The Dead Are Raised Up

But that is not all! Far from it! John, who has seen all the things the Lord Jesus did, tells us that the Lord did so many things while He was on earth that the whole earth could not hold all the books that would need to be written to tell about them all. Come with me just this one more time to see a marvelous thing.

A twelve-year-old girl, the only child of her parents, lay dying. Would the Lord Jesus be able to come in time to heal her? The crowd was pushing Him this way and that so that He could barely move forward. Just then came word that the child had died. Jesus would not need to come to the house now, the servant said. Oh, how wrong he was! Jesus needed to come now more than ever before! Only He could help now, for all life is in God's hands (Ps. 31:15).

How sad to think that the people at the dead girl's house did not believe He could raise her from death. They even made fun of Him. But they were in for a big surprise. Although they did not deserve it, the Lord Jesus made the girl come back to life as simply as if He had awakened her from sleep. They certainly found out that Jesus is the God who does wonders! So it was that everywhere He went, Jesus proved who He was and what He had come to do; God's Son from heaven came to earth to save sinners like you and me. His miracles and message proved that He is indeed who He said He was (John 8:25).

What God Wants Me to Know

You would think that everyone would be ready to believe in such a person as this One! He had shown and told them who He was; He had shown them the way to heaven. He had said that He came to seek and to save the lost, that He had power to forgive sins (Matt. 9:6), and power to raise us from the dead and give us eternal life (John 11:25). Well, did they believe in Him? Some did, but many more did not. Listen to what they said: "Where *did* this man *get* this wisdom, and *these* miraculous powers? Is not this the carpenter's son? Is not His mother called Mary, and His brothers, James and Joseph and Simon and Judas? And His sisters, are they not all with us? Where then *did* this man *get* all these things? And they took offense at Him" (Matt. 13:54b–57a). They only thought they knew who He was— the carpenter's son—a good man, but not God!

One day the Lord Jesus asked His disciples, who had been with Him during His mission on earth, "who do you say that I am?" (Mark 8:29a). Quick as can be, Peter answered, "Thou art the Christ" (Mark 8:29b). Yes, Peter had it right. Now that you, too, have been shown from God's Word that "Christ Jesus came into the world to save sinners" (1 Tim. 1:15*b*), who do you say He is? Do you mean it? Then believe in Him right now, and the greatest miracle of all will happen in your life—you will be saved!

Just before the Lord Jesus went back up to His home in heaven, He said that all who believed in Him were to share the good news of salvation with others. As God the Father had sent Him, so He was going to send us into the world (John 17:18). Believer, you are on a mission for your Lord. Can others see that you belong to Him and that you are glad and proud of it? Does your life back up your words? What a wonderful job He has given us to do, and best of all He has given us the power of God the Holy Spirit to help us all through life. Then, when we go to be with Him, we may hear Him say, "Well done, good and faithful slave [servant]; you were faithful with a few things, I will put you in charge of many things, enter into the joy of your master [Jesus Christ]" (Matt. 25:21).

Lesson Review

Can you quote our memory verse? "Christ Jesus came into the world to save sinners" (1 Tim 1:15*b*).

Do you know what two words I am leaving out of my next sentence? "Jesus Christ did not come to (heal) all sicknesses; He came to (save) sinners." There are three words which describe the things the Lord Jesus did to prove that He is God: wonders, miracles, and signs. The purpose of the miracles was to make the people listen to what He would say. What was His mission? Think of your memory verse, 1 Timothy 1:15*b*. Yes, to save sinners.

The Lord Jesus was offering Himself to be the Savior of the world. He said, "I am the way, and the truth, and the life; no one comes to the Father, but through Me" (John 14:6). He invited everyone to believe in Him and be saved. His invitation is for you as well. Have you done it? I do hope your answer is not "no." But if it is, listen well to our next lessons to learn what Jesus Christ did for you. After that, I am sure your answer will be "yes."

Memory Verse

"Christ Jesus came into the world to save sinners." (1 Tim. 1:15*b*)

Chapter Seventeen

God the Son: His Death

A. Subject: God the Son: His Death—Exodus 12; Luke 22:13–20

B. Lesson Titles:
1. Lesson One: The First Passover
2. Lesson Two: The Last Passover

C. Story Objective:

In God's mind the plan of salvation, which called for the Lord Jesus Christ to become true humanity and to die on the cross for all the sins of the world, was an accomplished fact from eternity past (Heb. 2:9; Rev. 13:8b). The way of salvation always being the same, by grace through faith in Jesus Christ (Acts 16:31; Eph. 2:8–9; Titus 3:5; cf. Gen. 3:15, 20–21; 15:6), God was free to accept the symbolic offering of sacrificial animals throughout the Old Testament. However, the shed blood of these animals—the innocent dying for the guilty—could not take away sin (Heb. 10:4). The animal blood was a symbol that merely illustrated Christ's *covering* or atonement for the guilty sinner. God passed over the sins of the people when He saw the blood (Ex. 12:13) until the coming of the Lamb of God who "takes away the sin of the world" (John 1:29).

The spotless lamb of Scripture portrayed the perfect Son of God; its shed blood stood for the spiritual death of Christ on the cross (2 Cor. 5:21; 1 Pet. 2:24). His physical death was both a voluntary act on His part and a direct result of His spiritual death as His mission on earth was finished (Luke 23:46; John 10:17–18).

With the fulfillment of Scripture, the Passover has given way to the Lord's Table. We now look back to the finished work of Christ, to that day when God the Father provided His own Lamb (Acts 2:23a; 1 Pet. 1:19–20). God the Son laid down His life willingly (John 10:18) and accomplished His mission—our so-great salvation (Heb. 2:3).

D. Vocabulary and Doctrinal Concepts:
1. Vocabulary: atonement, communion, condemn, Egypt, fat portion, firstborn, firstlings, flock, form (noun), forsaken, Israelites, Jerusalem, Jews, judgment, Lord's Table, millstone, New Testament, offering, Old Testament, Passover, Pharaoh, plague, slavery, spotless, wrath
2. Doctrinal Concepts:
   a. The doctrine of the blood:
      1) The blood of Jesus Christ is the basis of our redemption (Eph. 1:7; 1 Pet. 1:18–19).
      2) The blood of Jesus Christ is the basis of our justification (Rom. 5:9).
      3) The blood of Jesus Christ is the basis of cleansing (Heb. 13:12; 1 John 1:7; Rev. 1:5).
      4) The blood of Jesus Christ is the basis of forgiveness (1 John 1:7); mechanics: rebound (1 John 1:9).
      5) There can be no salvation apart from the blood of Christ (Heb. 9:22).
      6) The blood represents Jesus Christ's work on the cross, accomplishing our salvation (Col. 1:20; Heb. 10:19; 13:20; 1 Pet. 1:2); His work is the basis of our sanctification (Heb. 10:10–14).
   b. The Lamb of Scripture:
      1) Provided a covering for the first sinners (Gen. 3:21).
      2) The acceptable offering (Gen. 4:4).

3) A substitute provided by God (Gen. 22:8).

4) Male without blemish, to be killed, roasted, and eaten—Christ, perfect, judged, slain, received by faith (Ex. 12:5–8).

5) The blood applied, saves from judgment (Ex. 12:7, 13).

6) The Lord's Passover (Ex. 12:11; Lev. 23:5).

7) The lamb; a male, a voluntary offering (Lev. 1:3).

8) For our transgressions—as a lamb to the slaughter (Isa. 53:5, 7; Acts 8:32).

9) "He Himself bore our sins in His body" (1 Pet. 2:24).

10) "He laid down His life for us" (1 John 3:16).

11) "Worthy is the Lamb that was slain" (Rev. 5:12).

   c. The Passover:

1) A picture of salvation, redemption (Ex. 12:1–13; cf. 1 Cor. 5:7*b*)

2) To be remembered (Ex. 12:14; Luke 22:19–20: 1 Cor. 11:23–26)

3) The last Passover (Luke 22:14–15)

4) The first Passover: the lamb's blood painted on the door (Ex. 12)

5) The last Passover: the Lord's Table—the bread, His perfect person; the cup, His work (Luke 22:19–20)

E. *Source Book* Keywords: blood of Christ, Christ (Lamb without spot), communion, cross, Passover, salvation

F. Activities:
1. Suggested Visuals: none
2. Games, Songs, Worksheets
3. Memory Verse: "But God demonstrates His own love toward us, in that while we were yet sinners, Christ died for us." (Rom. 5:8)
4. Opening and Closing Prayer

LESSON ONE
THE FIRST PASSOVER

*H*ave you ever noticed your shadow as you walked outdoors on a sunny day? With the sun striking you in the face, your shadow would be cast behind you; with the sun at your back, your shadow would go before you. Your shadow has your form, your shape; my shadow has mine. Yet your shadow is not the real person, the real you, is it? It just shows that you have either passed or that you are coming in sight.

Did you know that God used shadow forms to show the death of the Lord Jesus long before His coming? John knew what these shadows pictured. When He saw the Lord Jesus coming, he called out, "Behold, the Lamb of God who takes away the sin of the world!" (John 1:29). Can you think whose shadow God used? Your clue is found in what John said. Yes, the lamb; in fact, the death of countless lambs down through the years, since the beginning of time. Today, we will stand on this side of the cross, before it actually occurred and we will see the shadow of the cross (Heb. 10:2–9).

The Shadow of the Cross

Who were the first people to see the shadow of the cross? Adam and Eve. God told them of the coming and death of the Savior, and they accepted God's way of salvation. Then God clothed them in coats of skins, and the first sinners understood that the innocent little lambs had given their lives and shed their blood that Adam and Eve might be covered (Gen. 3:15, 21). They understood that this was a picture of what the Savior would one day come to earth and do and that He would give His life so that the sins of all would be covered. They had learned that "without shedding of blood there is no forgiveness" for sinners (Heb. 9:22). This they taught their children, and we read that Abel showed God his faith by offering a lamb from his flock, but that Cain refused God's way of salvation (Gen. 4:3–4): "So it came about in the course of time that Cain brought an offering to the LORD of the fruit of the ground. And Abel, on his part also brought of the firstlings of his flock and of their fat portions. And the LORD had regard for Abel and for his offering."

The death of the lambs was only a shadow picture of the death of God's own Lamb, the Lord Jesus Christ. But we know that where a shadow is there must also be the real thing or the real person. Because God the Son was sure to come at the right time, God the Father could accept the blood of the lambs as a sign of faith on the part of the offerer. Do you remember what the Lamb of God was going to do about our sins? Take them away. Do you think the shadows could do that? No! A shadow can cover, but that is all it can do. So it was that sin was still there, but it was now covered, hidden by the blood (Heb. 10:4). When Jesus Christ would shed His blood, that is, die spiritually on the cross for our sins, sin would be removed altogether. Until then, believing parents told their children how God's plan of salvation worked, that the spotless little lambs were being put to death to picture the Lord Jesus dying in the sinner's place. Someday the shadows would become reality. They could surely trust God to keep His promise.

The Passover Lamb

Let me tell you about the night of the first Passover when the shed blood of many lambs saved the lives of all the firstborn of the Israelites. The Israelites had been slaves in the land of Egypt for about four hundred years. Soon God was going to send a leader, Moses, to take them out of Egypt. Oh, how they longed for that day when they would be free once more! But when Moses came to Pharaoh, the king of Egypt, he would not let them leave. God had to send plague after plague, bad things after bad things, as punishment and warning (Gen. 15:14; Rom. 9:17; cf. Ex. 7:5), and still Pharaoh's answer was "no."

At last God sent Moses and Aaron to the palace with a final warning. This was God's message: "About midnight I am going out into the midst of Egypt, and all the first-born in the land of Egypt shall die, from the first-born of the Pharaoh who sits on his throne, even to the first-born of the slave girl who is behind the millstones; all the first-born of the cattle as well" (Ex. 11:4–5).

All the firstborn in Egypt? Was God going to kill the firstborn of the Israelites as well? No, for we read on in verse 7 that God was going to spare their children and their animals. But there was something God wanted them to do. He told Moses that the Israelites were to take a spotless lamb for each home. It was to be a male, a boy lamb, in its first year. For three days they were to watch it to make sure it was perfect in every way. Then they were to kill their lambs, that is, to cut the lambs' throats. Do you know what God told His people to do with the lambs' blood? They were to paint their doors with it: first, the two sides of the door, then the top.

The lambs were to be roasted over a fire and eaten that very same night. This was the first Passover (Ex. 12:1–11). What was God going to do that night? Listen to what He said: "For I will go through the land of Egypt on that night, and will strike down all the first-born in the land of Egypt, both man and beast; and against all the gods of Egypt I will execute judgments—I am the LORD. And the blood shall be a sign for you on the houses where you live; and when I see the blood I will pass over you, and no plague will befall you to destroy *you* when I strike the land of Egypt" (Ex. 12:12–13).

What would you have done had you lived then? Would you have obeyed the Lord and killed the lamb and painted your door with its blood? Or would you have taken a chance, thinking, "Oh, I don't think the Lord will do it"? Not to obey would have been foolish; it would have cost the Israelites their firstborn! Just the same, God gave them a choice to do it or not, and I imagine there was not one house which did not have a blood-painted door where the Israelites lived.

The Judgment of Egypt

Then midnight came, and with it came God's judgment of Egypt's firstborn. From Pharaoh's oldest son in the palace to the firstborn of the prisoners in the deepest dungeon, to the firstborn of all cattle, all the males died, as the Lord had said (Ex. 12:29–30). Not one house escaped the judgment of God.

But what about the Israelites? They had done as they were told and none of their firstborn was hurt. Now they stayed in their houses and waited until morning (Ex. 12:22, 28). As the Lord passed through the land, He kept His promise. What would you have looked for if you had gone with Him? To see whether the firstborn of the Israelites had been good or bad? No! You would have looked for all the blood-painted doors.

The Shadow of the Cross on the Door

Now let's imagine the doors of Jews. Remember where God said to paint the blood? That's right, on the two sides and then on the top. Do you see now why God had said the blood must be put on the doors in this way? Right; it formed a picture of the cross. Again, this was not the real cross, only a shadow form; but it was to point the people to the cross of the Lord Jesus Christ.

When God saw the blood on the doors, He *passed over* the houses. The people inside those houses were *under the blood*. The blood saved them from judgment, and the following morning they marched out of Egypt and slavery as a free people (Ex. 12:51) as God had promised.

A Night to Remember

God told the Israelites to keep the Passover always. Year after year they celebrated that special day; year after year they told their children what God had done for them. They explained the killing and eating of the lamb. They explained the blood-painted doors. But as often happens, down through the years many things will change, especially when the same thing is done over and over, year after year; it soon loses its meaning. Before long, most of God's people, the Jews, looked back to the Passover in Egypt, but they forgot to look forward to the cross.

The Shadows Become Reality

Only a few remembered. They waited, they watched, and they understood. They recognized the Lord Jesus as God's Lamb. They watched all He did and listened to all He said. They understood that here was the perfect God-man who never did wrong, who had no sin. Here was God's Lamb on the cross. His mission was finished. Our sins were gone forever, for He had taken them out of the way. There was no need to keep the Passover any longer. They could move to the other side of the cross and remember that God *did* send His Son to be the Savior of the world.

What God Wants Me to Know

The Bible tells us that someday God's judgment will fall upon the unbelieving world as it once did upon the Egyptians. Who will be safe then? All who are under the blood of Christ. What do I mean? If we believe in the Lord Jesus Christ, we are safe from God's wrath, or anger. God will not condemn us because He knows that the Lord Jesus was judged for us (Rom. 5:9; 8:1). "In Christ" we are protected under the blood of Christ every bit as much as were the firstborn Israelites inside their houses. Nothing and no one can ever separate us from the love of God "in Christ Jesus our Lord" (Rom. 8:38–39). That is something we want to remember, not once a year, but every single day!

Jesus Christ died to save all sinners, so that includes you. Do you still remember what the Israelites had to do with the blood of the dead lambs? Yes, they had to put it on their doors. Just killing the lambs would not have kept them safe from God's judgment. They had to believe what God said; they had to apply the blood to the doors. Many people know that Jesus Christ died on the cross, but knowing this will never save them—only believing will. Pharaoh knew, too, what God was about to do. Did that help him any? No!

There is no need for you to go out and get a lamb. Right where you are, you can apply what you now know. Turn to John 3:36 and read God's promise and God's warning: "He who believes in the Son has eternal life; but he who does not obey the Son shall not see life, but the wrath of God abides on him." God means what He says. Now make your decision!

Lesson Review

Do you remember on which side of the cross we stood in this lesson? Yes, on the far side of the cross where we looked forward to the things which would happen someday. The cross was only a *shadow* in those long ago days. In what way was the first Passover a shadow picture of the cross? The lamb was a shadow picture of God's Lamb. The blood was a shadow picture of Christ's spiritual death. Painting the blood on the door was a shadow picture of believing in the Lord Jesus Christ.

Memory Verse

"But God demonstrates His own love toward us, in that while we were yet sinners, Christ died for us." (Rom. 5:8)

LESSON TWO
THE LAST PASSOVER

*H*ave you ever become so interested in something you were doing that you did not want to stop even long enough to eat? That's how important His mission was to the Lord Jesus Christ. One day when the disciples returned from buying some food, He said to them, "My food is to do the will of Him who sent Me, and to accomplish His work" (John 4:34; cf. Job 23:12). The disciples looked at each other in amazement. What did He mean, do the Father's will and finish His work? Do you know? Let's help the disciples find out, shall we?

The Work of the Trinity

What must we tell the disciples first? We must tell them about the work of the Trinity in salvation, that each person of the Godhead has a different job to do. What was the Fa-

ther's work? The salvation plan. What did the Son do? Work out the plan. And the Holy Spirit? Show the plan. When we remember this, we understand what the Lord Jesus was talking about that day. He was telling the disciples that He was going to the cross that we might be saved and that the Father's plan can come true.

Looking Back to the Cross

Of course it is easy for us to know these things from the Bible. From where we are, we can look back to the cross. We can read of all that happened in times past as the Holy Spirit teaches us the things of God (1 Cor. 2:9–13).

The cross stands for the finished work of Christ (John 19:30) and is proof of God's love for us. That's what Romans 5:8 tells us, along with many other verses in the

New Testament. It is a good verse for us to know, believe, and share with others: "But God demonstrates His own love toward us, in that while we were yet sinners, Christ died for us [as a substitute for us]." It was on that cross that the Lord Jesus Christ became our Mediator to bring God and us back together again by bridging the sin-gap!

His sinless, perfect life could never have saved us; His miracles, wonderful though they were, could only help people in this life. But to help us for all eternity, He had to die as our substitute. He had to become our sin-bearer and be judged in our place. How did the disciples learn these things even though they did not have the New Testament as we have? They had the Old Testament which told them about God's promised Savior, and they had the Lord Jesus Christ with them.

The Time of the Cross

Let's go back to the time of the Lord's mission on earth, the time of the cross. By now, the disciples had been with the Lord Jesus for three-and-a-half years. They had watched Him and had been taught by Him. Little by little, He had prepared them for His death. He had told them that He must suffer and die, that He must be buried and rise on the third day (Matt. 12:40; 17:12; Mark 9:9; Luke 9:22; 17:25). But perhaps the disciples were like some boys and girls I know who have heard so many times that Jesus died on the cross for our sins that they no longer pay attention! The Lord knew we must be reminded again and again of His work for us lest we become forgetful and thankless!

Keep On Doing This in Remembrance of Me

Turn in your Bible to Luke 22. Jerusalem was crowded with visitors from near and far who had come to keep the Passover. The Lord Jesus, too, had come with His disciples. Remember, the Passover was a very important holy day, for it was a picture of that great day when the Lamb of God would take "away the sin of the world" (John 1:29). God had commanded His people at that time to remember this day every year and think back to the day when God saved the Israelites from slavery in Egypt (Ex. 13:14). Soon God would do an even greater thing!

When the disciples had finished preparing the Passover meal, the Lord Jesus sat down and reclined on low couches with them (Luke 22:13–14). He told them that this would be His last Passover with them. Soon He would suffer and die on the cross (Luke 22:15). From then on, they need not keep the Passover any longer. The real Lamb would be killed (1 Cor. 5:7b) and they, like we, could look back to the cross and remember how much He loves us.

After the Passover meal, the Lord Jesus took the bread and gave thanks. The disciples watched Him break the bread and divide it among them. They heard Him say, "This [referring to the bread] is My body which is given for you!" (Luke 22:19). They saw Him hold the cup. Yet the Lord Jesus called it "My blood" which is "poured out for you" (Luke 22:20). He told them to take the bread and eat it (Matt. 26:26). He told them to drink of the cup (Matt. 26:27), and He commanded them, saying, "Do this [keep on doing this] in remembrance of Me" (Luke 22:19). Silently, and perhaps sadly, they obeyed. They did not want Him to leave them, for still they did not understand that He *must* die. He must finish the work the Father sent Him to do.

"I will come again," the Lord Jesus promised (John 14:3). Then He said to them that they should rejoice "because I go to the Father" (John 14:28). Soon the Holy Spirit would come and teach them what Jesus meant (John 14:26).

Just as He had said He would, the Lord Jesus went to the cross. The Bible tells us that "He Himself bore our sins in His body on the cross" (1 Pet. 2:24). God the Father had to judge Him for our sins. What was the penalty for sin? Spiritual death. God can have nothing to do with sin, and Jesus Christ screamed out, "MY GOD, MY GOD, WHY HAST THOU FORSAKEN ME?" (Matt. 27:46).

So awful was the suffering of our Lord that God the Father sent a deep darkness to cover the land and hide the judgment from those who would watch (Luke 23:44). Where were the disciples? All but John had scattered like frightened rabbits. Three hours later, John heard the most wonderful news. The Lord Jesus Christ called out, "It is finished!" (John 19:30; cf. 17:4). The darkness was gone, and the Lord Jesus had died. He had given His life gladly, willingly. How could anyone who loves Him forget that day?

What God Wants Me to Know

Did the Lord Jesus stay dead? Of course not! He rose on the third day and before long returned to His heavenly home. Did the disciples obey His command? Did they teach others to eat the bread and drink the cup? Indeed they did (Acts 2:42, 46; 1 Cor. 11:23–26), and so do we. When we come together for our communion service, the Lord's Table, we remember what He did for us. We look back to the cross. We eat the broken bread and think of the perfect God-man—His person. We drink of the cup and think of the work He came to do and finished—our salvation.

We think of the day when Jesus Christ Himself took the bread and the cup and thanked the Father. Jesus was thankful for the Father letting Him be our Savior. Think of that! How could we forget? How could we not be thankful? Eating the bread and drinking of the cup is a picture of faith. It is our way of showing that we have believed in the Lord Jesus Christ. Yes, we remember! The cross is not 'that same old stuff.' It's exciting, thrilling! We remember His promise to come again to take us to be with Him forever.

Before the Lord Jesus died, He prayed a long prayer. In it He prayed for all who would believe in Him after they heard what He came to do (John 17:20). Were you one of those for whom He prayed? In fact, if you were the only person in the world who would ever believe in Him, He would still have come. He would have suffered and died for you alone! That's how much He loves you. He proved His love. Will you accept it?

Lesson Review

The mission of God the Son had to end with His death on the cross. Listen to the statements I will make about the death of the Lord Jesus Christ. Then choose the right one out of the three which I will give you.

1. A shadow picture of the cross could be seen in (a) the promises of God, (b) the deaths of countless lambs in Old Testament times, or (c) in the Lord Jesus Christ. Answer: (b).
2. The first people to see the shadow of the cross were (a) Cain and Abel, (b) Satan and his angels, or (c) Adam and Eve. Answer: (c).
3. The Lamb of God was to (a) take away our sins, (b) cover our sins, or (c) stop us from sinning. Answer: (a).
4. On the night of the first Passover, the firstborn of the Israelites were spared (a) by the life of a perfect lamb, (b) by the death of a perfect lamb, or (c) by the lamb's blood applied to their doors. Answer: (c).
5. On the night of the first Passover (a) all, (b) some, or (c) none of the firstborn of Egypt were slain. Answer: (a).
6. God told the Israelites to put the lamb's blood on (a) their doors, (b) their roofs, or (c) their windows. Answer: (a).
7. The Israelites were to keep the Passover every (a) week, (b) year, or (c) five years. Answer: (b).
8. The shadows became reality when (a) the Lord Jesus was born, (b) the Lord Jesus died on the cross, or (c) when the Lord Jesus returned to heaven. Answer: (b).
9. We were saved by (a) the sinless life of Jesus Christ, (b) by the words of Jesus Christ, or (c) by His death on the cross. Answer: (c).
10. The Lord Jesus said that He (a) would rise from the dead in three days, (b) might rise from the dead in three days, or (c) would pretend to be dead for three days. Answer: (a).
11. When the Lord changed the Passover into the Lord's Table, He said that (a) the Passover need no longer be kept, (b) the disciples should keep the Passover every year, or (c) only the Jews should keep the Passover now. Answer: (a).
12. The bread and the cup of the Lord's Table are a reminder of (a) the person and work of the Lord Jesus Christ, (b) His resurrection, or (c) His coming into the world. Answer: (a).
13. Jesus Christ had to die (a) spiritually, (b) physically, or (c) eternally to pay the penalty for our sins. Answer: (a).
14. In order to be saved, we must (a) believe and be baptized, (b) believe and ask forgiveness for our sins, or (c) believe on the Lord Jesus Christ. Answer: (c).
15. Salvation (a) is a free gift from God, (b) must be earned and deserved, or (c) can be prayed for. Answer: (a).

Memory Verse

"But God demonstrates His own love toward us, in that while we were yet sinners, Christ died for us." (Rom. 5:8)

Chapter Eighteen

God the Son: His Death, Burial, and Resurrection

A. Subject: God the Son: His Death, Burial, and Resurrection—Matthew 27:27—28:8; John 19:38—20:9

B. Lesson Titles:
1. Lesson One: The Crucifixion and Burial
2. Lesson Two: The Resurrection

C. Story Objective:

As the unique person of the universe, Jesus Christ is both true humanity (Luke 1:32, 35; Gal. 4:4) and undiminished deity (John 1:1–2; 8:58). As God, He possesses eternal life and is therefore not subject to death (Ps. 90:2); as man, He died on the cross. Like all who have died, He, too, must now be buried; yet the grave had no power over Him.

The Scriptures reveal the death, burial, and resurrection of our Lord Jesus Christ, as well as anticipate the believer's resurrection (Ps. 16:8–11; Isa. 53:8–9; John 11:25; 1 Cor. 15:20). While He was on earth, Jesus Christ spoke frequently of the way He must die and of the three-day interval between His burial and resurrection (Matt. 20:17–19; John 2:19–21; 12:32–33). Not only is the resurrection of our Lord the guarantee that "the dead in Christ shall rise" (1 Thess. 4:16), it is also the demonstration that our justification was completed on the cross (Rom. 4:25). His death and resurrection make Jesus Christ "Lord both of the dead and of the living" (Rom. 14:9).

D. Vocabulary and Doctrinal Concepts:
1. Vocabulary: bidding, burial, condemnation, crucify, damnation, deceit, grave, Hades, light-years, mummy, Potter's Field, resurrection, Sheol, tomb

2. Doctrinal Concepts:
   a. "Three days and three nights in the heart of the earth" (Matt. 12:40b).
   b. The burial narrative (Matt. 27:57–61; cf. John 19:38–42).
   c. The sealing of the tomb (Matt. 27:62–66).
   d. The resurrection narrative (Matt. 28).
   e. Jesus reaffirms the prophecy of His resurrection (Luke 24:46).
   f. The resurrections of life and damnation (John 5:28–29).
   g. Death could not hold Him (Acts 2:23–24).
   h. The resurrection chapter (1 Cor. 15).
   i. "The dead in Christ shall rise first" (1 Thess. 4:16–17).
   j. We will be raised in His likeness (1 John 3:2; cf. Phil. 3:20–21).
   k. Charting the death, burial, and resurrection:
      1) Death (Matt. 27:27–50).
      2) Burial (Matt. 27:51–61); His body buried (Matt. 27:60); His spirit in the presence of the Father (Luke 23:46); His soul in Sheol (Ps. 16:10).
      3) Resurrection (Matt. 28).
      4) The risen Christ (God the Father, Rom 6:4b; God the Son, John 2:19; 10:17; God the Holy Spirit, Rom. 8:11).
      5) The risen Christ seen (Acts 1:3).

E. *Source Book* Keywords: cross (burial, resurrection, ascension, and session; physical death of Christ), resurrection

F. Activities:
1. Suggested Visuals: Christ on the cross, tomb sealed
2. Games, Songs, Worksheets
3. Memory Verse: "Christ died for our sins according to the Scriptures, and that He was buried, and that He was raised on the third day according to the Scriptures." (1 Cor. 15:3*b*–4)
4. Opening and Closing Prayer

LESSON ONE
THE CRUCIFIXION AND BURIAL

*H*ave you ever looked at the stars through a powerful telescope? If you have, you will have noticed that they were brought in so close to your eyes that you felt you could almost reach out and touch them. No longer did they seem to be millions of light-years away. In an even more wonderful way, God showed some of His servants in Old Testament times things which would happen hundreds, yes, thousands of years later. We might say God let them look through the telescope of time.

Three of these men were Job, David, and Isaiah. Although these men lived hundreds of years apart, God let them see into the future. Would you like to know what these men saw in their minds as clearly as if they were actually there at the time? Then listen as they describe to us the Lord's death, burial, and resurrection.

Let's take David first. He saw the Lord Jesus crucified. He tells us about it in Psalm 22. Open your Bible to that passage. He heard the very words the Lord Jesus would scream out on the cross: "My God, my God, why hast Thou forsaken me?" (Ps. 22:1). He saw the enemies of Jesus, shaking their heads and pointing to the cross, saying, "Commit *yourself* to the LORD; let Him [God] deliver him [Jesus]" (Ps. 22:8). He knew exactly how much pain the Lord Jesus would suffer in His body. He even saw the nail prints in His hands and feet and almost felt His terrible thirst (Ps. 22:13–17).

Next, David looked down on the Roman soldiers who sat at the foot of the cross. They had divided His few pieces of clothing and were now rolling dice for Jesus' robe (Ps. 22:18).

But now the sad scene changes. David sees an empty tomb or grave. Jesus had risen from the dead. David knows that although his own dead body would someday sleep in the grave, the glad day would come when the Lord would awaken him forever (Ps. 16:9–10).

Many years had passed when Isaiah saw the same picture. Someday you may want to read Isaiah chapter 53 for yourself. It tells how our Lord suffered pain and shame for our sakes and also of His death for sinful "us." Isaiah could even see the place where Jesus was buried. Let's read Isaiah 53:9: "His grave was assigned with wicked men, Yet He was with a rich man in His death, Because He had done no violence, Nor was there any deceit in His mouth." Who were these "wicked men"? Whose was the "rich man[s]" grave? Wait and see!

Then there was Job. Job had suffered a great deal. He had lost all he owned, and now he was terribly and painfully sick. God let him see that happy day when the Lord Jesus would come back to the earth. Because Job knew that Jesus had risen from the dead, he, too, knew he would live again (Job 19:26).

Was what these men saw really to come true? Could they trust their eyes as they saw through the telescope of time? Indeed so, and we will see how what they saw actually happened, for we are now ready to learn about our Lord's death, burial, and resurrection.

The Death of Jesus Christ
Matthew 27:26–50

After He had been cruelly beaten, the God-man-Savior was led away to a place called Golgotha, or Calvary. He wore a crown of thorns, and the sharp thorns dug painfully into His head and face. Because He had been so severely beaten, He was struggling up the hill, staggering under the heavy load of the cross. It was nine o'clock in the morning when the soldiers nailed Him to the cross. They lifted up the cross and set it into its place between two other crosses. Yes, Isaiah had seen right. The Lord Jesus *did* die between two wicked men—thieves, both of them.

Now, what David had seen came true. To be nailed on a cross was the most painful and slow kind of death a person could die. Oh, how the Lord Jesus suffered hanging there! His bones were pulled apart by His own weight. He cried out thirstily for water (John 19:28).

At the foot of the cross the Roman soldiers whiled away time. They had divided among themselves the pieces of clothing He had owned and were now throwing dice to see who of them would win the robe. Crowds of curious people stood about watching. Others walked past, shaking their heads and making fun of Jesus. "If You are the Son of God, come down from the cross," they yelled (Matt. 27:40*b*). "He saved others; He cannot save Himself" (Matt. 27:42*a*). "He trusts in God; let Him deliver *Him* now [Let's see if God will help Him now!]" (Matt. 27:43*a*).

Could our Lord have come down from the cross? Certainly He could have, but He knew He must not. He must bear the sins of the world in order to save us; He was God's Lamb which had been offered up to die. How long would He stay on the cross? Until it was time for Him to be buried. For three long hours God the Father judged our sins in the Lord Jesus. God can have nothing to do with sin; that's why the Father turned away from the Son. Yes, David had heard right; the Lord *did* scream out, "MY GOD, MY GOD, WHY HAST THOU FORSAKEN ME?" (Matt. 27:46).

First, Jesus died spiritually, just as Adam did after he sinned in the Garden. Spiritual death means separation from God the Father. Afterwards He died in His body. But remember: Jesus is also God, and God has eternal life! God cannot die! It was the man Jesus who died, and like all dead He must be buried.

His Burial
Matthew 27:57–61 and John 19:38–42

But where would they bury Him? Since He had died on the cross like a criminal, He should really be buried in the "Potter's Field" where the two thieves would be buried (Matt. 27:7). Had Isaiah been wrong? No, God knows the end from the beginning; He had shown Isaiah what was going to happen (Isa. 46:10).

It was early in the evening. A rich man from Arimathea, whose name was Joseph, had come to see the Roman governor, Pilate. What did he want? He had come to ask Pilate for the body of Jesus. The governor commanded it be given to him, and Joseph made his way to Calvary.

But he was not the only one who wanted to bury Jesus properly. Nicodemus, too, had come and had brought with him nearly one hundred pounds of sweet-smelling spices for the burial. Nicodemus had once gone to see the Lord Jesus by night, and both he and Joseph had become believers. Together they took the body of Jesus and wrapped it carefully in strips of linen, sprinkling the spices between the many layers of cloth, for this is the way the Jews buried their loved ones in those days.

Close to Calvary was a lovely garden. There Joseph had bought a tomb for himself. It was a new tomb where he hoped to be buried someday, a fine tomb in a fine setting such as only the very rich could afford. And Joseph was very rich indeed. In that tomb they placed the body of Jesus. Then they rolled a heavy stone over the opening and left. Sadly, Mary Magdalene and another Mary watched the burial of their beloved Lord Jesus. In fact, everywhere in the land, those who had loved Him wept and sorrowed over His death. Not one of them seemed to remember that He had told them this would happen, and that He must stay in the grave three days and three nights before He would rise from the dead.

The Sealing of the Tomb
Matthew 27:62–66

Now the Lord's enemies had not forgotten His words, and they began to worry about them. The very next day they went to see Pilate and said, "Sir, we remember that when He was still alive that deceiver [can you imagine anyone's calling the true God a "deceiver"? Why, that's one of Satan's names—Rev. 20:3] said, 'After three days I *am to* rise again.' Therefore, give orders for the grave to be made secure until the third day, lest the disciples come and steal Him away and say to the people, 'He has risen from the dead'" (Matt. 27:63–64).

Pilate agreed and told them to see to it themselves that the tomb was sealed and that guards were there on watch. This the Lord's enemies did at once. They thought that now they could relax; they were rid of Jesus once and for all. What a surprise they had coming! We will learn about the Lord's resurrection in our next lesson.

What God Wants Me to Know

After the Lord Jesus died, His body was laid in a grave. What do you think happened to His soul and spirit? Well, His spirit went up into the presence of the Father (Luke 23:46), and His soul went into Hades, Sheol, the place where the souls of the dead were once kept (Ps. 16:10).

Would you like to know what happens to us when we die? Must we be able to look into the future to find out? No, we have God's promise in writing in our Bibles. We read that when a believer dies, he is said to have "fallen asleep" (1 Thess. 4:13–14). You are not afraid to fall asleep at night, are you? Of course not. We awaken from sleep fresh every morning, ready to start a new day. Just so, the believer's body awakens from 'death sleep' to a bright, new, forever day with the Lord. Need anyone be afraid of that? I should say not!

But what about our souls and spirits? As soon as we take our last breath, the soul and spirit leave our bodies. They rise to be with God—in His presence—until the body is raised in new life. Truly, we have a wonderful future awaiting us.

Our memory verse for this lesson says, "Christ died for our sins according to the Scriptures, and that He was buried, and that He was raised on the third day according to the Scriptures" (1 Cor. 15:3*b*–4). If someone dies who has never believed in the Lord Jesus, it is said that he shall die in his sins (John 8:24). There is no excuse for anyone to die in his sins because Jesus has died for all our sins. He took our place that we might live forever with Him. If you have not believed in Him, the Bible says that you are dead even while you are still living; you are dead in sins (Eph. 2:1–5). You are dead to God and can have no relationship with Him, now or forever. But you can change that right now; you can be made alive in a second. First John 5:12 is God's promise to you: "He who has the Son has the life; he who does not have the Son of God does not have the life."

You can have new life simply by believing that Christ died for your sins, that He was buried and rose again—for you.

Lesson Review

Can you remember what the cross and the tomb stand for? Yes, the death and the burial of our Lord Jesus Christ. What had He said about His death and burial? That He must die on the cross and rise on the third day. Did God show this to anyone else? Yes, to David, Job, and Isaiah. Who had forgotten that He said He would come back to life, and who had remembered? His friends forgot; His enemies remembered. How did His enemies try to make sure He could not come out of the tomb and His friends could not steal the body? They sealed the tomb and had soldiers guarding it.

Memory Verse

"Christ died for our sins according to the Scriptures, and that He was buried, and that He was raised on the third day according to the Scriptures." (1 Cor. 15:3*b*–4)

LESSON TWO
THE RESURRECTION

*D*o you think that a sealed lock, or chains, or even the heavy stone could keep the Lord Jesus in the tomb? Do you think the true God could tell a lie? *Never!* All happened as He said it would. He had died for our sins; He had been buried, and He would rise according to His Word.

The Resurrection of Jesus Christ

Since you know the Easter story, we want to look at the resurrection of the Lord Jesus in a different way. We want to learn just how He was raised from the dead, what kind of a body He had, and how He proved He had risen as He said He would.

Isn't it wonderful that we can know from God's Word what happened inside that sealed tomb? Why, it's like having X-ray eyes that can see through the thickest stone, the deepest darkness, and yes, even a dead body! And what do we get to see?

Inside that cool, dark tomb of rock lies the dead body of Jesus, wrapped up like a mummy in linen strips and spices.

The first night passes, then the first day; the second night and day; the third night passes. The guards report to their officers that all is quiet at the tomb. No, they had not seen any of the disciples of Jesus or Jesus Himself. For that matter, neither would they nor anyone else!

On the third morning, long before daybreak, life returns to the still body. What had happened? The soul and the spirit of Jesus had slipped back inside His body. How did it happen? Jesus Himself and His Word, the Bible, tell us. He once said, "I lay down My life . . . I have authority to lay it down, and I have authority to take it up again" (John 10:17–18; cf. Job 9:12; Col 1:16). Jesus is God; He is eternal life. He is God and therefore omnipotent or all-powerful. It would have been easy for God the Son to raise up the body which had been specially prepared for Him (Heb. 10:5).

But we read that God the Father and God the Holy Spirit resurrected Jesus Christ. Romans 6:4*b* says, "Christ was raised from the dead through the glory [all that God is—His essence] of the Father," and Romans 8:11 says that "Spirit . . . raised Jesus from the dead."

When you wake up in the morning, do you stretch and yawn and sit up on the side of your bed? Most people do. Is that what the Lord Jesus did when His body awoke from the sleep of death? Would He begin to unwrap the linen strips and shake out the spices? Where would He begin, seeing His fingers had been wrapped separately first, then together, and His arms had been strapped to His body before it was wrapped all around again? He did nothing like that! He need not! He now had a glorified body, a resurrection body that was able to do the most amazing things.

The Resurrection Body of the Lord Jesus

No longer would His body feel pain or death, hunger or thirst. He could eat, but He needed no food; He could open doors or walk through them. He could come and go in an instant, appear or disappear as He wished. The risen Lord merely slid out of His grave clothes much as a butterfly leaves its ugly, brown cocoon after it has changed from a caterpillar to a lovely winged creature, or a cicada that leaves behind its empty, crusty shell. The Lord left the linen wraps undisturbed, still showing the shape of His body. He carefully folded the cloth which had been tied under His chin and around His head and laid it in a place by itself (John 20:7).

Then He left the tomb. In His glorious resurrection body, He walked right through the closed, sealed, stone door, right past the guards, unseen and unheard. They never knew what happened until they saw a bright angel, and then they fainted from fear (Matt. 28:4). Yes, the Lord had risen, even as He had shown Job, David, Isaiah, and those who loved Him while He was on earth.

Proofs of His Resurrection

The first one to see the resurrected Christ was Mary Magdalene (John 20:11–17). She and two other women had come to the tomb early Sunday morning and found the stone rolled away. "Someone must have stolen His body," she thought, and ran off to tell Peter and John. Then she returned and stood outside the tomb. Weeping sorrowfully, she bent down and looked in. Two angels sat where she had seen Joseph and Nicodemus place the body of Jesus. "Why are you crying?" the angels asked her. Mary Magdalene told them. Sadly, she turned away from the empty tomb and there stood Jesus!

At first she did not know Him. Her eyes were so full of tears that she could not see clearly; but also, she had never seen anyone in a glorified body. As soon as He spoke to her, she recognized the Lord. Her sadness turned to joy. He had risen from the dead, and she had seen Him with her own eyes! "Go quickly and tell His disciples," the Lord told her (Matt. 28:7a), and Mary Magdalene's feet barely touched the ground as she ran to do the Lord's bidding. What wonderful, wonderful news she carried!

Others saw Him, too. There were the women who had come with Mary Magdalene that morning. They had been told by the angel that Jesus had risen from the dead (Matt. 28:5–8). Now they, too, were running to share the good news. And whom did they meet as they ran? None other than the Lord Jesus! The women dropped to their knees and embraced His feet (Matt. 28:9). "Go and take word to My brethren to leave for Galilee, and there they shall see Me," He said (Matt. 28:10).

Then there was Peter. He, too, saw the risen Lord that same day (Luke 24:34). So did the two who walked to Emmaus later that afternoon (Luke 24:13). As they walked, they talked about the things which had happened in Jerusalem during the last three days. Their faces were long and sad. They did not notice someone walking up to them until the Lord asked, "What are these words that you are exchanging with one another as you are walking?"

"You must be a stranger in town," they said, "or else you would have known of it!" "Known what?" asked Jesus. "About Jesus and how we had hoped He would set the Jews free. Instead, He died on a cross, although some of the women surprised us this morning, claiming they had seen angels and that Jesus Himself had risen." They shook their heads in unbelief as if to say, "we don't believe it!"

"You are foolish and slow to understand that Jesus must first suffer and then come into glory," the Lord Jesus said to them. Then He began to teach them patiently what the Scriptures said about Him. By now they had reached Emmaus. It was late, and they begged Him to eat with them and spend the night. They still did not know who He was.

He went into the house with them. He could have surprised them by walking through the closed door or through the wall. You know He could, but He chose the open door instead. Later that night, He was going to come through a locked and bolted door (John 20:19), but not now. He was going to show them who He was in a different way. He picked up the bread, gave thanks to the Father, and broke it; He gave them each a piece. It was the way He did it and the words He said that reminded them of their Lord. Could it be? Yes, it was He, Jesus, their risen Lord! But as soon as they knew Him He disappeared. One second He was there, then He was gone. The two never touched their meal but rushed to Jerusalem to tell the eleven, who had always been with the Lord Jesus, that it was true!

They were still speaking, when all at once the Lord stood among them, saying, "Peace be with you" (John 20:21). They were terrified and thought they had seen a spirit or ghost. But the Lord said, "See My hands and My feet, that it is I Myself; touch Me and see, for a spirit does not have flesh and bones as you see that I have" (Luke 24:39; cf. John 20:27). They saw the nail prints in His hands and feet and touched them. They were overjoyed, yet wondered if they were imagining all this.

"Have you any food here?" asked the Lord Jesus. They handed Him a piece of fish and some honey. They watched Him eat and were no longer afraid. It was their beloved

Savior! "Didn't you understand these things would happen to me?" He asked them. He told them He had to suffer and die, to be buried and rise from the dead on the third day. "And now that you have seen it happen, you must tell others about this," He said (Luke 24:41–48).

Surely this should have been proof enough; yet the Lord showed Himself to those who loved Him many more times before He returned to heaven (Acts 1:3). Did any unbelievers see Him after He rose? It seems that only three of them did—His half-brothers James and Jude, who believed in Him then and became the writers of the Book of James and the Book of Jude (1 Cor. 15:7; Jude 1). Later, on the road to Damascus, Saul, or Paul as he came to be known, saw the resurrected Christ. Never again would any of the disciples doubt His resurrection. They would be willing even to risk their lives in the telling of it.

Only the Lord's enemies shook their heads, even when the soldiers told of the angel at the tomb and that Jesus had disappeared. His enemies decided they must act quickly. "Here, take this money and tell that the disciples came and stole the body while you slept," they said to the soldiers. Would the soldiers not be ashamed to admit they fell asleep on guard duty? What if Pilate heard of it? "Don't worry about that! We'll take care of that!" they were told. So the soldiers pocketed the large sum of money and did as they were ordered. Sad to say, many of the Jews believed their story.

What God Wants Me to Know

Whose story do you believe? That of the soldiers, or that of the Word of God? The Word says that He *did* rise. Had He not, we would still be dead in our sins. In raising up Jesus from the dead, God showed that He had accepted the work of His Son; that He was willing to save us. Because He was resurrected, we, too, shall live forever (1 Cor. 15:12–18). Someday we, too, will have a resurrection body just like that of the Son of God (Phil. 3:21). Should we die before He comes back for us, our souls and spirits will rejoin our bodies, and our bodies will be made over for heaven-life as we meet Jesus in the air to be with Him forever (1 Thess. 4:15–17). It may even be that some of us never need die before we are changed. Oh, how we long for that day! But until then, we have work to do. We must tell the Good News that "Christ died for our sins according to the Scriptures, and that He was buried, and that He was raised on the third day according to the Scriptures" (1 Cor. 15:3b–4). Did you notice how all who were told of the risen Lord *ran* to tell others? We, too, must be quick about it. There is no time to waste.

You have heard the wonderful news today. Perhaps it was your first time to hear it, and now you know that death is *not* the end of all things. It is only the beginning. For the believer, it is the beginning of eternity in the presence of our Lord in heaven; for the unbeliever it is the beginning of eternity without God, in a terrible place called "the lake of fire" (Rev. 20:15).

Someday the unbelievers, too, will hear the Lord calling; they, too, will be resurrected—but to the resurrection of damnation or condemnation. That means they will receive an indestructible body which will never wear out, but will suffer eternally in the lake of fire. Is God cruel for doing this? No, listen to what He says in His Word: "For God so loved the world, that He gave His only begotten Son, that whoever believes in Him should not perish, but have eternal life. For God did not send the Son into the world to judge the world, but that the world should be saved through Him. He who believes in Him is not judged; he who does not believe has been judged already, because he has not believed in the name of the only begotten Son of God" (John 3:16–18). We do not want to scare you into believing in the Lord Jesus Christ, but we do want you to know what to expect if you turn away from God's way of salvation. Right now, you, too, can be saved by believing in Him and can walk out of here *knowing* that you have eternal life and will live in the presence of the Lord forever (1 John 5:11–12).

Lesson Review

How long did the Lord Jesus stay in the tomb? Three days and three nights. Where were His soul and spirit during that time? His soul was in Hades, and His spirit was with the Father. What happened to His soul and spirit after the three days and nights had passed? They rejoined His body. Who raised Him from the dead? God the Father and God the Holy Spirit. How did He get out of the tomb, since it was sealed and guarded? He came through the stone. How was that possible? He now had a resurrection body.

Can you describe in what way the resurrection body of the Lord Jesus is different from the body He had when He came down to earth? He could not feel pain or death, hunger or thirst. He could eat, but needed no food. He could open doors or walk right through them. He could appear or disappear. Who else is to have a body like that of the Son of God? All believers. Will the unbelievers be resurrected as well? Yes. Where will they spend eternity? In the lake of fire. How can anyone keep from going there? By believing in the Lord Jesus Christ. Who saw the Lord Jesus after He rose from the dead? The three women who had come to the tomb; Peter; John; the two believers on the road to Emmaus; the Lord's two half-brothers, James and Jude; the eleven disciples; and Paul.

Was the Lord going to stay on earth now that His enemies could no longer hurt Him? No! He had told His disciples many times that He must return to His Father in heaven. How He did, when, and why is what we will find out next.

Memory Verse

"Christ died for our sins according to the Scriptures, and that He was buried, and that He was raised on the third day according to the Scriptures." (1 Cor. 15:3b–4)

Chapter Nineteen

God the Son: His Ascension and Session

A. Subject: God the Son: His Ascension and Session—John 14:2; Acts 1:9; Hebrews 1:13

B. Lesson Titles:
1. Lesson One: The Ascension of Christ
2. Lesson Two: The Session of Christ

C. Story Objective:

The ascension of Christ: Forty days after the Resurrection, during which time the Lord Jesus Christ "presented Himself alive, after His suffering, by many convincing proofs" (Acts 1:3), He departed from this earth visibly in His resurrection body and entered into heaven (Acts 1:2–3, 9). As our Great High Priest He entered into heaven to present the perfect Sacrifice for sinful humanity—Himself (Lev. 16:30; Heb. 9:16–28), where now He appears "in the presence of God for us" (Heb. 9:24).

The session of Christ: Upon entering heaven, Christ "sat down at the right hand of the Majesty on high" (Heb. 1:3*b*). The seating indicated the completion of Christ's work in salvation (Heb. 10:12) and His acceptability to God the Father as man (Ps. 110:1; Heb. 1:13).

Through His redemptive work, His ascension and session, the Lord continues to bring "many sons [believers] to glory [the right hand of the Father]" (Heb. 2:10; cf. Eph. 1:6). By means of his union with Christ, the Christian is said to be "raised up" and "seated" in "heavenly *places*" (Eph 2:6; current positional truth) even while he is still on the earth.

Christ's work in session: At God's right hand, the place of honor, our Lord's work still continues; He is the giver of gifts (Eph. 4:7–12); He makes intercession for us (Heb. 7:25); He is the believer's "Advocate with the Father"

(1 John 2:1); He is the Great High Priest, representing man before God (Heb. 9:24). His session will terminate with His return for His own—the Rapture of the Church—only to be resumed and continued throughout all eternity.

D. Vocabulary and Doctrinal Concepts:
1. Vocabulary: Age of Israel, ark of the covenant, ascension, atoning, Bible doctrine, breastplate, Day of Atonement, defend, defense lawyer, glorify, high priest, hosts, incense, intercede, intercession, mercy seat, Holy of Holies, priests, session, Tabernacle
2. Doctrinal Concepts:
   a. Ascension:
      1) Prophesied (Ps. 68:18; Prov. 30:4; Luke 22:69; John 3:13; 6:62; 14:2–3)
      2) Fulfilled (Luke 24:50–51; Acts 1:1–9)
      3) Reaffirmed (Acts 2:33; Eph. 4:8–10; Heb. 4:14; 1 Pet. 3:22*a*)
   b. Session:
      1) Prophesied (Ps. 110:1; Matt. 22:41–45)
      2) Fulfilled (Acts 2:33–34; Heb. 1:3*b*)
      3) Reaffirmed (Acts 7:55; Eph. 1:20; Col. 3:1*b*; Heb. 8:1; 10:11–12; 12:2; 1 Pet. 3:22*a*)
   c. Charting the Lord's ascension and session:
      1) Christ's death, burial, and resurrection (1 Cor. 15:3–4).
      2) Christ seen alive over a period of forty days (Acts 1:3).
      3) Christ's ascension (John 14:2; Acts 1:9).
      4) Christ's session (Heb. 1:13): He prays for us (Heb. 7:25); He helps us (Rom. 8:34*b*); He defends us (1 John 2:1).

E. *Source Book* Keywords: Christ (waiting in heaven); cross (burial, resurrection, ascension, and session); heavens, three; salvation; Tabernacle

F. Activities:
1. Suggested Visuals: ark of the covenant, Christ ascending, Christ in session, Christ's time line, golden altar, golden candlestick, golden table
2. Games, Songs, Worksheets
3. Memory Verse: "Christ Jesus is He who died, yes, rather who was raised, who is at the right hand of God, who also intercedes for us." (Rom. 8:34b)
4. Opening and Closing Prayer

LESSON ONE
THE ASCENSION OF CHRIST

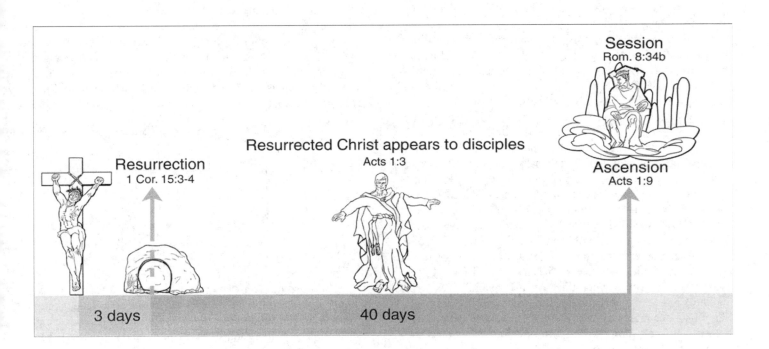

We live in an exciting age, called the space age by many. Once it seemed impossible that man could ever travel into space, even a short way up in an airplane. But now we think nothing about reading of satellites going into orbit and flying about the sky faster than we can imagine. We can watch manned spacecraft on our television screens as they take off, streaking across heaven or re-entering and landing again, and we are amazed at what man can do!

But wait a minute! Is space travel really new? Were our astronauts or Russia's cosmonauts the first "spacemen"? Would it surprise you to know that they were not? Would it surprise you to hear that others before them have traveled much farther into space thousands of years ago, and without the help of a rocket? Do you wonder who they were?

One was Enoch; the other, Elijah (Gen. 5:24; 2 Kings 2:11). Enoch and Elijah lived in the Age of Israel in the days of the Old Testament. Both went up alive from this earth, for God took them. We are told in God's Word that Enoch pleased God. One day he was walking on earth; then suddenly he was whisked off the earth and could not be found (Heb. 11:5). Just like that! Elijah, too, was taken up in a wonderful way—in a chariot of flames drawn by fiery horses. Neither of them needed a spacecraft, nor a space suit, nor any of the cumbersome things that go along with travel into space. God saw to that.

As a believer in the Lord Jesus Christ, you, too, will be a space-traveler someday! God will see to it that you'll travel safely, up, up, up, through the clouds, beyond the moon, beyond the planets and stars, right into the very presence of God. And who do you think made this possible? Yes, the Lord Jesus Christ, the Creator and Lord of space (Col. 1:16)! Let's hear about it, shall we?

My Father's House

Beyond time and space lies God's heavenly home. The prophet Isaiah had described to us how he saw the Lord, high and lifted up upon His throne, surrounded by six-winged angels. Their voices rang out God's praises: "Holy, Holy, Holy, is the LORD of hosts, The whole earth is full of His glory" (Isa. 6:1–3).

In the Book of Revelation, the last book in our Bible, the Apostle John tells us that he, too, was allowed to see this marvelous sight and to hear the angelic voices. Looking into God's throne room, he saw God on His throne, dazzling with the brightness of jewels. An emerald-colored rainbow shone about the throne, and out of the throne came flashes of lightning and thunders and sounds.

Around God's throne stood twenty-four smaller thrones upon which God's highest angels sat clothed in white, and wearing golden crowns on their heads (Rev. 4:2–8). What a sight! For neither Isaiah nor John were actually there in person. We know that from the Lord Jesus Himself. He said that "no one has ascended into heaven, but He who descended from heaven, *even* the Son of Man [meaning Himself]" (John 3:13). Ascend means to go in an upward direction, or to go up; descend means to go down. When the Lord Jesus Christ ascended to heaven, we call this "His ascension."

The Lord Jesus Christ was going to *ascend* to this place too marvelous really to describe that He simply called "My Father's house" (John 14:2). "In My Father's house are many dwelling places; if it were not so, I would have told you" He said. "I go to prepare a place for you" (John 14:2). But before He could go back up to heaven, the Lord Jesus had to die on the cross for our sins, be buried, and rise from the dead.

The Forty-Day Interval

For the next forty days, the Lord Jesus "presented Himself alive, after His suffering, by many convincing proofs" (Acts 1:3). Who all had seen Him alive right after the crucifixion? Let's name them once more: the three women who had come to the tomb; Peter; John; the two believers on the road to Emmaus; the Lord's two half-brothers, James and Jude; and the eleven disciples. How did they know He was really alive? They had seen Him come and go, appear and disappear; they had heard Him speak and had watched Him break bread and eat. They had touched

Him; there could be no doubt about it. He *was alive*! Even doubting Thomas was convinced of it!

After that, more than five hundred believers saw the risen Christ at the same time (1 Cor. 15:6). Could that many people be wrong? Never! In fact, so sure were they that the Lord had risen from the dead that they were even willing to die for Him!

But now the forty-day period was almost over. He was teaching the disciples many things they still had to learn. On the last day He met with them outside the city of Jerusalem and together they climbed the Mount of Olives. I wonder if the disciples suspected that this was the last time they would see their Lord on the earth?

The Ascension

What do you think were the Lord's last words to His faithful followers? "'You shall receive power when the Holy Spirit has come upon you; and you shall be My witnesses both in Jerusalem, and in all Judea and Samaria, and even to the remotest part of the earth.' And after He had said these things, He was lifted up while they were looking on, and a cloud received Him out of their sight" (Acts 1:8–9).

The Lord had kept His promise; they had seen Him ascend (John 6:62). Wouldn't you have stood and stared open-mouthed to see Him go up? The disciples did. They just could not take their eyes off the wonderful sight, even when a cloud hid Jesus from them.

But what was that? Two angels stood next to the disciples. They were bringing a wonderful message: When the right time came, the Lord Jesus would return in the cloud as they had seen Him go (Acts 1:10–11; cf. Zech. 14:4; John 14:2–3). In the meantime the disciples had work to do. They returned to Jerusalem to wait for the coming of the Holy Spirit whom Jesus had promised to send to take His place (John 14:16; Acts 1:4–5).

What God Wants Me to Know

How good a disciple of the Lord Jesus are you? A disciple is one who learns God's Word, Bible doctrine, and applies or uses it daily (John 8:31; James 1:22a). Do you know that you should tell others about the Lord Jesus Christ? Do you ever tell anyone? You have learned three verses which you can share with those who do not know the Lord Jesus as their Savior. What are they? "For God so loved the world, that He gave His only begotten Son, that whoever believes in Him should not perish, but have eternal life" (John 3:16); "But God demonstrates His own love toward us, in that while we were yet sinners, Christ died for us [as a substitute for us]" (Rom. 5:8); "Christ died for our sins according to the Scriptures, and that He was buried, and that He was raised on the third day according to the Scriptures" (1 Cor. 15:3–4). Now we are adding another one, Romans 8:34*b*: "Christ Jesus is He who died, yes, rather who was raised, who is at the right hand of God, who also intercedes for us."

Isn't it wonderful to know that Christ died for our sins and rose again, and that He ascended to heaven? Do you know what that means to you and to me? It means that because He went up, all those who belong to Him will go to be where He is to live with Him forever (John 14:3).

The Lord Jesus wants everyone to be with Him in heaven. Does that include you if you have never believed in Him? Indeed it does. He died for you because He loves you. But if He remained dead, He could not help anyone; that's why He rose on the third day. Why did He go back to heaven? To prepare a place for all who will trust in Him. Will you be one of them? Will you go up with Him when He returns in the clouds for His own? Only you can decide; no one can do it for you. Why not do it now?

Lesson Review

What was the new word we learned that means to go up? Right, the new word was ascend. Who ascended? The risen Lord. To what place? Heaven. How many days after His resurrection was His ascension? Forty days. How did He ascend into heaven? In a cloud. Who saw Him go? The eleven disciples. Who told them the Lord would return the same way they had seen Him go up into heaven? Two angels. What had the Lord commanded His disciples to do after He ascended to heaven? Witness about Him.

Memory Verse

"Christ Jesus is He who died, yes, rather who was raised, who is at the right hand of God, who also intercedes for us." (Rom. 8:34*b*)

LESSON TWO
THE SESSION OF CHRIST

Why did our Lord come down from heaven in the first place? To save sinners (1 Tim. 1:15*b*), to be God's 'show and tell' to the world, and to become our Great Mediator (1 Tim. 2:5–6*a*). On the cross He finished the work the Father had sent Him to do. Then He was buried, rose on the third day, and proved Himself to be alive forevermore. Wouldn't it be enough for all to know this? Why couldn't Jesus have stayed on earth and made things right for us here? Why did He have to ascend to heaven?

God the Father had a far greater plan; He wants us to live in heaven, in His presence and in the presence of His holy angels (Heb. 12:22–23)! Remember, that's why the Lord Jesus said, "I go and prepare a place for you . . . that where I am, *there* you may be also" (John 14:3). Now, while the disciples watched and stood staring into heaven, the Lord Jesus was on His way to God's throne room. He had to appear in God's presence for us!

His Arrival in Heaven

What a thrilling day that must have been for God's holy angels! They had seen Him in heaven as the Son of God; they had watched Him as the God-man-Savior on the earth, and now He was coming back as the God-man, the first true man to enter into God's throne room. As God, all heaven and earth belonged to Him, but as man He must have God's permission to come near Him. Would God allow a man into heaven where only God and His holy angels lived?

I am sure the angels watched and waited to hear what God the Father would say. So much depended on His words! If He let Jesus Christ come into the throne room, then other human beings would be allowed to come to heaven as well, for it would show that God was satisfied with His Son's work on the cross. But if the Father turned Him away, all human beings would be hopelessly lost forever.

Another Shadow Picture Comes True

The scene I have just described to you is very much like what happened once every year on earth in a place called "the most holy place" or the Holy of Holies (1 Kings 8:6). That was in the days of the Old Testament when God still showed His people shadow pictures of the Lord Jesus. In those long-ago days, before our Mediator came to bridge the sin-gap between God and us, the priests represented the people before God and God to the people. They wore special clothes and served God in a special place, in the Tabernacle, God's dwelling place on earth.

There were two golden-walled rooms inside the Tabernacle: a larger one called "the holy place" (Heb. 9:2) and a smaller one called "the Holy of Holies" (Heb. 9:3). These rooms were beautifully furnished. In the first room stood a golden candlestick (Ex. 25:31), a golden table (Ex. 25:23–24), and a golden altar (Ex. 30:1–5); in the second room was a golden box and above it the mercy seat or the ark of the covenant (Ex. 25:10–21). But do you know what could not be found anywhere in the Tabernacle? Chairs! There was not one chair to be seen. That meant that the priests had to serve God standing every day (Heb. 10:11).

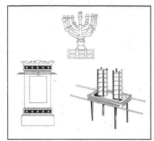

Over and over and over they brought the blood of sacrificed animals so that God might see they believed God's own Lamb would come someday. They knew that the blood of the animals could never take away sins, but only do what? Picture Christ's saving or atoning work on the cross.

Once every year on the Day of Atonement the high priest laid aside his lovely robes and the breastplate with glittering stones to put on a plain white robe. He took a basin with blood and a bowl of sweet-smelling incense, pushed aside the heavy, embroidered curtain, and walked into the Holy of Holies to stand and sprinkle the blood of the animal on the mercy seat. On that day God accepted the blood as the shadow picture of the Lord Jesus Christ paying for the sins of the world on the cross.

Outside the Tabernacle the people watched and waited. Would they ever see the high priest again? They could not go near the Holy of Holies; only the high priest could enter in for them. Would God accept their sin-offering from him? If only he would come out all dressed up again in his high priestly robes and breastplate they would know all was well.

Do you see now how it must have been in heaven the day the Lord Jesus ascended? He had brought the one perfect sacrifice on the cross—Himself, and now He had gone alone into God's heavenly Tabernacle, into the heavenly Holy of Holies—God's throne room. He is our own Great High Priest, not the shadow, but the real person behind the shadow; He was appearing in the presence of God for us where you and I could never have gone!

His Session

So important was this moment that God wanted us to know the exact words He said to the Lord Jesus. They were "SIT AT MY RIGHT HAND [the place of honor], UNTIL I MAKE THINE ENEMIES A FOOTSTOOL FOR THY FEET" (Heb. 1:13; cf. Ps. 110:1). When Jesus Christ sat down at the right hand of God the Father, we call this His session, meaning to sit.

What a shout of praise must have been heard in the throne room as the God-man sat down next to the Father on His throne! The angels may well have called out, "Worthy is the Lamb that was slain to receive power and riches and wisdom and might and honor and glory and blessing . . . To Him who sits on the throne, and to the Lamb, *be* blessing and honor and glory and dominion forever and ever" echoed their praises from heaven and earth and seas (Rev. 5:12–13).

Wouldn't you like to have been there? The Apostle John tells us what a breathtaking sight the seated Lord is. He shares his vision with us in Revelation 1:10–18. He says that he heard the voice of the Lord, and it was as powerful as the sound of a trumpet and as mighty as the rush of many waters. He saw the Lord as our Great High Priest, dressed in a long flowing robe of purest white and wearing the golden breastplate. He looked into our dear Lord's face. His hair was white as snow, and His eyes burned as a flame of fire. His face shone with the brilliance of the noonday sun.

Then John glanced down to see the Savior's feet. They shimmered like melted bronze. John's eyes scarcely could take in such beauty, such majesty! He fell down limp at the Lord's feet and fainted. But wonder of wonders, Jesus reached out and touched John with His right hand and said, "Do not be afraid; I am the first and the last and the living One; and I was dead, and behold, I am alive forevermore, and I have the keys of death and of Hades" (Rev. 1:17*b*–18).

No wonder the angels worshiped Him! No wonder heaven rings with His praises! God the Father had answered Jesus' prayer (John 17:1*b*). He had "highly exalted Him," raised Him up and seated Him at His right hand; He had given Jesus "the name which is above every name, that at the name of Jesus EVERY KNEE SHOULD BOW, of those who are in heaven, and on earth" (Phil. 2:9–10). Yes, God had "glorified," made great, His Son (Acts 2:32–34; 3:13); He had asked Him to sit down at His right hand!

Why Jesus Sat Down

Do you wonder why Jesus sat down? Did He need a rest? No, a resurrected body never gets tired. Jesus sat down for the same reason that God "rested" on the seventh day from all the work which He had done (Gen. 2:2). God rested then because His work of creation was finished, and Jesus sat down because His work of salvation was complete. There was simply nothing more to be done; the cross is forever, a once-and-for-all sacrifice (Heb. 10:12). The way to God was open, and "whoever believes" in the Lord Jesus Christ can now come to the Father through Him (John 3:16; 14:6).

The Work of Session

Although Christ's work of salvation is finished, and our place in heaven is sure, the Lord has much work to do. As in the days of long ago when the high priests on earth prayed to God for the people, so now our own Great High Priest prays for all who have believed in Him. "He always lives to make intercession for them [for *us*]" (Heb. 7:25*b*), or as our memory verse says, "Christ Jesus is He who died, yes, rather who was raised, who is at the right hand of God, who also intercedes for us" (Rom. 8:34*b*).

As you pray on earth in Jesus' name, He takes your prayers to the Father and asks the Father for your needs. His Father will refuse the Son nothing that He asks for you (John 15:16*b*). Isn't that wonderful to know? See how very important your prayers are to Him? Because He is also a human being like you and I, He knows better than anyone else what problems and troubles we might be having. He alone can help us (Heb. 2:18).

There is another very important thing He does for us in heaven. Do you wonder what it is? He is our "defense lawyer." What do I mean? Well, as you have learned, we have a great enemy, Satan, who keeps tattling on us to the Father. "God," he says, "did You just see what Jane Smith or Charlie Brown did? They're sinning, and they call themselves Christians! Now what are You going to do?" (Rev. 12:10*b*).

I'll tell you what God is going to do when the devil accuses you. He listens instead to the Lord Jesus defend us. Jesus will say, "I died for Jane's sins and for Charlie's sins. My blood has cleansed them and will keep on cleansing them. Why, even now they are confessing their sins" (1 John 1:9; 2:1)! The moment you name your sins to the Father, He forgives and forgets them. He dismisses your case, and Satan has lost another battle against God and God's people. Aren't you glad to have the Lord Jesus at God's right hand to be your defense lawyer?

The End of Christ's Session

Will the Lord Jesus Christ stay at God's right hand forever? No! If you have listened attentively, you will have noticed two things that were said: (1) God the Father said to the Lord, "SIT AT MY RIGHT HAND, UNTIL . . . ." (Heb. 1:13), meaning there would be a time when Jesus would once again leave; and (2) Jesus promised that after He had prepared a place for us in heaven, He would come and take us to be with Him (John 14:3). We will learn about that glad day in our next lesson.

What God Wants Me to Know

Now, while the Lord Jesus is in heaven speaking up for us, we who are still on the earth are to speak up for Him. We represent Him on the earth, that is, speak for Him and in His place. If we who know and love Him keep silent, who will make known God's way to heaven? It's not a matter of "do we want to?" He has commanded us to go and tell of Him. Have you obeyed that command?

Did you know that even now, while you are still sitting right here, God already sees you seated in heaven with Christ at His right hand? Turn in your Bible to Ephesians 2:6. So sure is your place in heaven, as a believing boy or girl, that the Father is said to have "raised us up with Him, and seated us in the heavenly *places*, in Christ Jesus."

The right hand is the place of acceptability, where someone can be received. Do we deserve such an honor? Not at all! But Christ does, and we are accepted "in the Beloved" (Eph. 1:6). The Father loves the Son; therefore, He loves us "in Him." That means He sees us as one with Jesus, even seated on His throne. Isn't that something!

It makes sense, then, that those who sit in heavenly places should not wade through mud puddles of sin, doesn't it? True, Jesus defends us when we sin, but that does not give us an excuse for sinning! So when you sin, and you will, be sure to get cleansed immediately by using 1 John 1:9 and not bring shame to our wonderful Lord.

Then there is another place where God wants you to 'sit down'—on His promises. Trust Him, no matter what. He knows, He cares; He will help you! Will you remember that?

If you are not "in Christ," I want you to know that you are not accepted by God. There is no welcome, no place for you in God's throne room or in any part of heaven. You are either in Christ or not in Christ! You are either in this room or not in here. Well, just the same, God allows you to choose if you want to go to heaven or not. How does anyone get there? Jesus said, "I am the way, and the truth, and the life; no one comes to the Father, but through Me" (John 14:6). It's entirely up to you. Jesus Christ is waiting right now. "He is able to save forever those who draw near to God through Him" (Heb. 7:25*a*). "Believe in the Lord Jesus, and you shall be saved" (Acts 16:31)!

Lesson Review

What happened forty days after the Lord Jesus rose from the dead? He ascended to the Father. What do we call this? Ascension. What happened when He arrived in heaven? He was seated at the Father's right hand. What do we call this? Session. Who was the first man ever to come into the Father's presence in heaven? Jesus Christ. Why was it so important that He be accepted in heaven? Until then no human being was allowed in heaven. Since His acceptance we, too, are accepted in Him. Why did God the Father tell Jesus to sit down? His salvation work was completed. What does Jesus Christ do in heaven for us? He prepares a place for us, makes intercession for us, defends us, cares for us, and helps us. What did the Lord Jesus command believers to do during His absence from the earth? Represent Him here; witness for Him. In which way are believers seated "in the heavenly *places*" while they are still on the earth? God sees us "in Christ," at His own right hand, so sure is our place in heaven. How long will the Lord stay at the Father's right hand? Until the Lord comes for us.

Memory Verse

"Christ Jesus is He who died, yes, rather who was raised, who is at the right hand of God, who also intercedes for us." (Rom. 8:34*b*)

Chapter Twenty

God the Son: His Coming at the Rapture

A. Subject: God the Son: His Coming at the Rapture—John 14:3; 1 Thessalonians 4:16–17

B. Lesson Titles:
1. Lesson One: The Rapture Promised
2. Lesson Two: The Rapture Fulfilled

C. Story Objective:

The Lord Jesus Christ prophesied not only His ascension and session, but also His subsequent return, first for His own—the Rapture, then with His own—the Second Advent. Thus, He graciously outlined for us God the Father's plan for the ages.

The term "Rapture" is not found in the Bible but indicates that moment of time when all believers of the Church Age, dead or living, shall be caught up together to meet the Lord in the clouds to ever be with Him (1 Thess. 4:16–17). The divine timetable of this great event, however, remains a mystery. As all Christians are gathered "together unto him" (2 Thess. 2:1), their bodies will be changed (1 Cor. 15:52) into the likeness of His glorified resurrection body (Phil. 3:21), ultimately sanctified (Jude 24*b*) for everlasting fellowship with God and the Savior.

The Rapture is the Christian's blessed hope, his comfort and assurance of being reunited with loved ones who have gone on before to be with the Lord (2 Thess. 2:1). Immediately following the Rapture, all believers must appear before the judgment seat of Christ at which time their service, or works, shall be evaluated to be rewarded or burned, as the case may be (1 Cor. 3:11–15; 4:5; 2 Cor. 5:10). With the Rapture being imminent, the child of God may look forward with eager anticipation to the Lord's summons. He should live each moment so as to "have confidence [of reward], and not shrink away from Him in shame [loss of reward] at His coming" (1 John 2:28).

D. Vocabulary and Doctrinal Concepts:
1. Vocabulary: archangel, Church Age, Hebrew and Greek texts, judgment, Rapture
2. Doctrinal Concepts:
   a. The Rapture:
      1) Promised (John 14:2–3)
      2) Imminent (James 5:7–8)
      3) Eagerly awaited (Phil. 3:20; 1 Thess. 1:10; Titus 2:13)
   b. Events at the Rapture:
      1) Events summarized (1 Thess. 4:13–17).
      2) All made alive at His coming (1 Cor. 15:22–23).
      3) Some will never see death (1 Cor. 15:51).
      4) An instantaneous change in us; the dead "raised incorruptible," the living made immortal (1 Cor. 15:52–53, KJV).
      5) We are given bodies like unto His glorious body (Phil. 3:21; 1 John 3:2).

E. *Source Book* Keywords: dispensations (Church Age), Elijah, judgment seat of Christ, the Rapture

F. Activities:
1. Suggested Visuals: Rapture time line
2. Games, Songs, Worksheets
3. Memory Verses:
   a. "For the Lord Himself will descend from heaven with a shout, with the voice of *the* archangel, and

with the trumpet of God; and the dead in Christ shall rise first." (1 Thess. 4:16)

    b. "Then we who are alive and remain shall be caught up together with them in the clouds to meet the

Lord in the air, and thus we shall always be with the Lord." (1 Thess. 4:17)

4. Opening and Closing Prayer

LESSON ONE
THE RAPTURE PROMISED

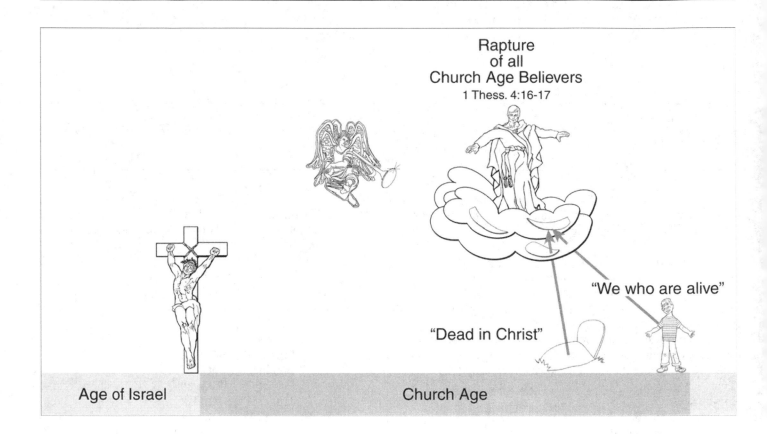

Age of Israel   **Church Age**

Whe call that special moment when the Lord comes back for us "the Rapture." Can you tell me what Rapture means? Well, we certainly do not want you to grow up to be ignorant, especially where the Word of God is concerned! Did you know that God has told us all but one thing about the Rapture? Don't you want to know what He says? I do! So, first of all, let's get the meaning of two important terms that we will be using. The first is our word "Rapture"; the second is the phrase "to be taken up."

The word "Rapture" means a change of form and place; "to be taken up" means a change of form. When the translators of the Bible translated the words of the Hebrew and Greek texts, they gave them to us in our own language. Actually, the word "Rapture," like the word "Trinity," is not found in our Bibles at all. Instead, we read words like

"caught up," or "was not," or "God took him," or "taken up." The reason why we use the word "Rapture" is that it combines all the other words into one and best tells us what that special moment will mean to us.

The Example of Enoch

We talked about the first 'spacemen' at the beginning of our last chapter on the Lord's ascension into heaven. Do you still remember their names? Enoch and Elijah. What happened to Enoch will someday happen to an entire generation of believers, those who are alive at the time. But just what was that? Open your Bible to Genesis 5:24 where we read, "And Enoch walked with God [was in fellowship]; and he was not, for God took him."

"What had become of Enoch?" wondered his friends and family. Only a few minutes ago they had talked to him, and now he had disappeared without a trace. Had he died? If so, where was his body? No, the Bible says that Enoch had not died like Adam, Seth, Enosh, Kenan, and Mahalalel before him (Gen. 5:5, 8, 11, 14, 17). He had been "taken up." Turn to Hebrews 11:5 and see for yourself what had become of Enoch: "By faith Enoch was taken up so that he should not see death; AND HE WAS NOT FOUND BECAUSE GOD TOOK HIM UP; for he obtained the witness that before his being taken up he was pleasing to God." God had moved him from one place to another, in less than a second. This is a perfect picture of what the Rapture will be like.

The Rapture Promised

Now this is not the only place where God promises this wonderful event. Let me remind you of the words of the Lord Jesus Christ to His disciples on the night before He died. He said, "And if I go and prepare a place for you, I will come again, and receive you to Myself; that where I am, *there* you may be also" (John 14:3).

When He spoke of "going," He meant His ascension. "I will come again" is the promise of His return, and His words "receive you to Myself" is the promise of the Rapture.

The disciples were not the only ones to whom this promise was made. All believers, from the time of the cross to His coming in the air, will go up to be with the Lord at the Rapture. What do you think will happen when God's promise of John 14:3 comes true?

The Events of the Rapture

Find 1 Thessalonians 4:16 in your Bible, and let's read that verse together. "For the Lord Himself will descend from heaven with a shout, with the voice of *the* archangel, and with the trumpet of God; and the dead in Christ shall rise first."

The Lord Descends

The day will come when the Lord Jesus Christ will get up from the Father's right hand to descend from heaven with a shout. He could have chosen to send an angel for us and wait for us in heaven. But no, He is coming Himself to take us to heaven. Remember what He said in John 14:6? "I am the way, and the truth, and the life; no one comes to the Father, but through Me." Only Jesus can save us and take us to heaven—not the angels, not even God the Father or God the Holy Spirit. There is only one person in whom we must trust—Jesus Christ (Acts 4:12). Have you believed in Him? Then you, too, will go up at the Rapture.

The Moment of the Rapture

You and I live at a time that we know as the Church Age. The Church Age began ten days after the Lord Jesus

had returned to heaven, when the Holy Spirit came down to the earth. You will learn more about the coming of the Holy Spirit soon. As we said, all who have believed in the Lord Jesus Christ during this time will be taken up when He comes back for His own.

Let us suppose that right now is the moment of the Rapture and that the Lord has just descended from heaven. What can we expect? What should we look and listen for? How would we and all other Christians throughout the world know that He has come? Our memory verse tells us exactly what will happen: "For the Lord Himself will descend from heaven with a shout, with the voice of *the* archangel, and with the trumpet of God; and the dead in Christ shall rise first" (1 Thess. 4:16).

At first we will all hear a mighty shout. We have already found out that the voice of the Lord is greater than the loudest trumpet sound, stronger than the rush of many waters. No matter whether you are asleep or even dead, there is no fear of missing the Lord's call! The only ones who will not be able to hear Him are the unbelievers; neither will they be able to see Him at the Rapture.

Next you will hear the voice of an archangel. An archangel is a high ruling angel. The Bible gives us the name of only one archangel, Michael. Gabriel is a very great angel, but we do not know whether or not he is an archangel. Archangels are God's special messengers who are sent out only on very important errands (Dan. 8:16; 9:21; 10:13, 21; 12:1; Luke 1:19, 26; Jude 9; Rev.12:7). Our memory verse does not tell us the name of the archangel whom the Lord Jesus is taking along.

What else do you remember from 1 Thessalonians 4:16? Yes, the trumpet of God. In the days of the Old Testament, trumpets were used to call people together. That's just how it will be in that moment. Believers everywhere will recognize the sound of that trumpet even though they have never heard it before.

The Dead in Christ Rise First

Now, a most amazing thing takes place. Shortly before all living believers are called to go up, those who are in their graves, "asleep in Christ," leave their graves (1 Cor. 15:18). Do they come out as skeletons? Many of them have been dead and buried hundreds upon hundreds of years! No! God has promised them bodies just like that of the Son of God (Phil. 3:21). When they rise from the dead, they have perfect resurrection bodies; they come out of their burial places and never leave a mark anywhere. The unbelievers will never know these graves are now empty.

What about those of us who may still be alive? Well, you will find out what happens to us in our next lesson.

What God Wants Me to Know

Are you, like Enoch, walking with God in fellowship moment by moment? Are you trying to please Him and serve Him? You know what the Lord Jesus wants you to do for Him until He comes for you, don't you? He wants you to tell others about Him.

Let us suppose your father had to leave for quite a while. Before he left, he told you to do several things for him. "When I return," he promised, "I will give you a nice reward if you have obeyed me." Perhaps you put off doing what you knew you should, thinking, "Oh, there's still plenty of time left." Then suddenly your father surprised you and walked in the door. Would you be glad or ashamed to see him?

Had you only obeyed him, how different things would be! Every day you would have looked for him to come home, watching and waiting, hoping this would be the day of his return. And wouldn't you rush into his arms, ready to meet him? How glad you would be had you done what you should when he hands you the promised reward!

At the start of our lesson I told you that there is one thing about the Rapture God did not tell us—when the Lord Jesus will come in the clouds. It may be any moment—even now before this lesson is over. Will you be rewarded or lose your reward when He comes? Well, that will depend on whether or not you obeyed God's Word. You will want Him to come quickly, if you do what He said. He promises, "Behold, I am coming quickly, and My reward *is* with Me, to render to every man according to what he has done" (Rev. 22:12).

The Lord Jesus could call any time. If He came to take us up now, would you be ready? Remember, only those who have trusted in Him will hear and see Him. They will be caught up to "meet the Lord in the air" (1 Thess. 4:17). Will you tell the Father right now, if you have never done so before, that you are believing in Christ for your salvation?

Lesson Review

I want you to think of 1 Thessalonians 4:16, your memory verse, as I ask you some questions. The first six

may be answered in the words of your memory verse. Here we go.

Who shall come for us at the Rapture? "The Lord Himself." What will He do when He leaves the Father's right hand? "Descend from heaven." Will we hear Him say anything? We will hear Him "shout." What else shall we hear? "The voice of *the* archangel." What instrument will be used to call us? "The trumpet of God." Then what will happen? "The dead in Christ shall rise first."

Very good. Can you tell me the meaning of the word "Rapture"? A change of place and form. Do we find this word in our Bibles? No, but it describes well all the things that will happen when the Lord returns for His own.

The first to go up at the Rapture are "the dead in Christ," all believers who have died since the Church Age began: those whose bodies are in graves or at the bottom of the ocean; those who have died in wars or in plane crashes; those whose bodies have never been found—all will be made alive again when the trumpet sounds. What an awakening that will be! All those dead bodies will suddenly be changed into resurrection bodies, exactly like that of the Son of God. In our next lesson we will see what happens to those who are still alive on the earth.

Memory Verse

"For the Lord Himself will descend from heaven with a shout, with the voice of *the* archangel, and with the trumpet of God; and the dead in Christ shall rise first." (1 Thess. 4:16)

LESSON TWO
THE RAPTURE FULFILLED

*D*o you like surprises? I am sure we all do. The most wonderful of all surprises is the Rapture. Think of it—one generation of believers on the earth will never even die! Who will they be? That depends on when the Lord Jesus returns. God has kept that date a secret from us. He will surprise us some day or some night, but He wants us to look for the Rapture at any moment. Every day when you awaken you may wonder, will it be today? Let's

suppose once more it *is* today, and that the dead in Christ have already received their resurrection bodies. Their change of form has taken place and now ours begins.

Again, open your Bible to 1 Thessalonians 4, this time to verse 17. We will read it together: "Then we who are alive and remain shall be caught up together with them in the clouds to meet the Lord in the air, and thus we shall always be with the Lord."

Caught Up Together

Would we have time to finish learning about the Rapture if we heard the trumpet right now? Of course not. It will be much greater to be in the Rapture than to learn of it! Every believing boy and girl, man and woman, all over the world will suddenly be changed. They wil rise together, right through the ceiling, right through the roof just like the Lord Jesus did through the sealed stone.

But what about the lame and the crippled, those who are sick in hospitals, or helpless in wheelchairs? What of those who are deaf? Will they hear? Or those who sleep, will they miss the Lord's call? Never! There will not be one believer left behind at the Rapture, not even the dawdlers and slowpokes. As soon as the dead and the living Christians have changed forms into resurrection bodies, they are "caught up together."

And that is where our change of place comes in. When both dead and living believers have their resurrection bodies, they will go up the same way the Lord Jesus did. Do you remember? In clouds. Then we will meet the Lord Jesus in the air and again be with our own loved ones who have died. Think of the joy there will be when families and friends meet again never to part! Think how great it will be to be made exactly like the Lord Jesus, free from sin and the sin nature, and to have a resurrection body (Phil. 3:21; 1 John 3:2*b*)! We will have a body which can never hurt or be sick and die again, a body that will be able to walk through solid objects and soar through heaven like a bird!

How Shall We Know Him?

But you may well wonder, "If we are to be exactly like the Lord Jesus, how will we know Him among those many people caught up at the Rapture?" We will have no trouble recognizing the Lord. He alone will have the nail prints in His hands and feet and the deep scar in His side. Those scars will remind us forever how much He loved us "while we were yet sinners" (Rom. 5:8).

Not only will we know Him, we will also recognize each other. Think how much we will enjoy each other once our sin natures are gone! Most of all, we will love being with the Lord Himself. Our memory verse tells us how long we shall be with Him. How long? "Thus we shall always be with the Lord." If you are a believer in the Lord Jesus Christ, a whole eternity of gladness is waiting for you!

The Twinkling of an Eye

It took us two lessons to learn about the coming of the Son of God at the Rapture. But how long will the Rapture actually take? Let's count off the events as they take place. First the Lord shall descend from heaven with a shout. Next the archangel calls and the trumpet sounds. The dead in Christ will rise from their graves; after them we who are still alive will go up. We are given resurrection bodies and will meet the Lord in the air, in the clouds. Wouldn't you

think all this would take hours, even days? Not at all. Jesus Christ is God. He is omnipotent, all-powerful. Distance means nothing to Him, for He is also omnipresent, in all places at once. If He snapped His fingers and countless stars, suns, moons, and planets came into being (Ps. 8:3), could He not work just as fast at the Rapture?

That is exactly what He will do. Turn in your Bible to 1 Corinthians 15, and let's read verse 51. "Behold, I tell you a mystery; we shall not all sleep, but we shall all be changed." In this verse Paul shares a secret with us. The secret is God's surprise to us—the Rapture. He says that not all believers will die, but that all believers will someday be changed. How long will that take? Paul tells us at the beginning of verse 52 that it will only take a moment, just as long as it takes to blink an eye: "In a moment, in the twinkling of an eye, at the last trumpet; for the trumpet will sound, and the dead will be raised imperishable, and we shall be changed." Try it! Blink your eyes! There, now you know how long the Rapture will take. What a mighty God we have!

What Became of Charlie Brown?

Now I want you to think back to a verse we read about Enoch: Hebrews 11:5. "By faith Enoch was taken up so that he should not see death; AND HE WAS NOT FOUND BECAUSE GOD TOOK HIM UP; for he obtained the witness that before his being taken up he was pleasing to God."

Just imagine, if the Lord comes for His own during the night, the next morning someone might ask in school, "Where's Charlie Brown? Where are Jane, and Joe, and Mary?" No one knows why you do not come to school anymore; even the principal cannot find out. Your house is empty, perhaps not locked, and your unbelieving friends and families cannot understand why you left all your belongings behind. Maybe they will call the police and report you missing. Like Enoch of old, you, too, will have disappeared without a trace.

Put your name in place of Enoch's name in Hebrews 11:5. Now read it: "By faith *Charlie* was taken up so that he should not see death; AND HE WAS NOT FOUND BECAUSE GOD TOOK HIM UP; for he obtained the witness that before his being taken up he was pleasing to God." Multiply this thousands of times until all living believers of the Rapture have been named. In addition to them, there are the millions of resurrected dead. Perhaps this will give you an idea of how great a meeting there will be in the air. And what is that great meeting called? Right, the Rapture.

The Judgment Seat of Christ

What happens after the Rapture? When we arrive in heaven, we must all stand before the judgment seat of Christ. The Lord will look over all we have done for Him. Will our works stand the test? All that we have done while we were in fellowship in the power of the Holy Spirit will be rewarded, and all we did in our own strength will be burned (1 Cor. 3:11–15). There is no place for our own good works in heaven, and we cannot take them with us. But our own place in heaven is sure for us, according to God's promise.

What God Wants Me to Know

Do you know what the Bible calls the Rapture? In Titus 2:13 it is called "the blessed hope." What does that mean? When we say, "I hope," we are not sure something will happen, are we? But the way the Bible uses the word "hope" is different. Hope in the Bible means confidence; all that we long for and wait for is wrapped up in God's promises. God always keeps His Word. The Rapture is certain to come, and you, believer, will be in it. Look for Him, wait for Him, and see to it that you stay in fellowship and make every day count for the Lord (2 Pet. 3:11b, 14).

Do you know what happened soon after God took Enoch off the earth? The flood came and wiped away all the wicked. Do you know what will happen after the Lord takes believers off the earth at the Rapture? God will send judgment after judgment upon the earth. There will then be only seven years left for those who remain on earth—seven years during which they can still decide to take Jesus as their Savior. Who will be left behind when the Rapture comes? All living unbelievers will stay on the earth, and all dead unbelievers' bodies will stay in their graves. Oh, what terrible times will be on the earth then!

Will you be here to see and feel these awful things? You need not be. The Rapture will not come until the last person in the Church Age who will believe in the Lord Jesus Christ has done so. Are you that person? Whether you are or not, if you will accept God's Son right now, He will reserve a place for you which no one else can take (Eph. 2:6; 1 Pet. 1:4). The Father is waiting for your decision. What will it be?

Lesson Review

Today we will answer some questions from 1 Thessalonians 4:17. Who is said to be "alive and remain[ing]" when the Lord comes at the Rapture? We are. Who are "we"? Believers. What shall happen to all living believers at that time? They shall be caught up together with those believers who have died. Where shall we be caught up? "In the clouds." Why? "To meet the Lord in the air." How long shall we be with Him? Forever.

Can you tell me what happens to the unbelieving dead and living at the Rapture? The dead remain in their graves, the living remain on the earth. What can they expect for the next seven years? A time of great trouble. What will the Lord do after He has taken us to be with Him? He will evaluate our works. What shall be rewarded and what burned? Our own good works done in our own strength are burned; all good works done while in fellowship and in the power of the Spirit will be rewarded.

Memory Verse

"Then we who are alive and remain shall be caught up together with them in the clouds to meet the Lord in the air, and thus we shall always be with the Lord." (1 Thess. 4:17)

Chapter Twenty-One

God the Son: His Second Coming

A. Subject: God the Son: His Second Coming—Zechariah 14; Matthew 24; Revelation 19:11–16

B. Lesson Titles:
1. Lesson One: The Promise of the Second Coming
2. Lesson Two: The Events of the Second Coming

C. Story Objective:

At His first advent, God the Son came into the world as the baby in the manger (Gal. 4:4). Then He came in humility, having emptied Himself of the outward expression of His deity (Phil. 2:5–8). In contrast, at His second advent He shall appear in great power and glory (Matt. 24:30*b*; Col. 3:4) in His resurrection body (Acts 1:11).

The second coming or advent of our Lord Jesus Christ is the greatest point of eschatology. It will take place seven years after the Rapture of the Church (Dan. 9:24–27; Rev. 11:3; 12:6; 13:5), at the end of the Tribulation (Dan. 12:1; Zech. 14:3–5). His coming will mark the beginning of the final phase of human history on this present earth—the millennial reign of Christ and His resurrected saints (Rev. 20:4).

Some marvelous changes shall be brought about which have been eagerly anticipated by creature and creation alike. Believing Israel shall be delivered, regathered, and restored to the Promised Land (Isa. 11:12). Religion and war will be abolished (Isa. 2:2–5; Rev. 17—18), and Satan is bound for a thousand years (Rev. 20:1–3). All creation shall be freed from the curse of sin (Isa. 11:35; Rom. 8:18–23). However, in all its perfection, the Millennium is but a prelude to the blessings of eternity which are yet to come.

D. Vocabulary and Doctrinal Concepts:
1. Vocabulary: advent, millennial kingdom, Millennium, Tribulation
2. Doctrinal Concepts:
   a. The Lord's second coming:
      1) Described in the words of Jesus (Matt. 24)
      2) The purpose of His coming (Matt. 25:31–46)
   b. With His own:
      1) With all His saints (1 Thess. 3:13; cf. Col. 3:4)
      2) With His saints to execute judgment (Jude 14–15)
   c. To the earth:
      1) He will stand upon the Mount of Olives (Zech. 14:4–5).
      2) Two armies with the Lord; raptured believers and His angels (Matt. 16:27; Acts. 1:11; Rev. 19:14).
      3) He will reign (Micah 4:7*b*).
      4) Every eye will see Him (Rev. 1:7).
      5) To set up His kingdom (Rev. 19:11–16).
   d. One-thousand-year reign (Rev. 20:6); Satan bound for one thousand years (Rev. 20:2–3)
   e. Bible terminology:
      1) *The Day of Christ*: the Rapture and gathering up of the Church (1 Cor. 1:8; Phil. 1:6; 2:16)
      2) *The Day of the Lord*: the period of the Tribulation (seven years), Second Coming, Millennium (one thousand years), and judgment (1 Thess. 5:2; 2 Pet. 3:10)

E. *Source Book* Keywords: dispensations (Tribulation, Millennium), Second Advent

F. Activities:
    1. Suggested Visuals: Christ at Second Advent, escha-
        tological time line
    2. Games, Songs, Worksheets

3. Memory Verse: "BEHOLD, HE IS COMING WITH THE
    CLOUDS, and every eye will see Him." (Rev. 1:7a)
4. Opening and Closing Prayer

LESSON ONE
THE PROMISE OF THE SECOND COMING

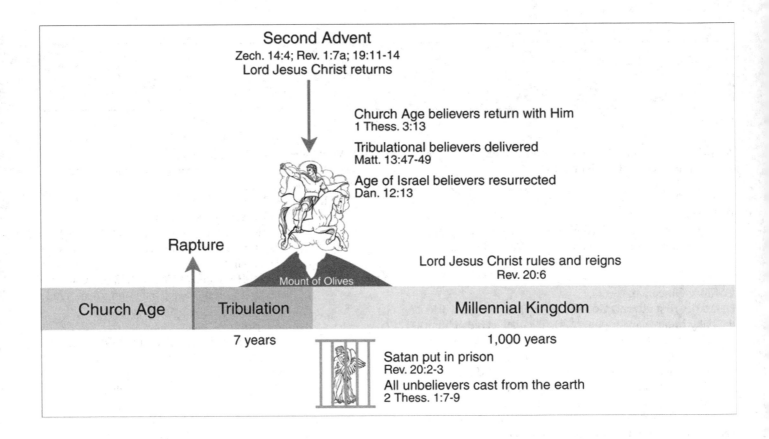

Second Advent
Zech. 14:4; Rev. 1:7a; 19:11-14
Lord Jesus Christ returns

Church Age believers return with Him
1 Thess. 3:13

Tribulational believers delivered
Matt. 13:47-49

Age of Israel believers resurrected
Dan. 12:13

Rapture

Lord Jesus Christ rules and reigns
Rev. 20:6

Mount of Olives

Church Age   Tribulation   Millennial Kingdom

7 years   1,000 years

Satan put in prison
Rev. 20:2-3
All unbelievers cast from the earth
2 Thess. 1:7-9

Can you still remember how many years this time of great trouble, the Tribulation, will last? Seven years. Have you wondered and asked yourself, "Then what?" Well, if you have, I can answer your question today. The Lord Jesus will come down once more, this time all the way down to the earth. We call this the second coming or second advent of the Lord. Advent means "a coming." When was the Lord's first coming or advent? When He came to earth as the baby in the manger. When the Lord comes the second time, will He be born all over again? Of course not; the Second Coming will be altogether different, different even from the Lord's coming at the Rapture.

Today many believers are all mixed up about the Rapture and the Second Coming, although God tells us how different these comings will be. Let me see how sharp you are about the events of the Rapture; then listen as I tell you what we can expect at the Second Coming.

Contrasting the Rapture and the Second Advent

Rapture	Second Advent
(1) For His own (1 Thess. 4:16–17)	(1) With His own (1 Thess. 3:13)
(2) Seen by believers (Heb. 9:28)	(2) Seen by all (Rev. 1:7a)
(3) Believers taken (John 14:3)	(3) Unbelievers taken (Matt. 24:37–39; 2 Thess. 1:7–9)
(4) Comes in the air (1 Thess. 4:17)	(4) Comes to earth (Zech. 14:4)
(5) We don't know when (Mark 13:32)	(5) We know when (Matt. 24:29–30)
(6) Believers to heaven (1 Thess. 4:16–17)	(6) Believers to earth (Col. 3:4)

1. For whom does the Lord Jesus come at the Rapture? For His own, Church Age believers. When He comes back the second time, He will bring us with Him; with His own. Where does it say so? In 1 Thessalonians 3:13: "So that He may establish your hearts unblamable in holiness before our God and Father at the coming of our Lord Jesus with all His saints."

2. The second way in which His comings are different is this: At the Rapture only one group of people can see the Lord. Who are they? Only believers can see Him. But at the Second Coming "every eye will see Him" (Rev. 1:7a): "BEHOLD, HE IS COMING WITH THE CLOUDS, and every eye will see Him."

3. The third difference is in who is taken off the earth and who is left behind. Tell me, who is taken off the earth at the Rapture? Yes, all believers. In contrast, at the Lord's second coming all unbelievers will be taken off the earth.

4. How far down does the Lord come at the Rapture? He comes in the air. At His second coming He will come down all the way to the earth.

5. Do we know when the Rapture will occur? No. But God told us when the Second Coming will be. Seven years later.

6. At the Rapture believers are taken to what place? To heaven. At the Second Coming, the Lord brings us back with Him to the earth.

There are many more such contrasts, but these will do for now, and they will help us understand better what God is planning to do when the right time comes.

The Tribulation

After we have left this old earth at the Rapture to be with our wonderful Lord, He will reward us for all we have done for Him while we were in fellowship on earth. Then the Lord will make us ready for our return trip to the earth (1 Thess. 3:13; Rev. 19:14). Let's pretend we can look down from heaven to see what happens on earth while we are gone. Of course, we don't need to do that, nor will we even want to; God has it all written down for us to read right now.

How dreadful those seven years will be! The Bible says they will be the most horrible years this world has ever seen. We read, "For then there will be a great tribulation, such as has not occurred since the beginning of the world until now, nor ever shall" (Matt. 24:21).

What does "tribulation" mean? It means a time of trouble. There will be wars and crimes, sickness and hunger, cruelty and suffering as never before. In fact, it will be so bad that we read in Matthew 24:22 that unless God would shorten the time to seven years, no one would be left alive: "And unless those days had been cut short, no life would have been saved; but for the sake of the elect those days shall be cut short." Many thousands upon thousands shall die, but also many shall turn to the Lord Jesus Christ and be saved. Oh, how those who believe in the Lord Jesus will long for His return! They will count the days I am sure; they will pray for His coming. Perhaps during the last year they will even look up hopefully into the sky, seeking for the cloud in which they know the Lord will return to the earth.

Awaiting the Lord's Return

But how will they know all these things? The same way we do—from the Word of God. God's enemy, Satan, would love nothing better than to see God's Word destroyed, twisted, and never taught again. But he won't have his way. God promised that we shall always have His Word in writing (Matt. 24:35; 1 Pet. 1:25). Even now, while we study our lesson, many Bibles have been hidden away in caves in the land of Israel or Palestine. Someday, after we have gone to heaven, people will find these books and read them and discover God's plan for themselves.

Mount of Olives

Yes, those believers of the Tribulation will have studied the many verses which tell of the Lord's second advent. They will know from the Book of Acts what the angels promised the Lord's disciples: that the Lord Jesus will come back in a cloud and stand on the top of the Mount of Olives (Zech. 14:4; Acts 1:11). They will also know the Lord's warning: "See to it that no one misleads you" (Matt. 24:4). What did the Lord mean?

Well, just shortly before the Lord's second coming there will be a terrible battle fought in Jerusalem. Some Jewish believers will flee to the mountains. Probably most of them will be women and children and people too old to fight, or too sick to fight any longer. Other believing Jews will be fighting the enemy in the streets of Jerusalem. Their enemies will try to trick the fighting men into surrendering to them; they will tell them that the Lord Jesus has come back. But they must not be deceived; they must not believe what they hear. Instead, they must remember what God says in His Word: "Then if anyone says to you, 'Behold, here is the Christ,' or 'There *He is*,' do not believe *him*" (Matt. 24:23).

Why must they not listen and come out of hiding? Think of your memory verse! That's right, Revelation 1:7 says that "every eye will see Him." No one will need to call out, "The Lord has come, the Lord has come!" Every unbeliever and every believer will see Him, no matter where they might be.

Just when all looks hopeless for the believers, when it seems they cannot possibly hold out against their enemies a minute longer, the Lord is already on His way. In our next lesson we will find out how exciting His return will be, for remember you, too, will be there with Him in the clouds.

What God Wants Me to Know

As a believer, do you know the Word of God well enough to know a lie from the truth? If someone tells you that the Lord will not really come back down to earth, nor will He come to meet us in the clouds, would you believe him? I certainly hope not! You have learned differently, right from the Word of God.

If someone told you that God will not really forgive your sins unless you feel sorry for them, would you fall for that? That, too, is a lie! First John 1:9 is a part of God's Word and says, "If we confess our sins, He is faithful and righteous to forgive us our sins and to cleanse us from all unrighteousness."

Just remember this always, believers: Trust God's Word above the words of man (Rom. 3:3–4). If what you hear lines up with the Bible, you may safely believe it; if not, pay no attention to it. Know God's Word; trust and obey it always.

Unbelieving boys and girls, too, can trust the words of the Bible. Those words you see and hear are God's words. God always means what He says. God offers you a choice. Believe on the Lord Jesus Christ and be saved forever; or refuse God's way of salvation and be eternally condemned. Believe in Him, and you will be among those who return to the earth with the Lord at His second advent; or say "No" and spend all eternity in the lake of fire. Which will you choose—safety in Christ or judgment from Him? Tell the Father your decision in silent prayer.

Lesson Review

What are the six contrasts we learned between the Rapture and Christ's second coming? (1) At the Rapture, He comes *for His own*; at the Second Coming, He comes *with His own*. (2) At the Rapture, He is *seen by believers*; at the Second Coming, He is *seen by all*. (3) At the Rapture, *believers are taken*; at the Second Coming, *unbelievers are taken*. (4) At the Rapture, the Lord *comes in the air*; at the Second Coming, He *comes to earth*. (5) We *don't know when* the Rapture will occur; we *do know when* the Second Coming will be. (6) At the Rapture the *believers go to heaven*; at the Second Coming the *believers go to earth*.

Who will look eagerly for the Lord to return to the earth? Believers of the Tribulation. Why? Because it is a time of such terrible trouble. There will be wars and crimes, sickness and hunger, cruelty and suffering as never before. Many thousands upon thousands shall die, but also many shall turn to the Lord Jesus Christ and be saved.

Memory Verse

"BEHOLD, HE IS COMING WITH THE CLOUDS, and every eye will see Him." (Rev. 1:7a)

Are you afraid of the dark? You laugh, thinking that only little kids fear darkness. Well, let me tell you about a day of darkness which will strike terror in the hearts of the bravest of men.

A Day of Darkness

The land of Palestine is in total darkness. The sun refuses to shine by day and the moon and stars by night. There is not the faintest ray of light to be seen anywhere. Throughout the land all activity has stopped, even the fighting in the streets of Jerusalem. And not only is it dark there, but throughout all the earth. What is happening? What can this awful darkness mean? Mighty men tremble, for this is something they do not understand. But those who know God's Word are glad. They know that at any moment now the Lord is coming back. Then the dark skies will be brighter than noonday, and every eye will see the Lord return in power and glory (Isa. 13:9–10; Ezek. 32:7–8; Joel 2:10–11; 3:15–16).

Can you think of another time when it was darker than midnight, although it was actually noonday? Yes, at the time when the Lord Jesus, bearing our sins, hung on the cross (Matt. 27:45). What a warning that was to the unbelievers then, and now God was warning them to believe in the Lord Jesus Christ, the last warning anyone would have! What if this is the last warning God is giving you? What if He has decided to take you from the earth today? Would you know where you are going to spend eternity? None of us knows how long we will live. Decide now, before it is forever too late!

The Lord Returns

Do you know how fast lightning travels? I'm sure you have seen it streak across the sky. That's how fast and how suddenly the Lord will come. One moment the heavens will be pitch dark; the next moment they will be all aglow with the glory of God the Son (Matt. 24:27). God's heaven will open wide, and a dashing white horse, carrying a rider on its back, will speed through the skies. Who is this rider? Revelation 19:11 tells us His name is "Faithful and True." Can you guess? Think of the Essence Box and the words "immutable," unchangeable, and "veracity," truth! Yes, the Lord Jesus Christ is the faithful and true God; now He is returning as He promised. This time He is not coming to seek and to save the lost, but to judge and to make war. Of course, we know that in all that He does, He is fair and just.

His Appearance

What a wonderful sight the Lord will be! His eyes will blaze as "a flame of fire," and on His head will be many crowns to show that He is the Sovereign of heaven and earth (Rev. 19:12). He will wear a long, flowing robe of white dipped in blood. Remember, He has come to make war, and war cannot be fought without bloodshed! And so that all will know who He is, the words "KING OF KINGS, AND LORD OF LORDS" are written on His robe (Rev. 19:16).

The Lord's Armies

Is the Lord coming alone? Think back to what we learned when we contrasted the Rapture and the Second Advent. No, He is not coming alone; all raptured Church Age believers will come with Him. Let's read Revelation 19:14: "And the armies which are in heaven, clothed in fine linen, white *and* clean, were following Him on white horses." We will be one of the two armies, but who is in the other army of the Lord? Hold your place here and turn to Matthew 16:27*a*: "For the Son of Man is going to come in the glory of His Father with His angels." Can you tell me? You are right, the angels will make up the second army of the Lord.

Both armies will ride spotless white horses and will wear snow-white uniforms. Surely these horses will be the fastest horses that ever were ridden. But have you ever heard of a soldier going to war dressed in white? And we *will* go to war, for there is a dreadful war being fought on earth. The unbelievers are fighting against those few faithful believers who are now making their last stand in Jerusalem. Only miracles can save them now. And the first miracle has already happened—darkness which hides them from their enemies. Now the second miracle is on the way, for the God of heaven and earth is coming to be their Deliverer (Zech. 14:4). He alone will fight, and we, the believers and angels, will be His honor guard.

A Mountain Splits Apart

"BEHOLD, HE IS COMING WITH THE CLOUDS" (Rev. 1:7*a*). We can almost hear the glad shout when the believers see the long-awaited Lord. No doubt they rush toward the mountain where they know the Lord will soon stand. What a happy day this will be for them! The very second the Lord's feet touch the mountaintop, a most amazing thing will happen: "And in that day His feet will stand on the Mount of Olives, which is in front of Jerusalem on the east; and the Mount of Olives will be split in its middle from east to west by a very large valley, so that half of the mountain will move toward the north and the other half toward the south" (Zech. 14:4).

Does that amazing thing remind you of another miracle which the Lord worked for His people long ago, when there seemed to be no way of escape for them from their enemies? What other place was divided right down the center for the Israelites to walk through? The Red Sea. Surely, if the Lord can make a sea split down the middle, He can also split a mountain in two! And through that opening the trapped believers, who have fought so bravely against their strong enemies, walk to safety.

Even now there is a crack in the Mount of Olives. How do we know? A well-known geologist, a man who studies the structure of the earth, discovered a crack in the earth's crust in the mountain. Are you surprised? You should not be. God's Word is true, and when He tells us that this mountain will split apart at the second coming of Christ, we can be sure it will—just that day and not a minute before then. In the meantime, God's faithfulness holds the mountain together.

The Judgment of Living Unbelievers

How do you think the Lord will fight that war? Will He use cannons, bombers, submarines? No, He does not need earthly weapons. Do you remember how the Lord fought against Satan in the wilderness? With the sword of the Spirit, which is the Word of God (Matt. 4:4, 7, 10). That is exactly how the Lord will fight now. Go back in your Bible to Revelation 19:15: "And from His mouth comes a sharp sword, so that with it He may smite the nations; and He will rule them with a rod of iron; and He treads the wine press of the fierce wrath of God, the Almighty." The Lord need only speak a word, and His enemies will drop dead at His feet, so powerful is His Word! You know what Hebrews 4:12 says: "The Word of God is alive and powerful, and sharper than any two-edged sword" (corrected translation). It is your best weapon, too, Christian soldier, now and ever!

Do you think that the unbelievers will be glad to see Him? Certainly not; they will be terrified. They have refused to believe in the Lord Jesus Christ when He offered them His love-gift of salvation, and now they see that He has come to punish them. Do you know what they will do? They will try to hide themselves from omniscient, all-knowing God.

Turn in your Bible to Revelation 6:15–17: "And the kings of the earth and the great men and the commanders and the rich and the strong and every slave and free man, hid themselves in the caves and among the rocks of the mountains; and they said to the mountains and to the rocks, 'Fall on us and hide us from the presence of Him who sits on the throne, and from the wrath of the Lamb; for the great day of their wrath has come; and who is able to stand?'" Will that do them any good? Of course not. God knows where they are hiding. He will cast off every unbeliever from the earth (2 Thess. 1:7–9). Now, only believers in the Lord Jesus Christ are left, and they will stay on the earth (Matt. 13:47–49).

The Resurrection of Old Testament Believers

At His second advent the Lord will raise up the dead believers of the Age of Israel. Then David's view into the future will come true (Ps. 16:9–11), and he will live again on the earth. Daniel, too, will be resurrected (Dan. 12:13), and so will countless others of the Old Testament.

The Millennial Reign of Christ

Now the Lord is ready to set up His millennial kingdom over the earth. Millennium means one thousand years. The Lord will give the Jewish people the land which He had promised them so long ago, and the happiest one thousand years the world has ever known will begin (Rev. 20:6). The Lord Jesus will reign in righteousness and justice. And wonder of wonders, we will reign with Him!

We will see some great changes on the earth. There will be no more religion. Religion is man trying to get God's attention by his own works. Satan, who started all religion, is chained and put in prison for a thousand years (Rev. 20:2–3a). There will be no more wars, nor any weapons. All animals will be tame. Who knows, you might even have a lion or a tiger for a pet! You will see small children play with snakes and never get bitten. Roses will lose their thorns; and the deserts will no longer be dry, but will blossom and grow grass and juicy fruits. There will be no more storms or earthquakes, no floods, no more sickness, and no one ever need be afraid. No one will be poor or needy. All will be perfect and good because the Lord Jesus is King of kings (Isa. 11:5–8; 35:1–2; Micah 4:3).

What God Wants Me to Know

Just think of it, you will help the Lord rule in His perfect kingdom! Does He need your help and mine? No, He does not, but He will let us help Him then, even as He lets us help Him now. Every little or big thing you do for Him while you are in fellowship counts. The more you do now to bring honor and glory to Him, the greater your place will be in the Kingdom.

What are some of the things you can do now? Obey His Word, trust Him moment by moment, tell others about the Lord Jesus, obey your parents and teachers—all these the Lord will reward. But even if you have never done more than just believe in Jesus Christ, you will still be in the Lord's heavenly army. You will come back with Him in your resurrection body and see His glory when He returns to the earth.

But pity the ones who have not believed in the Lord Jesus Christ! All unbelievers, rich and poor, the mightiest kings as well as the poorest beggars, men, women, children will tremble at the Lord's second coming. There is no hiding place from the anger and judgment of God. They will think, "What have I done? Why did I not believe in Him when I heard of God's gift of salvation? Oh, I wish I had, I wish I had!" But it will be too late then.

Maybe you have not made up your mind about the Lord Jesus Christ. Do you know who He is? He is the second person of the Trinity, God the Son. Do you understand what He has done for you? He has given His perfect life to pay the price for your sins. He was punished so that you may go free and your sins might be forgiven. It is not too late for you to believe right now! Don't put it off. God's Word says, "Now is 'THE ACCEPTABLE TIME,' behold, now is 'THE DAY OF SALVATION'" (2 Cor. 6:2). Believe in the Lord Jesus Christ now, and you will be saved and given a place in the Lord's army this very moment!

Lesson Review

Until His second advent, the Lord Jesus Christ has given us the power of the Holy Spirit to help us live the kind of life He wants us to live, and to help us tell others about Him and God's way of salvation. How can we be saved? By believing in Jesus Christ. Seven years after the Rapture the Lord Jesus is going to return to the earth. Who will He bring with Him? Yes, believers and angels. Where will He stand when He comes the second time? On the Mount of Olives. And what will happen to the mountain? It will split in two.

Then begins the Lord's reign on the earth. How long will it last? One thousand years. What is the word that means one thousand years? Millennium. Satan will be bound and thrown into prison, and all living unbelievers will be cast off the earth. Where will you and I be during those wonderful years? We will reign with Him, won't we? Can you tell me some of the wonderful changes that will happen then? There will be no more religion. There will be no more wars, nor any weapons. All animals will be tame. You will see small children play with snakes and never get bitten. Roses will lose their thorns; and the deserts will no longer be dry, but will blossom and grow grass and juicy fruits. There will be no more storms or earthquakes, no floods, no more sickness, and no one ever need be afraid. No one will be poor or needy. When the thousand years are over, eternity, the forever happy time, will begin. All believers will be with their Lord in heaven, even as He has promised, but all unbelievers will be forever separated from God in the lake of fire. Do you know someone who does not know the Lord Jesus as his Savior? Would you do as He commanded and tell them how they may be saved?

Memory Verse

"BEHOLD, HE IS COMING WITH THE CLOUDS, and every eye will see Him." (Rev. 1:7*a*)

Chapter Twenty-Two

God the Holy Spirit: His Ministry in the Old Testament

OVERVIEW

A. Subject: God the Holy Spirit: His Ministry in the Old Testament—Genesis 1:2 and 41:38; Psalm 104:30; 2 Peter 1:21

B. Lesson Titles:
   1. Lesson One: His Person and His Work
   2. Lesson Two: The Power of the Holy Spirit and Old Testament Leaders

C. Story Objective:

The Holy Spirit is a person in the same sense that God the Father and God the Son are persons or personalities. He is the third member of the Trinity and one in essence with the other two (Matt. 28:19). The fact that He is said to have the same divine attributes as the Father and the Son attests to His deity and personality. In speaking of the Holy Spirit, Scripture uses personal pronouns (John 16:13).

The Holy Spirit has always been in the world and has always had a relationship with mankind, but there is a marked difference between His work in the Old Testament and in the New Testament. Throughout the Old Testament days, God chose certain individuals by His sovereign will and according to His own purposes to whom He gave the enduement of the Holy Spirit. However, upon continued sin in those believers' lives, the Holy Spirit could be taken from them (Ps. 51:11). The various ministries of the Holy Spirit in the lives of some of the Old Testament believers shall provide the basis for this lesson.

D. Vocabulary and Doctrinal Concepts:
   1. Vocabulary: bidding, doctrine, enduement, garment, indwell, idols, judges, prophets

2. Doctrinal Concepts:
   a. The person of the Holy Spirit:
      1) He is God (Acts 5:3–4; 1 Cor. 2:14).
      2) He has distinct personality and the very essence of God (John 15:26).
      3) He is sovereignty (1 Cor. 12:11); "holiness," righteousness and justice combined (Rom. 1:4); love (Rom. 15:30; Gal. 5:22); eternal life (Heb. 9:14); omniscient (1 Cor. 2:10–11); omnipresent (Ps. 139:7–8); omnipotent (Acts 1:8); immutable (John 14:16; Gal. 5:22); veracity (John 15:26).
   b. The function of the Holy Spirit as declared in the Old Testament:
      1) His work in creation and restoration (Gen. 1:2; Ps. 104:30).
      2) His work of conviction (Gen. 6:3).
      3) He endued a limited number of believers: Joseph (Gen. 41:38); Moses and the seventy elders (Num. 11:17, 25); the workmen who constructed the Tabernacle (Ex. 31:3); those who made the priestly garments (Ex. 28:3); Joshua (Num. 27:18); the judges (Judg. 3:10; 6:34; 11:29; 13:25; 14:6; 15:14); the kings, Saul and David (1 Sam. 10:9–10; 1 Sam. 16:13); prophets, such as Daniel (Dan. 4:8; 5:11); leaders, such as Zerubbabel (Zech. 4:3; 4:12–14).
   c. The Holy Spirit could be asked for and received (2 Kings 2:9–10).
   d. The Holy Spirit was given by God and could be removed for carnality (Ps. 51:11).

e. The Holy Spirit inspired the writers of Scripture (Job 32:8; Jer. 1:9; 2 Pet. 1:21).

f. The Holy Spirit taught divine truths (Neh. 9:20).

g. The Holy Spirit upheld believers (Ps. 51:12).

E. *Source Book* Keywords: God the Holy Spirit (deity of, enduement of, Old Testament ministry of), verbal plenary inspiration

F. Activities:

1. Suggested Visuals: Joseph, Joshua, King Saul

2. Games, Songs, Worksheets

3. Memory Verse: "'Not by might nor by power, but by My Spirit,' says the LORD of hosts." (Zech. 4:6*b*)

4. Opening and Closing Prayer

LESSON ONE
HIS PERSON AND WORK

We have already learned in our study of the Trinity about God the Father and God the Son. Now we are getting ready to learn some of the doctrines concerning God the Holy Spirit. He is the third person of the Trinity. That means He is as much God as God the Father and as God the Son; He has the same divine essence as have the other two members of the Trinity. He is sovereignty, righteousness, justice, love, eternal life, omniscience, omnipresence, omnipotence, immutability, and veracity.

As His name tells us, the Holy Spirit is invisible. But that does not make Him unreal. Have you ever seen the wind? You have not! What you saw were the effects of the wind, what the wind did—the swaying leaves on a tree, the rippling waters, a piece of paper skipping down the street, a swirl of dust, the clouds sailing across the sky. But you never saw the wind itself. Yet the wind is real; you must admit that. Even more real is God the Holy Spirit, especially to those who know the Lord Jesus as their Savior and know His Word. In fact, were it not for the Holy Spirit, we would have no Bible at all, for He is the one who caused the Bible to be written. Do you still remember what 2 Timothy 3:16*a* says? "All Scripture is God-breathed and profitable for teaching, for reproof, for training, for instruction in righteousness" (2 Tim. 3:16*a*, corrected translation).

If you turn to 2 Peter 1:21, you will find out that it was God the Holy Spirit who inspired the writers of God's Word: "No prophecy was ever made by an act of human will, but men moved by the Holy Spirit spoke from God." And it is God the Holy Spirit who teaches us the things of God and His Word (Job 36:22; 1 Cor. 2:13), as well as the things concerning Himself.

The Holy Spirit as a Person

The very first thing we want to notice is that the Holy Spirit is a real person, not just a thing—an influence for our good, although He does influence or move us. Whenever the Bible mentions the Holy Spirit, words such as "He," "His," or "Him" are used, never "it." Let's see an example of what I am speaking of in John 16:13: "But when He, the Spirit of truth, comes, He will guide you into all the truth; for He will not speak on His own initiative, but whatever He hears, He will speak; and He will disclose to you what is to come." Sometimes the translators of the Bible have used the words "Holy Ghost" in place of the words "Holy Spirit." But there is no "Holy Ghost," and we should always read "Holy Spirit" instead. Will you remember that? Just keep in mind that God is a very real person, not an unreal 'spook.'

Now, where in the Bible are we first introduced to the Holy Spirit? In the second verse of Genesis 1. Let's read both Genesis 1:1 and 1:2 together, shall we? "In the beginning God created the heavens and the earth. And the earth was formless and void, and darkness was over the surface of the deep; and the Spirit of God was moving over the surface of the waters."

His Work in Creation and Restoration

As you know, all persons of the Trinity have their separate functions or work to do. The Father planned all of creation; the Son made all things; and the Holy Spirit restored all things when Satan's sin brought ruin to the original earth God had created. When we read that God said, "'Let there be light'; and there was light" (Gen. 1:3), those were the Father's words, and the work was that of the Holy Spirit. But long before that time, God the Son had created, or made out of nothing, those same lights. Those lights had gone out when everything had become dark and empty (Gen. 1:2). Now the Holy Spirit 'turned the lights back on again' and brought order back upon the world.

When the earth was ready for human beings to live on it, the Holy Spirit stayed to continue His own special work on earth. Do you wonder what it was, apart from "inspiring" the writers of the Bible? Then listen carefully as we move quickly through the Old Testament passages which tell of His work.

His Work in the Days of the Old Testament

Down through the ages, God saw to it that His perfect plan would always be carried out. In heaven, the angels of God serve Him and do His bidding. But here on earth, God uses believers, and sometimes even unbelievers to work out His plans. To make sure of this, the Holy Spirit's own power is needed, for God's work must always be done God's way. That's why the Lord says to us in Zechariah 4:6b that it is "'Not by might nor by power, but by My Spirit,' says the LORD of hosts." The "Spirit" is, of course, the Holy Spirit, and the word "hosts" is a word you have already learned. Do you remember? It means heavenly armies, or angels.

Just as God, the Lord Jesus Christ, is called by many names other than God the Son, so is God the Holy Spirit. Perhaps the name which best describes what He does is the one found in the New Testament—"the Helper" (John 14:26). It means the one who has come alongside to help, or better yet, inside to help, for that is exactly what the Holy Spirit does for believers.

The Enduement of the Holy Spirit

The Old Testament tells us that the Holy Spirit was given by God to certain Old Testament believers whom God had chosen to do some difficult task. In every case, He came unseen and unfelt, and in every case His work could be plainly seen.

The Holy Spirit Was in Joseph

The first man recorded to have the Holy Spirit endue him was Joseph. Turn in your Bible to Genesis 41:38: "Then Pharaoh said to his servants, 'Can we find a man like this, in whom is a divine spirit?'" Can you think back

to the lessons you have learned about God's omniscience and Joseph? What was the job for which God had chosen Joseph? To save the children of Israel during the great famine (Gen. 45:7; 50:20). It was God the Holy Spirit who had shown Joseph the meaning of Pharaoh's dream and what should be done about it. Pharaoh could not see the Holy Spirit, but he could recognize that God Himself must be in

Joseph to give him such wisdom—the very wisdom Joseph would need to become prime minister of Egypt.

The Holy Spirit Was in Moses

Can you think of another well-known believer of the Old Testament whom God made a great leader? He was put in the river as a baby and was raised in the palace. Right! It was Moses. God had asked Moses to lead more than two million stubborn people out of Egypt and through the wilderness for forty long years. No one needed the Holy Spirit's power and wisdom more than Moses. God always knows just what we need to do the job He has given us to do: "Then I will come down and speak with you there, and I will take of the Spirit who is upon you, and will put *Him* upon them; and they shall bear the burden of the people with you, so that you shall not bear *it* all alone" (Num. 11:17).

Jethro, Moses' father-in-law, had come to visit Moses and the Israelites in the wilderness. As he watched Moses leading such a great people, he thought that surely Moses was working too hard. He advised Moses to find helpers (Ex. 18), and then he returned to his own country, Midian. Moses listened to Jethro and thought the idea was good indeed, yet for a while he did nothing about it.

But the Israelites were a troublesome and complaining people. Time and time again, God had to punish them for their unbelief. Moses, too, became discouraged. He told God that the job he had been given to do was much too hard for one man; he would rather be dead than lead the Israelites alone another minute (Num. 11:10–15).

Do you think God gives a believer more than he can bear? Never! "No temptation has overtaken you but such as is common to man; and God is faithful, who will not allow you to be tempted beyond what you are able, but with the temptation will provide the way of escape also, that you may be able to endure it" (1 Cor. 10:13). Do you know how much power God had given Moses? Power enough to be seventy-one leaders. How do I know? "The LORD therefore said to Moses, 'Gather for Me seventy men from the elders of Israel, whom you know to be the elders of the people and their officers and bring them to the tent of meeting, and let them take their stand there with you. Then I will come down and speak with you there, and I will take of the Spirit who is upon you, and will put *Him* upon them; and they shall bear the burden of the people with you, so that you shall not bear *it* all alone" (Num. 11:16–17). You will know this, too. God allowed Moses to share his heavy burden with others, yet he could have done it alone because the all-power of the Holy Spirit was in him.

The Workmen of the Tabernacle, Furniture, and Robes

When God gave instructions for the building of the Tabernacle in the wilderness, He insisted that it be made exactly like the pattern He showed to Moses on the mountaintop

(Ex. 25:40). Would Moses be able to explain what he had seen to the workmen? God would make sure that all was done as He wished. The Holy Spirit would give wisdom and special skill or know-how to the builders of the Tabernacle and its furnishings and to those who made the priestly robes (Ex. 31:1–11). Did they deserve getting the Holy Spirit any more than Moses or Joseph? They didn't; no one ever deserves the presence of the Holy Spirit. He is a gift from God.

What God Wants Me to Know

Do you think that Joseph, Moses, or any of the others ever bragged about what they did for God? They did not! They knew what they had done was done in the power of God the Holy Spirit. Do you ever look around in a classroom to see if others have noticed that your answers to questions are mostly right? Are you proud of being good at certain things, and that you make better grades than others? Do you look down your nose at other Christian boys and girls who don't have as fine a house as your parents have, as pretty dresses as you wear?

Then remember what the Bible says: All that you have you have received as a gift from God (1 Cor. 4:7). The same Holy Spirit who endued the Old Testament believers now lives in or indwells you if you are a believer in the Lord Jesus Christ (1 Cor. 3:16). What gifts or abilities He has given you are to be used to please the Lord, not yourself. Will you remember that?

Perhaps you have not received the Holy Spirit. How can you have Him indwell you for the rest of your life? Can you pray for Him? No! Should you just sit around and wait until God might possibly choose you to do something big for Him? Of course not! The Holy Spirit is yours simply for believing in the Lord Jesus Christ. He is the gift of God the Father and God the Son to all who will believe in the Son (John 14:16; 16:7). Will you receive Him right now?

Lesson Review

What do you remember about the Holy Spirit? He is God, the third person of the Trinity, invisible and of the same essence as the Father and the Son. He inspired the writers of the Bible, teaches us spiritual truths, and shows the unbelievers their need of salvation. Where in the Bible do we first read of the Holy Spirit? In Genesis 1:2. What did He do after the earth became dark and empty because of Satan's sin? He restored it. What name given the Holy Spirit in the Bible best describes His work for the believer? The Helper—one who comes alongside to help. How did the Holy Spirit help believers in the days of the Old Testament? He endued some believers to give them power to carry out God's plans. This is different from the New Testament when He indwells and fills all believers.

Memory Verse

"'Not by might nor by power, but by My Spirit,' says the LORD of hosts." (Zech. 4:6*b*)

LESSON TWO
THE POWER OF THE HOLY SPIRIT AND OLD TESTAMENT LEADERS

*A*s you go through school, you will come across helpful pointers which will make it easier for you to remember lessons you have learned, like this little rhyme: "Columbus sailed the ocean blue, in fourteen hundred ninety-two." Well, here's another rhyme to help you remember the work of the Holy Spirit throughout the Old Testament, including His work in those few believers whom He endued for one reason or another. Listen: "Leaders, judges, prophets, kings, through God the Spirit did great things. He could be asked for in that day, was given or was taken away."

Let's make a chart of what we have already learned about the Holy Spirit's enduement of certain leaders of the Old Testament. Divide your paper into three columns; head them PERSONS, BOOK, WORK. Now, listen to my clues: I am thinking about the first recorded man who was said to have the Holy Spirit within him. Who was he, and in what book can we read about him? Joseph, in Genesis. What was his work? He was Pharaoh's Prime Minister.

Do you wonder how God helped believers before the time of Joseph? He sent the Angel of the Lord, Jesus Christ, or other angels to help them and to protect them. He dealt with His own, "Person to person." Only when God's promise to Abraham—to make of him a special nation—had come true, did God choose a human leader for them. That first leader was to be Joseph, Abraham's great-grandson. The Holy Spirit endued him and made him a great and wise leader who could take care of God's people in Egypt.

Next, we meet the man whose story is found in Exodus, Leviticus, Numbers, and Deuteronomy. Who was he? Moses. How did he manage to do signs and wonders in Egypt? How did he lead more than two million Israelites for forty years in the desert? Endued with the power of the Holy Spirit. God had given Moses just the measure of strength he would need for the job of leadership, yet Moses thought he should have human helpers as well. What did we call them, and how many of them were there? Seventy elders. God gave the Spirit to them so that there were more men to do the job. Each had the same amount of power—the all-power of God the Holy Spirit.

There were some others, too, who needed special know-how for the job God had given them to do. Who were they? The workmen of the Tabernacle and those who made the priestly robes. To them the Holy Spirit was given (Ex. 31:3–6) until their work was finished. Then, as our little rhyme says, He "was taken away." There was also another reason why the Holy Spirit was sometimes removed—sin in the life.

Joshua and the Holy Spirit

God had told Moses to train Joshua to take over the leadership of the Israelites after his death. Young Joshua was a general. He was faithful to God and to Moses. It was brought to Joshua's attention that there were two men who had begun to preach, even though they had not been at the Tabernacle when God put His Spirit in the elders. Joshua wondered whether they might be trying to take away Moses' leadership. "Moses, my lord, restrain [forbid] them," he begged. He must have been surprised to hear Moses answer: I wish that "the LORD would put His Spirit upon them [all of God's people]" (Num. 11:25–29).

Was it God's plan for all believers in the Old Testament days to receive power from the Holy Spirit? No, He would be given only to those who had some special job to do for the Lord. Who do you think would be the next in line to receive power from the Holy Spirit? Why, Joshua, of course! We are told in Deuteronomy 34:9 that Joshua was "filled with the spirit of wisdom"—God the Holy Spirit. Joshua was the one who brought the Israelites into the Promised Land. But before Joshua died, he reminded the Israelites that God was their true Leader and King, and that they were to obey Him always. The story of Joshua is recorded in the book named after him.

The Judges and the Holy Spirit

Not long after Joshua's death, God's people turned away from serving the Lord and began to worship idols instead.

Joshua and his helpers had all died, and the Israelites felt there was no need to obey their words any longer. They forgot the true God of heaven, but He had not forgotten them.

God allowed strong enemies to make war against His people, and when they began to pray to God for help, He gave them new leaders—judges—to rule over them and fight their wars. The Book of Judges is full of interesting stories of what the judges, endued with the power of the Holy Spirit, did: stories about Othniel, Gideon, Jephthah, and Samson.

The Kings and the Holy Spirit

Isn't it a pity that most of us have to learn our lessons the hard way? The Israelites certainly did! God had wanted them to be His own special people; they were to be different from all other nations around them (Deut. 7:6). But as we continue to read their history, we soon find out that this did not suit the Israelites at all. They no longer wanted to have judges rule over them. Other nations had kings; so they, too, wanted a king whom they could see, instead of the invisible, heavenly King (1 Sam. 8:5b).

How often have you wanted something other boys and girls had? You begged your parents to let you have it also, and you argued, "But Mother, Father, *everybody* has one." Shouldn't you stop to think, "Perhaps God doesn't want me to have this because it won't be good for me, or make me happy"?

The Israelites were often very unhappy with the kings who ruled over them, for most of them were bad kings, selfish and unjust, who brought sorrow to the land because they did not obey God's Word. Time and time again, we read from 1 Samuel through 2 Chronicles that the king did that which was "evil in the sight of the LORD." Let's look at just two kings: one who was good, the other who was bad—David and Saul.

King Saul and the Holy Spirit

We'll take Saul first, because he was the first king of Israel. Saul was the finest, tallest, handsomest man in the land. The last of the judges, Samuel, had anointed him king according to God's Word (1 Sam. 9:2, 15–17). But Samuel was sad, very sad indeed, that the Israelites wanted a king other than God (1 Sam. 12:12b). He warned them that things would go badly for them if they and their king should ever stop serving the Lord God (1 Sam. 12:24–25).

Saul could have been a wonderful king. The Holy Spirit had been given to him to "be changed into another man" (1 Sam. 10:6). You see, Saul was the son of a wealthy, powerful rancher. There had never been a king in Israel before him. Who would teach him what a king was to do? God the Holy Spirit, Sovereign of heaven and earth, would teach Saul from within.

Saul's reign had begun well enough. He was a brave king and a good leader to his soldiers. He won great victories over his enemies, but Saul's real trouble came from his inside enemy—from his sin nature. Sin piled upon sin as he disobeyed God's Word, and in the end, God the Holy Spirit had to be taken away, as was Saul's kingdom (1 Sam. 13:13–14; 15:28; 16:14). God chose David to be king in Saul's place.

David and the Holy Spirit

From the day that David also was anointed king by Samuel, the Holy Spirit endued Him to help him (1 Sam. 16:13). King David was the greatest king the Israelites ever had. When he sinned against God, he was quick to confess his sins, for he remembered that the Holy Spirit had been taken away from King Saul before him. Once David prayed, "Do not take Thy Holy Spirit from me" (Ps. 51:11*b*). God answered David's prayer; the Spirit stayed with David as long as David lived. David's last words were: "The Spirit of the LORD spoke by me, And His word was on my tongue" (2 Sam. 23:2).

The Prophets and the Holy Spirit

Now that there were no more judges in Israel, but kings, God appointed them helpers—the prophets. The prophets were to pass on God's messages and warnings to their kings. There were many great and well-known prophets. Some of the books in the Bible are named after them: Isaiah, Jeremiah, Ezekiel, Daniel—all the way to Malachi. There was Elijah, God's messenger to wicked King Ahab and Queen Jezebel; there was Elisha, who did twice as many wonderful things as Elijah had done before him. Shall I tell you how Elisha received the Holy Spirit? He asked for Him! Remember our little rhyme? "He could be asked for." Elisha did just that, and God listened and answered his wish (2 Kings 2:9*b*, 15).

Often, when bad kings sat upon the throne of Israel, they treated God's prophets cruelly. Do you remember what King Jehoiakim did to Jeremiah? He put him into the deepest prison and nearly starved him to death. Do you remember what Jehoiakim did with the warning message Jeremiah sent him? He cut the scroll into little pieces and burned it in the fireplace.

At last Samuel's terrible warning came true. The kings and their people, for the most part, had not listened to God's Word. Their land was taken away from them in warfare, their kings were killed, and those who survived were taken into faraway lands as prisoners (1 Sam. 12:25; 2 Chron. 36:15–21).

But God had not forsaken His people. He is faithful even if they were not. After their time of punishment was over, God raised up leaders once again—not kings now, but prophets, priests, and leaders. He gave them back their homeland and helped them rebuild it. So, down through the years, the Holy Spirit continued to carry out God's plans for God's people.

What God Wants Me to Know

Do you remember my telling you that although we cannot see the Holy Spirit, the results of His presence can be seen? Because the Holy Spirit endued Joseph, there was none as wise as he. Because the Holy Spirit endued Moses, the mighty leader of God's people did signs and wonders and became a great prophet (Deut. 34:10). Because of the enduement of the Holy Spirit, the elders could preach and prophesy (Num. 11:25). Because of the enduement of the Holy Spirit, King Saul was courageous at first (1 Sam. 11). Because the Holy Spirit spoke through David, we have the Book of Psalms. David wrote more than half of the Psalms. It was "not by [their own] might nor by power," but by God's Spirit that these men could do God's work, God's way. Today every believer is indwelt by the Holy Spirit for as long as he lives. Every believer is also filled with the Spirit every time he confesses his sins. Are you allowing the Holy Spirit to have His way in your life by keeping your sins confessed?

Let's look at one more verse—Romans 8:9*b*: "If anyone does not have the Spirit of Christ, he does not belong to Him." Are you the person this verse is talking about? You are, if you have not believed in the Lord Jesus Christ. Therefore, the Holy Spirit is not in you. You cannot even understand the lesson we have just learned. But you can understand that you have to believe in the Lord Jesus Christ to be saved. Will you do it now? Then the Holy Spirit will be given to you to teach you God's Word and to help you carry out God's plan for your life.

Lesson Review

We have learned of the work of God the Holy Spirit in the days of the Old Testament. See whether you still remember who some of the believers were to whom the Holy Spirit was given. I will name the books of the Old Testament in which we read about them; you will tell me their names. Ready? Genesis—Joseph; Exodus—Moses, workmen, and those who made priestly clothes; Numbers—elders; Deuteronomy and Joshua—Joshua; Judges—Othniel, Gideon, Jephthah, and Samson; 1 Samuel—Prophet-priest Samuel, King Saul, and King David; Psalms—David; Isaiah through Malachi—the prophets. Can you name any of the prophets we talked about? Elijah, Elisha, Isaiah, Jeremiah, Ezekiel, Daniel. Can you name the king from whom the

Holy Spirit was taken? King Saul. Why was that? Continued, unconfessed sin in his life. Can you name the prophet who received the Holy Spirit by asking for Him? Elisha. All of these, and many more, did mighty things, not in their own strength—but how? "'Not by might nor by power, but by My Spirit,' says the LORD of hosts" (Zech. 4:6*b*).

Memory Verse

"'Not by might nor by power, but by My Spirit,' says the LORD of hosts." (Zech. 4:6*b*)

Chapter Twenty-Three

God the Holy Spirit: His Coming in the Church Age

OVERVIEW

A. Subject: God the Holy Spirit: His Coming in the Church Age—Acts 1:10—2:8; John 14

B. Lesson Titles:
1. Lesson One: The Promise of the Spirit
2. Lesson Two: The Coming of the Spirit at Pentecost

C. Story Objective:

Before His ascension, the Lord Jesus Christ promised that He and the Father would send the Holy Spirit to indwell all believers in the Church Age (John 14:16–17; 16:7; Acts 1:8). He referred to the Holy Spirit as "the Helper," meaning one who comes alongside to help. The Spirit's coming took place fifty days after the Resurrection, or ten days after the ascension of the Lord Jesus Christ (Acts 2:1–4).

Although the Holy Spirit's ministries differ from age to age, they are nevertheless essential in every dispensation. The work of the Holy Spirit in the Church Age (John 16:1–16) constitutes a manifestation of the grace of God unequaled in ages past, and the Christian today has the fullest spiritual privileges. It is the primary purpose of the Holy Spirit in the present age to glorify Christ.

D. Vocabulary and Doctrinal Concepts:
1. Vocabulary: foreign, harvest, native, Pentecost, shadows, sheaf, witness
2. Doctrinal Concepts:
   a. Dispensational orientation: The Church Age Pentecost to the Rapture is covered in the following Scripture passages: John 14—17 and the Epistles. Church truths were not revealed in the Old Testament. The first mention of the Church was made by the Lord in Matthew 16:18.
   b. The Church Age may be divided into two periods: pre-canon and post-canon. The pre-canon period extended from A.D. 32 to the close of the first century with the death of the Apostle John. During that time the Apostles headed the churches, and temporary spiritual gifts were in operation to focus attention on the hearing of the Gospel (Book of Acts). The Epistles have become the textbook of the modus operandi for the post-canon period, and temporary spiritual gifts have ceased to function.
   c. The 'problem passage' of Joel 2:28–32, as quoted in Acts 2:17–21, needs clarification:
      1) Peter uses the Joel passage as an illustration of what happened on the day of Pentecost.
      2) Establishes a parallel.
      3) Uses the parallel phenomenon to refute the charges made in Acts 2:13.
      4) Joel 2:28–32 is a millennial prophecy.
      5) Church doctrines are declared in the Epistles (Eph. 3:1–5; Col. 1:25–26).
   d. Characteristics of the Church Age: universal; positional sanctification; indwelling of Christ and the Holy Spirit; priesthood of all believers; canon of Scripture completed; a supernatural way of life, superseding the Mosaic Law, which is executed in the filling of the Spirit; ambassadorship, the personal responsibility of every believer; spirituality by filling of the Spirit; salvation by faith in Jesus Christ.

e. The doctrine of spiritual gifts:
   1) Every believer receives at least one gift from the Holy Spirit at salvation (1 Cor. 12:11).
   2) Each spiritual gift is necessary for the function of the Church (1 Cor. 12:15–21; 27–31).
   3) There are temporary and permanent spiritual gifts (Acts 19:11; cf. Phil. 2:27; 1 Cor. 13:8–10).
   4) All spiritual gifts operate on the filling of the Spirit (1 Cor. 13).
   5) In the local church, the permanent spiritual gifts are to function; the temporary cease to function (1 Cor. 14).

E. *Source Book* Keywords: dispensations (of the hypostatic union, Church Age), God the Holy Spirit (baptism of, filling of, indwelling, salvation ministry), spiritual gifts

F. Activities:
   1. Suggested Visuals: none
   2. Games, Songs, Worksheets
   3. Memory Verse: "You shall receive power when the Holy Spirit has come upon you; and you shall be My witnesses." (Acts 1:8*a*)
   4. Opening and Closing Prayer

LESSON ONE
THE PROMISE OF THE SPIRIT

Now I want you to think back to another lesson we have learned—the lesson on how the Lord Jesus ascended or went up into heaven. After the Lord Jesus rose from the dead, He showed Himself alive on the earth for forty days. Then He took His disciples with Him to the top of the Mount of Olives. He spoke to them for the last time, and He returned to His heavenly home.

The disciples could scarcely take their eyes off heaven. Perhaps they hoped to see their Lord in the cloud just once more, for they kept right on staring into the sky. Instead they saw two angels who told them the Lord would return someday (Acts 1:9–11). That brought the disciples back down to earth, and they remembered the Lord's command to wait in Jerusalem for the promised Holy Spirit to come to them (Acts 1:4–5). Quickly, the eleven came down from the mountain and hurried back to Jerusalem. They went to a friend's house to wait along with some other believers in an upstairs room (Acts 1:12–14).

If you were promised a visit from the president, wouldn't you be excited about it? Wouldn't you be sure to be there and not miss his coming? Wouldn't you talk about his coming with all your friends? You'd want to tell them exactly what he wrote or said, wouldn't you? You'd wonder how and when he was to come and what would happen when he arrived. I am sure the disciples discussed the coming of the Holy Spirit as they waited for Him. Let's pretend we can peek in and watch them, shall we?

The Promise Remembered

"I remember," Peter was saying now, "how the Lord Jesus sat down with us on the last Passover. How sad we all were to think that He would leave us so soon. I can still hear Him say, 'In my Father's house are many mansions . . . I go to prepare a place for you . . . I will come again!'"

Thomas spoke softly, "That's when I asked Him, 'Lord, we don't know where You are going; how can we know the way?' And He answered, 'I am the way . . . no one comes to the Father but by Me.'"

John, leaning forward, said that Christ had promised to send the Holy Spirit right after He ascended to heaven. "I will ask the Father, and He will give you another Helper, that He may be with you forever; *that is* the Spirit of truth, whom the world cannot receive, because it does not behold Him or know Him, *but* you know Him because He abides with you, and will be in you" (John 14:16–17).

Open your Bible to John 14:16–17. Who is this Helper? The "Spirit of truth," God the Holy Spirit. Do you remember what the word "Helper" means? One who comes alongside to help. How long did He stay with the Old Testament believers? Until their work was finished, or until sin in the life caused Him to be removed. How long does verse 16 say the Holy Spirit would indwell believers in New Testament times? Right! Forever. That means always. No matter how terrible our sins may be, the believer today will never lose the indwelling of the Holy Spirit. He need not pray, like David once did, "Do not take Thy Holy Spirit from me" (Ps. 51:11*b*), for in the New Testament times the Spirit indwells every believer forever!

Did you hear that? *In every believer*—not just in a few special believers! Do unbelievers have the Holy Spirit in them? Look at verse 17 for your answer: "the world [unbelievers] cannot receive [Him], because it does not behold [understand] Him or know Him [because they do not know Jesus as their Savior]." And where shall the Holy Spirit be? "He abides [lives] with you, and will be in [indwell] you," in our innermost beings, in our real selves.

The disciples knew that some wonderful things would happen when God the Holy Spirit came to make His home within them; they would do the same great things, even miracles, which the Lord Jesus had done in the power of the Holy Spirit (John 14:12). The Holy Spirit would guide them and teach them and glorify or make great the Lord Jesus in their lives. He would help them to tell others about the Savior (John 15:20–27), and remind them of the doctrines and promises they had learned (John 14:26). Truly the Holy Spirit would be a perfect replacement for the absent Christ. But when would He come, and how? What did Jesus mean when He promised the Spirit's coming "not many days from now" (Acts 1:5*b*)?

Day after day passed, and still the Holy Spirit had not come. But the disciples knew the Lord would keep His promise; they kept on waiting, wondering what to expect. Would they be able to see the Holy Spirit? Would they feel anything when He came? How would they know for certain that He had really come to give them power to be His witnesses? For that was what Jesus Christ had repeated on the mountaintop, on the day of His ascension: "You shall receive power when the Holy Spirit has come upon you; and you shall be My witnesses" (Acts 1:8*a*). In our next lesson you will find out what the coming of the Holy Spirit was like and what He did for the disciples that day.

What God Wants Me to Know

Do you sometimes become impatient when your mother or dad try to show you how to do something? I know many boys and girls who can hardly wait, and they beg, "Let me do it; I want to do it myself!" Once a girl about your age wanted to learn to knit. She couldn't wait for her mother to finish explaining and showing her how to hold the needles properly and pull through the stitches. Mother shrugged her shoulders and handed her the knitting. Do you know what happened? In no time, the needles and the yarn were in a hopeless mess.

That's what believers would be like without the power of the Holy Spirit in their lives. God knew it. Once the disciples were a fearful group of men. They had scattered like frightened rabbits when the Lord Jesus had been led away to be nailed to the cross. They had huddled behind closed doors after His death. It was a good thing they listened to the Lord's words to do nothing but wait until the Holy Spirit came to give them power. There's no telling what a mess they would have made, trying to witness (to tell what you know) in their own strength.

God's work must be done God's way. He cannot use our strength and power. That's why He has given us the Holy Spirit, to strengthen us from within, to help us live the sort of lives God wants us to live. Have you ever thanked the heavenly Father for the Holy Spirit who indwells you, who teaches and guides you, and who is your Helper?

There is one thing which we can never do for ourselves, no matter how hard we may try, and that is to work for our salvation. The Bible says, "He saved us, not on the basis of deeds which we have done in righteousness, but according to His mercy" (Titus 3:5*a*). Salvation is a gift. God the Father planned it; God the Son died so that we may be given it; and God the Holy Spirit shows us how badly we need to be saved.

Along with the gift of salvation comes the gift of God the Holy Spirit and the power He alone can give us. You need not sit around and wait and wonder when He might come; He is yours the very moment you believe in the Lord Jesus Christ. This can be the moment for you! Believe in the Lord Jesus Christ, and the Holy Spirit will make you over into a child of God and indwell you forever (Gal. 3:26; Titus 3:5*b*). It is entirely up to you.

Lesson Review

Who planned to send the Holy Spirit after God the Son's ascension? God the Father. Who promised to ask the Father to send the Holy Spirit to be the Helper? Jesus Christ. Who asked the Lord, "How shall we know the way?" Thomas. Who took the disciples to the top of the Mount of Olives? Jesus Christ. Who came to give believers power? God the Holy Spirit.

Who were the first to speak to the disciples after the Lord ascended up to heaven? The two angels. Who hurried back to Jerusalem? The eleven disciples. Who waited with the disciples in an upstairs room? Other believers. Who wondered how and when the Holy Spirit would come? All the believers in that room.

Memory Verse
"You shall receive power when the Holy Spirit has come upon you; and you shall be My witnesses." (Acts 1:8*a*)

LESSON TWO
THE COMING OF THE SPIRIT AT PENTECOST

*W*e all like to have visitors. When someone comes whom we love very much, we beg him not to leave, but stay a little longer. That was the way the Old Testament believers felt about having the Holy Spirit staying with them. To most of them He was given only as a visitor, and they never knew just how long He would be with them. No wonder David begged God not to take the Holy Spirit away from him. But we have also seen that if the Holy Spirit was not made welcome in someone's life because of continued, unconfessed sin, the Holy Spirit would leave very quickly.

The Lord Jesus had promised all believers that from now on things were to be different. Once the Holy Spirit had come down from heaven, He would no longer be a visitor; He would come to stay. While the disciples and the other believers waited in that room in Jerusalem, they kept thinking, "When, oh when, will that be?" Perhaps they all counted and marked off the days on their calendar. Forty-nine days had passed since the Lord rose from the dead; those first forty days they had seen Him alive on the earth and He had fellowshipped with them, and then He had gone back up to heaven, and nine days more had passed since. Just how much longer must they wait?

Why the Disciples Had to Wait

We'll have to go way back into the Old Testament to see why the disciples had to wait until the fiftieth day, the day of Pentecost, before the Holy Spirit came upon them. I told you once before that the sacrifices with their offerings and all of the Old Testament holy days were only *shadows* of the real thing. The real thing, or rather, the real person they had looked for then was the Lord Jesus Christ. We know that He came to make the shadows become reality, but let us see just once more what some of those shadow pictures meant.

What did the perfect lambs of the Old Testament foreshadow? The perfect person of the Lord Jesus Christ. What did the death of the lambs show? The death of Christ on the cross. With the shadow sacrifices, the covering or atonement of sin could only be pictured. What would the death of Jesus Christ, God's Lamb, do? Pay the penalty for sin. Of what was the Passover a shadow picture? Salvation. What did the blood-painted doors show? Faith in Christ.

I will tell you why the Holy Spirit came down when He did. He came on the day of Pentecost. I will tell you in a moment what that word means.

Apart from the Passover, there were other special holy days which God told His people to keep every year. All holy days were shadows pointing to something far greater which would happen at a future day. For instance, there was the Feast of First Fruits. Once the Israelites were in the land God had promised to give them, they were to bring to the priest a sheaf or bundle of the first-ripe grain which they had cut. The priest would take the sheaf and wave it before the Lord. It was a reminder to God's people that God had given them a plentiful and safe harvest, as He had promised. Now He would let them bring it all into their barns (Lev. 23:10–11a).

Now I ask you, what must a farmer do before he can harvest or gather anything at all? First, he must plant or bury the seed in the ground. If God gives the right amount of rain and sunshine, new life will come out of those seeds. Each kernel of grain will grow and ripen and bear "much fruit." Then comes harvest time.

To be our Savior, the Lord Jesus had to die and be buried and rise from the dead in new life. Before He went to the cross, He said, "Truly, truly, I say to you, unless a grain of wheat falls into the earth and dies, it remains by itself alone; but if it dies, it bears much fruit" (John 12:24).

When the right time came, the Lord Jesus was "cut off out of the land of the living" (Isa. 53:8). He was nailed to the cross to die for our sins. Then He was buried, but He did not stay in the grave, did He? No, He rose in new life on the third day. That day was a Sunday. The Feast of First Fruits always fell on a Sunday, too (Lev. 23:11b). Can you tell me now what the real meaning of the Feast of First Fruits was? Yes, it pointed forward to the resurrection of the Lord Jesus Christ. We can see this from 1 Corinthians 15:23: "But each in his own order: Christ the first fruits, after that those who are Christ's at His coming."

But wait, if Jesus Christ is just the first to be raised, there must be others. Who will they be? You and I, every believer in the Lord Jesus Christ. His resurrection is a reminder to us that we, too, will live forever.

Now God told the Israelites to start counting the days; "You shall also count for yourselves from the day after the Sabbath, from the day when you brought in the sheaf of the wave offering; there shall be seven complete Sabbaths [Saturdays]" (Lev. 23:15). How many days are seven complete weeks? Forty-nine days. That's how many days had passed since the Lord's rising from the dead. Then they were to count just one more day; they were to wait until the morning after the last Saturday—fifty days in all (Lev. 23:16a). On the fiftieth day, the Jews were to bring two loaves of bread, freshly baked from newly harvested grain which had been ground into flour.

The Coming of the Spirit on the Day of Pentecost

It was on that fiftieth day the Father and the Son had chosen to send the Holy Spirit. When He came, He would begin to gather in a new harvest for God. What would that harvest be? Believing men, women, boys, and girls! And just like all the grain had once been put together and ground into flour to be mixed and baked into bread, so now the Holy Spirit would take all believers and make them "one in Christ." We call this gathering in of believers the Church Age. It will last from the day of the coming of the Holy Spirit to the day when we are taken up at the Rapture.

Find Acts chapter two in your Bible, and let's read verse 1: "And when the day of Pentecost had come, they were all together in one place." The day of Pentecost, the fiftieth day since the Lord's resurrection, had come. Suddenly the waiting disciples and other believers in that upper room looked up. They listened in amazement. What they heard was a sound from heaven, like a rushing mighty wind, perhaps something like a tornado. It filled all the house (Acts 2:2), but that wasn't all. "And there appeared to them tongues as of fire distributing themselves, and they rested on each one of them" (Acts 2:3). After the sound there came something like fire which separated into many small split flames and scattered into every part of the room where they sat, so that a part of this strange heavenly fire rested upon each person there.

The wind and the flames of fire were not the Holy Spirit Himself. They were God's way of showing that the Holy Spirit had indeed come and that His new work in them could begin. If the disciples had wondered just how the power of the Holy Spirit might show in their lives, they need wonder no more. Although the wind and the flames had soon disappeared, the Holy Spirit had come to indwell them and fill them, even as the Lord Jesus had said He would. Remember, we spoke about not being able to see the wind, but only its work? Well, that was true of the Holy Spirit. Verse 4 tells us what the result of the filling of the Holy Spirit was that day: "And they were all filled with the Holy Spirit and began to speak with other tongues, as the Spirit was giving them utterance." All believers in that room began to speak "with other tongues." What does that mean? They suddenly spoke languages they had never studied before. Could you speak Spanish or French or Chinese if you had never learned these languages? Of course not. This was a miracle! It was a gift that the Holy Spirit gave to those believers of long ago.

The Work of the Holy Spirit in the Church Age

Remember what the Lord Jesus had promised His disciples, and all other believers of the Church Age? "You shall receive power when the Holy Spirit has come upon you; and you shall be My witnesses" (Acts 1:8a). They were to receive power after the Holy Spirit came to them. What kind of power? Power to do what they could never do on their own. How were they to use this power? They were to be witnesses. The amazing gift of languages had been given to the early Christians so that the Gospel, the good news of salvation, could spread quickly.

At this time, foreigners and Jews from many lands filled Jerusalem, and they spoke languages different from that of the Jews born and reared in Jerusalem. How surprised those people were when the disciples began to tell each person, in his own language, that Jesus Christ had died and risen for him, and that he could be saved by believing in Him (Acts 2:5–8)! Do you know how many souls were saved that day? "About three thousand" (Acts 2:41)! And who had done this great work? No one but the Holy Spirit. Sure, He had used the bodies and the mouths of the believers, but it had been His power, not theirs, that won them over to the Lord. And this was only the beginning—only the first day of God the Holy Spirit's work in the Church Age. In His power, the Gospel was preached to the ends of the earth, right up to our time.

What God Wants Me to Know

You heard the Gospel, too, didn't you? That's why you believed and were saved. Did the Holy Spirit come to you with the sound of a rushing, mighty wind? Did He rest on your head like a small, split flame of fire? Did you hurry out into the street, speaking some foreign language as though you had always known it? Of course not. None of those things happened to you when the Holy Spirit entered your life. He came in and indwelt and filled you gently, silently, without your feeling anything at all.

Does that mean that He gave you no power? No! You, too, have the all-power of God within you, but you can make use of it only when you are filled with the Spirit. Be sure that all your sins are confessed so that He can work unhindered in your life. You will learn more about the filling of the Spirit as we go along.

Acts 1:8a is meant as much for you as it is for all other believers. The power is yours to glorify or make great the Lord Jesus Christ. You, too, are to be His witnesses. Many of your friends do not know that Jesus died to save them. You must tell them. The Holy Spirit will give you the right words to say to them—words right from His Bible—like 1 Corinthians 15:3–4: "For I delivered to you as of first importance what I also received, that Christ died for our sins according to the Scriptures, and that He was buried, and that He was raised on the third day according to the Scriptures" or John 3:16: "For God so loved the world, that He gave His only begotten Son, that whoever believes in Him should not perish, but have eternal life." He saw to it that God's Word is all complete now in the pages of our Bibles.

Do you know why God the Holy Spirit no longer gives gifts such as being able to suddenly speak in a foreign language? He need not. The Bible now has all the information anyone needs about God. It has been translated into many other languages—in fact, almost every language. Now all may read it for themselves. Should you want to serve the Lord as a missionary in foreign lands, you will have to learn those languages before you can hope to speak to the natives. In the meantime, let the Holy Spirit teach you and use you right here to tell of the wonderful things God has done for you (Acts 2:11*b*).

The Holy Spirit can do none of these things for you until you have believed in the Lord Jesus Christ. But when you decide to believe in the Lord Jesus you will also receive the Holy Spirit (John 7:39).

Perhaps while you listened to this lesson, something inside of you kept tugging away, making you want to please God. In ourselves we can never please God, because we are all born sinful. We are unrighteous, but God is righteous. How can we come to Him? Only through the Lord Jesus (John 14:6). If you have this desire to come to God, to get to know Him and His Word, then God the Holy Spirit is speaking to you right now. He is making you understand your need to believe in the Lord Jesus Christ. Listen to Him (Heb. 3:8*a*). Believe in the Lord Jesus Christ right now (Acts 16:31).

Lesson Review

I want to ask you several questions about the coming of the Holy Spirit. When did the Holy Spirit come to indwell and fill all believers? On the day of Pentecost. When was that? Fifty days after the Resurrection, or ten days after the ascension of our Lord. Where did He first come down to the earth? Jerusalem. Where were the disciples and the other believers waiting for Him? In an upper room. What did they hear when the Spirit came? The sound of a mighty wind. What did they see? Flames of fire. What place did the wind fill? The whole house where they were sitting. What did the fire do? It rested on everyone's head. Why did God choose such a spectacular way to send the Holy Spirit? To show that He had really come. Why did He wait until the day of Pentecost before the Spirit was sent? To fulfill shadow pictures of the Old Testament. How did these believers know they were filled with the Spirit? They began to speak in foreign languages which they had not known before. How did they know the Holy Spirit would indwell them permanently? Because the Lord had said so. Who went out into all the city and told all the foreigners in their own language God's way of salvation? These believers. Who is promised power through the Holy Spirit, and is to be the Lord's witnesses today? Every Church Age believer.

Memory Verse

"You shall receive power when the Holy Spirit has come upon you; and you shall be My witnesses." (Acts 1:8*a*)

Chapter Twenty-Four

God the Holy Spirit in Regeneration

A. Subject: God the Holy Spirit in Regeneration—John 3:1–18

B. Lesson Titles:
1. Lesson One: The New Birth
2. Lesson Two: The Serpent of Brass

C. Story Objective:
Regeneration is a supernatural work of God whereby eternal life is imparted from the Father (James 1:17–18) to the believer in the Lord Jesus Christ by the agency of the Holy Spirit (John 3:3–7; Titus 3:5). Three illustrations describe regeneration in Scripture: (1) the new birth (John 3:7); (2) positional sanctification (Rom. 6:1–11); (3) new spiritual species (Eph. 2:10; 2 Cor. 5:17). The new birth is the impartation of eternal life through the divine Parent, as contrasted to the impartation of physical life through human parents. Spiritual regeneration is essential. Apart from it, we would still be dead in trespasses and sin and therefore unable to "see [know and enter into] the kingdom of God" (John 3:3). Through regeneration we are made spiritually alive. A new nature is created in the believer which is capable of fellowship with God and gives him a desire to do God's will.

D. Vocabulary and Doctrinal Concepts:
1. Vocabulary: abide, fast, imperishable, perishable, Pharisee, physical birth, regeneration, religion, renewing, Sanhedrin, spiritual life, wrath
2. Doctrinal Concepts:
   a. General Scripture references:

1) Children and heirs of God by faith (Rom. 8:14–17; Gal. 3:26)
2) Sonship certified by the Holy Spirit (Gal. 4:6)
3) "Of the household of faith" (Gal. 6:10*b*)
4) Of the household of God (Eph. 2:19)
5) The Father of dead and living believers of the Church Age (Eph. 3:14–15)
6) "One God and Father" (Eph. 4:6*a*)
7) Children of God (1 John 3:1–2, 10)

b. The new birth:
1) Born of God (John 1:12–13)
2) Made alive (John 5:21; Eph. 2:1; 4:24)
3) Begotten by the resurrection of Jesus (1 Pet. 1:3)

c. Results of the new birth:
1) Indwelling presence, guidance, teaching ministry of the Holy Spirit (John 14:16–17; 16:13–15)
2) A place with the Lord Jesus (John 14:2; 17:24)
3) An appreciation of the things of God (1 Cor. 2:9–12)
4) Eternal security (John 10:28–29; 1 Pet. 1:5)
5) Called out of darkness into light (1 Pet. 2:9–10)
6) "Partakers of *the* divine nature" (2 Pet. 1:4)

d. The ministry of the Holy Spirit in our lives:
1) At salvation: convicts of sin, righteousness, and judgment (John 16:8–11); is the agent of regeneration (John 3:3–7; Titus 3:5); indwells the believer, seals (Eph. 1:13); and baptizes the believer into Christ (1 Cor. 12:13)
2) In our Christian lives: produces the life of Christ in the believer (Gal. 4:19; 5:22–23)

3) At the Rapture and for all eternity: provides the resurrection body (1 John 3:2)

E. *Source Book* Keywords: Adam's original sin, the barrier (regeneration), God the Holy Spirit (salvation ministry), Moses, Nicodemus

F. Activities:
1. Suggested Visuals: Christ on earth, Nicodemus
2. Games, Songs, Worksheets
3. Memory Verse: "Do not marvel that I said to you, 'You must be born again.'" (John 3:7)
4. Opening and Closing Prayer

LESSON ONE
THE NEW BIRTH

*T*his lesson will teach the very first and most important thing that God the Holy Spirit does for everyone at the moment of salvation. What might that be? The new birth, which He gives every believer.

Have you ever seen a birth certificate? Everyone in our country is required to have a birth certificate. It is the record telling when and where you were born and that you are a member of a certain family, such as the "Jones" family. You had to show your birth certificate when you entered school, and boys will need it again when they enlist in the armed services of our country.

Girls may change their names someday, when they get married. They will then have a new name; one may be known as "Mrs. Smith," but her birth certificate is still hers and proves that she is one of the Jones' girls. No one has more than one birth certificate, for no one was born into more than one family here on earth. This birth is called physical birth.

Did you know that the Bible says that physical birth is not enough to get you to heaven? Jesus said, "You must be born again"! God means what He says, you can be sure of that. But, you may wonder, why isn't our physical birth enough? Let's find out, shall we?

The Necessity of the New Birth

Since the Lord Jesus said that we *must* be born again, there must be a good reason why we need another birth. Let's call our physical birth our first birth. What happened when we were born? We were given a body and a soul. Our body is designed to live here on this earth.

You know that when we go deep sea diving we need special equipment to survive in the water or else we will drown. If we were to go up into the air, or into space, we would need machinery to get us there and back. Why? Because we have earthly life. That means we are made to live here, at best, a few years, and at death our bodies end up in the grave.

Do you remember what our souls can do for us? Understand the things of the world in which we live. What happened to the spirit that God had given the first man, Adam? It had died because of Adam's sin. When we were born

physically alive, we were also born spiritually dead (Rom. 5:12; Eph. 2:1). Adam was perfectly created, not only with a body and soul, but also with a human spirit that allowed him to enjoy a relationship and fellowship with God. Adam was complete and perfect. However, when Adam sinned, his spirit died and he became an imperfect person. He had no way to have a relationship or fellowship with God now, and because we are all the children of Adam—human beings—neither have we. We need to be made spiritually alive and complete. There is only one way this can be done—in Christ. "In Him you have been made complete, and He is the head over all rule and authority" (Col. 2:10).

Turn in your Bible to John 3:7: "Do not marvel that I said to you, 'You must be born again.'" We must be born again; we need a second birth. In our first birth we received a body and a soul. What will we receive in our second birth? A human spirit. Our first birth puts us into our human families, but our second birth puts us into the family of God. Our first birth gives us earthly life; our second birth gives us spiritual or heavenly life. Without spiritual life we could never live in heaven. Can you see now why the Lord Jesus said these words? To whom do you think He said them? We find the answer in John chapter 3. Let's turn to that passage now.

Nicodemus and the Lord Jesus

One dark night, when most of the people in the city had gone to sleep, a man walked quickly toward the house where the Lord Jesus was staying. His name was Nicodemus, and the Bible tells us that he was a ruler of the Jews (John 3:1–2a); that means he belonged to the Sanhedrin, a council of seventy important Jewish people that judged over the Jews, something like our Supreme Court.

Nicodemus was a very busy man, and a most religious one. We say that he was religious because he made special efforts to pray seven or more times every day, and he went to the Temple to worship at least three times daily. He belonged to the Pharisees, a group which boasted of spending hours in prayer, of giving great sums of money to the poor, of doing many good works, and of keeping all the Jewish holy days and feast and fast days. These Pharisees could quote many Bible verses about the promised Savior, but instead of trusting in Him they would rather trust in their own works. Do you remember learning about a proud Pharisee and how he came to praise himself before God in the Temple?

Do you know what God says about anyone trying to work for his salvation? Titus 3:5–6 says, "He saved us, not on the basis of deeds which we have done in righteousness, but according to His mercy, by the washing of regeneration and renewing by the Holy Spirit, whom He poured out upon us richly through Jesus Christ our Savior." There is a big difference between religion and Christianity. Religion is all on the outside. It is man trying hard to do nice things to please God, but ignoring the fact that Jesus Christ has already done everything for us on the cross. A religious man wants to get to heaven his own way, not God's way. Christianity is being related to God only through faith in the Lord Jesus Christ (John 1:12–13).

Nicodemus was still trusting in himself as he made his way to Jesus that night. He was curious about Jesus. He had heard so much about Him; now he must find out for himself who this Jesus really was. He found the Lord Jesus awake and alone in the open room on top of the house. No doubt the Lord Jesus, who knows all things, was expecting Nicodemus. "Rabbi [teacher], we know that You have come from God *as* a teacher; for no one can do these signs that You do unless God is with him," Nicodemus began politely (John 3:2).

What were the miracles of the Lord Jesus to prove to the world? That Jesus is the one He claimed to be—God. Nicodemus had been greatly impressed with the miracles, but he had missed the real point—Jesus was not a teacher sent from God; He *is God*. Nicodemus needed to know this.

The Lord Jesus ignored the nice things Nicodemus tried to say. He looked right into Nicodemus (1 Sam. 16:7), and He saw what it was Nicodemus needed far more than anything else in the world. John 3:3 tells us what that was: "Jesus answered and said to him, 'Truly, truly, I say to you, unless one is born again, he cannot see the kingdom of God.'" Yes, Nicodemus needed to be born again. He needed to be born from above. So surprised was Nicodemus to hear these words that he hardly knew what to say. Why, he had come to find out who Jesus was, not to hear that he needed to be born all over again. After all, he was a grown man; there could be no doubt that he had been born. Must he become a baby once more? Nicodemus must have

shook his head. He didn't understand what Jesus was trying to say, nor could he (1 Cor. 2:14).

Let's think about Nicodemus as he looked to the Lord Jesus that night. It was true, Nicodemus had been born the first time. He had a body and a soul. He could love, hate, be curious; he could understand things and people. But he could not understand the things of God. He had earthly life, but no spiritual life. There are three *musts* for Nicodemus. You know the first must. What is it? Yes, he must be born again. Where does the Lord Jesus say so? Think of your memory verse. Second, he must be told how he can be born again. Third, Nicodemus must make a decision.

What God Wants Me to Know

What Jesus said to Nicodemus that day He still says to every man and woman, boy and girl in the world—"You must be born again." Everyone of us is born spiritually dead—that is, dead to God. In ourselves, we have no life that can have a relationship or fellowship with God now, nor can we share His life in heaven.

Can a dead man bring himself back to life? No, nor can anyone who is spiritually dead do anything to get spiritual life. But "God so loved the world [and that includes you], that He gave His only begotten Son, that whoever believes in Him should not perish, but have eternal life" (John 3:16). Jesus has done everything there was to be done that you and I might be born again to eternal life. Our only part is to receive it. And notice, the new birth is for everyone who will believe in the Lord Jesus Christ. God plays no favorites. "Whoever" includes every member of the human race—good or bad, black, yellow, white, or brown. Put your name in the place of "whoever believes." Believe and live! In our next lesson, we will hear what else the Lord Jesus told Nicodemus that day, and what Nicodemus decided to do about what he had heard.

Lesson Review

What did the Lord Jesus say must happen to all of us? We must be born again. How many births did we talk about? Two: the first birth and the second birth. Which one puts us into the human family and which into God's family? The first birth puts us into the human family and the second birth puts us into God's family. Why isn't the first birth enough? It gives us only earthly life. What are we given when we are born? A body and a soul. What must we have before we can understand and fellowship with God? A human spirit. How can we be made spiritually alive and born into God's family? By believing in the Lord Jesus Christ.

Who heard the Lord say the words of our memory verse? Nicodemus. Can you tell me what kind of a person he was? He was a ruler of the Jews, very busy, and very religious. He was a Pharisee. When did he come to see the Lord? By night. Who did he think that the Lord Jesus was? A teacher sent from God. What must he be told? That Jesus *is* God. We talked about three musts for Nicodemus. What were they? (1) He must be born again. (2) He must be told how. (3) He must make a decision. Nicodemus found out the first must. In our next lesson we will learn the answer to his question "How can a grown man be born all over again?" And also, we will learn what Nicodemus decided to do.

LESSON TWO
THE SERPENT OF BRASS

*D*o you remember anything about the moment when you were born? How it felt to be born? What happened when you were born? Whom you saw first? No, you do not! Perhaps your mother told you about it, but you, yourself, cannot remember a thing about it. You only know that you were born, for that is a fact. This was the birth Nicodemus was thinking about. But was Jesus really talking about the first birth? He was not. Listen to His words.

Nicodemus Learns How He Can Be Born Again

What the Lord Jesus had to say was very important. "Truly, truly, I say to you," He said, "unless one is born of water and the Spirit [Holy Spirit], he cannot enter into the kingdom of God" (John 3:5). Now Nicodemus is told how to be born again—of water and of the Holy Spirit. Still Nicodemus is shaking his head. What does the Lord mean? He cannot understand it; do you?

Jesus is using the word "water" as a picture of the Word of God; He is not talking about drinking water or water in which Nicodemus must wash. Water can never wash away sin, only dirt. Let's look up two verses that tell us how to be born again: "You have been born again not of seed which is perishable but imperishable, *that is*, through the living and abiding word of God" (1 Pet. 1:23), and "He saved us, not on the basis of deeds which we have done in righteousness, but according to His mercy, by the washing of regeneration and renewing by the Holy Spirit" (Titus 3:5). The words "regeneration" and "renewing" are both words for the new birth.

What Jesus is telling Nicodemus, and us, is that while our mothers gave us our physical or first birth, God the Holy Spirit gives us our second birth into the family of God "through the living and abiding word of God" and "the washing of regeneration and renewing of the Holy Spirit." Nicodemus now knew that he must be born again; that he must hear the Word of God about the Savior; and that he

must believe it. Then he, and we, can be made complete once more—body, soul, and spirit (Col. 2:10; 1 Thess. 5:23).

John 3:6 says, "That which is born of the flesh is flesh, and that which is born of the Spirit is spirit." Can you tell me which is the first and which is the second birth, as the Lord talks about them both? Right! The birth in the flesh or body is the first birth; the birth through the Holy Spirit is our second birth that gives us eternal life and a human spirit so that we can have a relationship and fellowship with God and understand His Word. Then Jesus said the words of our memory verse. Can you say them without looking at your Bible? "Do not marvel that I said to you, 'You must be born again'" (John 3:7).

Can we feel the second birth? Not any more than we felt the first birth. We have a birth certificate to prove that we had the first birth. How do we know that the second birth is real? Would you like to see the spiritual birth certificate God gave us? Then turn to 1 John 5:11–12*a*. "And the witness is this, that God has given us eternal life, and this life is in His Son. He who has the Son has the life." Isn't that proof enough—God's Word in writing? I should say it is!

Nicodemus Need Not Understand, but Believe

Nicodemus was still having trouble understanding what the Lord was telling him. You see, until we have spiritual life, we cannot understand spiritual things. Nicodemus prided himself in knowing the Old Testament, yet he really did not understand it. That's what the Lord Jesus was telling him now: "Are you the teacher of Israel, and do not understand these things?" (John 3:10). Maybe Nicodemus would be made to see it this way: The Lord asked Nicodemus if he understood the wind: "The wind blows where it wishes and you hear the sound of it, but do not know where it comes from and where it is going; so is everyone who is born of the Spirit" (John 3:8). No, you don't know where it came from nor where it is going. But you can see that the wind is real because of what the wind does. We talked about that, remember? The Holy Spirit producing the new birth in us is like the wind. You do not see Him, nor can you tell when He comes, but He will make changes in your life so you will know that you can understand God's Word.

No, Nicodemus cannot and need not really understand. What matters is that he must first believe. That is why salvation is so simple. Afterwards he will have no trouble understanding the things of God, for the Holy Spirit will teach him all things (John 14:26). In the meantime, the Lord Jesus would remind Nicodemus of a wonderful Old Testament story. It is found in Numbers 21:5–9. Let's turn to it and see what it says.

The Serpent of Brass

One time when the Israelites complained against God's provision for them in the wilderness, God punished them by sending fiery, poisonous snakes among them. Many were bitten and died. Soon the Israelites confessed their sin and begged Moses to help them. God told Moses to set up a pole in the camp and place on it a serpent made of brass. Any person who had been bitten by a poisonous snake could look at the snake of brass and be healed completely of the deadly bite. But those who refused to look at the brass serpent would die.

What kind of first aid was this? How could just looking at a brass snake save them from dying? Many people could not understand this. But you notice, God had not asked them to understand; He had asked them to do what He said, and to believe what He had promised them. It was a picture of looking to God in faith.

Nicodemus, of course, knew this story. Now, for the first time, he heard what it really meant, for Jesus explained it to him: "And as Moses lifted up the serpent in the wilderness, even so must the Son of Man be lifted up; that whoever believes may in Him have eternal life" (John 3:14–15).

The pole set up in the middle of the Israelite camp was a shadow of the cross upon which the Lord Jesus Christ was soon to die for the sins of the world. Nicodemus was listening carefully to what Jesus said. Jesus was telling Nicodemus very plainly now that He was God's Son who had come to take away the sins of the world. By faith in Him, Nicodemus might be born again (John 3:16–18).

The Jewish people had always believed that someday the Savior, the Messiah, would come into the world, but only a few believed that Jesus was He. Nicodemus had come to ask who Jesus really was; now he knew. Would Nicodemus receive Him or reject Him? That is the third must Nicodemus has to face.

The Decision of Nicodemus

John chapter 3 does not tell us whether Nicodemus believed in Jesus Christ at this time or not. Maybe it wasn't until the cross, to which Jesus had been nailed, was lifted up from the ground and set up on Calvary that Nicodemus looked up to Him in faith. But we are quite sure that he did

believe in the Lord. Nicodemus was one of the two men who tenderly took the body of Jesus down from the cross and prepared it for burial before they placed it in the tomb of Joseph of Arimathea (John 19:38–39).

Nicodemus' decision gave him his second birth into the family of God. By the power of God the Holy Spirit, he was made spiritually alive with a human spirit so that he had no more trouble understanding what God's Word had to say. He now had eternal life, life which would allow him to live in heaven in God's presence forever.

What God Wants Me to Know

Like Nicodemus, you do not have to understand what the new birth is all about. God only asks you to *believe* that Jesus Christ died to give you eternal life and then the Holy Spirit will give you the new birth when you have believed.

When the poisonous snakes bit the Israelites in the wilderness, the Israelites were not told to put on ointments or to do some *work* for their healing. They were not told to kill the serpents, get rid of their sins first, nor even to make an offering to the brass serpent to pay for salvation. They were not to look at their wounds, to feel sorry for their sins, or to pray—they were only to look and live! They were to believe God's Word and let God do the work to make them whole.

God offers to make us whole and complete through the second birth when we believe in Jesus Christ. How do I know? I know what He promises in Isaiah 45:22: "Turn to Me, and be saved, all the ends of the earth; For I am God, and there is no other." The moment you accept by faith God's offer of salvation by placing your belief in Christ you will be born again. You, too, have heard the three musts; you must be born again, you were told how your new birth comes about, and now you must decide for yourself what you will do with the information you have received. "He who believes in the Son has eternal life; but he who does not obey the Son shall not see life, but the wrath of God abides [remains] on him" (John 3:36).

As we have learned, the new birth is not something that we can see or feel. It is entirely an act of God the Holy Spirit. When we are born again, the Holy Spirit gives us new life. By the miracle of His power, He makes us "a new creature" in Christ Jesus (2 Cor. 5:17). The new birth, which we did not feel, is just the beginning of many new and marvelous things that will happen to us. Just as a blind man who has been made to see can notice the beauties and wonders of the world around him, so the one who has been given new life in Christ can now see and understand things from God's Word and enjoy fellowship with God which he never had before.

When you were born the first time into the Jones family, you cried for milk so that your body might grow. Now that you have been born again into God's family, you need spiritual food. God the Holy Spirit will feed your human spirit: first with the milk of the Word, the easy things, the

ABC's of the Bible; then as you grow in the knowledge of the Word, He will feed you meat or solid food, the deeper things of the Word (1 Pet. 2:2; 1 Cor. 3:2).

Just as we eat daily to help our bodies grow and stay healthy, so we need to take in spiritual food daily. God has provided spiritual food for all His children and this food is in the Bible, the Word of God. He has given us the Holy Spirit to teach us the Word. Do you read and study it daily? Do you listen as it is taught?

Lesson Review

What was the name of a teacher of the Old Testament we learned about? Nicodemus. He could not understand what the Lord Jesus was trying to tell him about who? God the Holy Spirit. What he needed, of course, was the new what? New birth. He was a grown man; his first birth had placed him into his parents' family. But his second birth would put him into what family? The family of God. His first birth had given him what kind of life? Physical life. But what he needed now was what kind of life? Spiritual life. Only who could give him this new life? Only God the Holy Spirit. Nicodemus, and all of us, were born what? Spiritually dead. The second birth makes us what? Spiritually alive to God. When we are born again we can have a relationship and fellowship with God and understand the truths of His what? His Word.

Can you quote John 3:16? "For God so loved the world, that He gave His only begotten Son, that whoever believes in Him should not perish, but have eternal life." Can you explain what the new birth is and how you may receive it? Our first birth puts us into our human families, but our second birth puts us into the family of God. Our first birth gives us earthly life; our second birth gives us spiritual life.

We receive a human spirit in our second birth. We are made spiritually alive by the power of God the Holy Spirit.

We have seen that God the Holy Spirit shows us God's plan from God's Word. We learned of His work in the days of the Old Testament, when He came to endue certain believers. Why did He come to them? To help them do some special job. How long did the Holy Spirit endue Old Testament believers? Until their work was finished, or until sin removed Him. Would He ever come to indwell believers forever? Yes. When? Ten days after the Lord's return to heaven. What was that fiftieth day, counting from the Resurrection to the Spirit's coming, called? The day of Pentecost.

Acts 1:8a says "You shall receive power when the Holy Spirit has come upon you; and you shall be My witnesses." This memory verse tells us three things that would happen when the Holy Spirit came down to start the Church Age. What were they? We would receive power; the Holy Spirit would come indwell and fill us, believers, and we should be the Lord's witnesses. What else had the Holy Spirit come to do? He did this for Nicodemus, when Nicodemus believed in the Lord Jesus Christ. The Holy Spirit gives believers a new birth. Yes, regeneration, or the new birth, is the work of the Holy Spirit for all who will believe in the Lord Jesus Christ as their Savior.

Memory Verse

"Do not marvel that I said to you, 'You must be born again.'" (John 3:7)

Chapter Twenty-Five

The Indwelling of the Holy Spirit

OVERVIEW

A. Subject: The Indwelling of the Holy Spirit—Exodus 25:8; 1 Corinthians 6:19; Matthew 26:31–35; Acts 4:10–19

B. Lesson Titles:
1. Lesson One: The Old and the New Sanctuary
2. Lesson Two: The Story of Peter

C. Story Objective:

In contrast to His ministry in the Old Testament where certain believers were endued with the Holy Spirit temporarily in order to perform certain tasks, the Holy Spirit permanently indwells every regenerated person during the Church Age (Rom. 5:5; 8:9). After the glorification of Christ, His resurrection to His session, the Holy Spirit was given to every believer at the moment of salvation (Gal. 3:2; 4:6) to indwell him forever (John 14:16).

The indwelling of the Holy Spirit cannot be lost through any sin or failure on the part of the believer. The indwelling is as permanent as is the believer's salvation and is the foundation of the many ministries of the Spirit to believers in this age. The indwelling of the Spirit makes the body of the believer the temple of God (1 Cor. 3:16–17; 6:19) and demands a holy life.

The filling of the Holy Spirit, however, can be lost through sin. Only through confession of sin by means of 1 John 1:9 can the believer recover the filling of the Holy Spirit, for the filling of the Holy Spirit empowers the believer to witness for his Lord (Acts 1:8) and to glorify Christ by living a supernatural life, the Christian way of life (John 16:14; 1 Cor. 6:20).

D. Vocabulary and Doctrinal Concepts:
1. Vocabulary: dwell, indwell, mercy seat, offering, pillar, sacred, sacrifice, sanctuary, substitutionary, Tabernacle
2. Doctrinal Concepts:
   a. The indwelling Spirit prophesied (John 7:37–39).
   b. "He abides with you, and will be in you" (John 14:17).
   c. The Holy Spirit's ministry of guidance (John 14:26; 1 John 2:27).
   d. The Spirit is a gift (Acts 11:17; 1 Thess. 4:8).
   e. Statements of the indwelling of the Holy Spirit (Rom. 8:11; James 4:5).
   f. Assurance through the indwelling Holy Spirit (1 John 3:23–24; 4:13).
   g. The old and the new sanctuary (Ex. 25:8; 1 Cor. 6:19).

E. *Source Book* Keywords: God the Holy Spirit (filling of, indwelling, sustaining ministry), Peter, Tabernacle

F. Activities:
1. Suggested Visuals: indwelling of God the Holy Spirit, Peter, Tabernacle
2. Games, Songs, Worksheets
3. Memory Verse: "Do you not know that your body is a temple of the Holy Spirit who is in you, whom you have from God, and that you are not your own?" (1 Cor. 6:19)
4. Opening and Closing Prayer

LESSON ONE
THE OLD AND NEW SANCTUARY

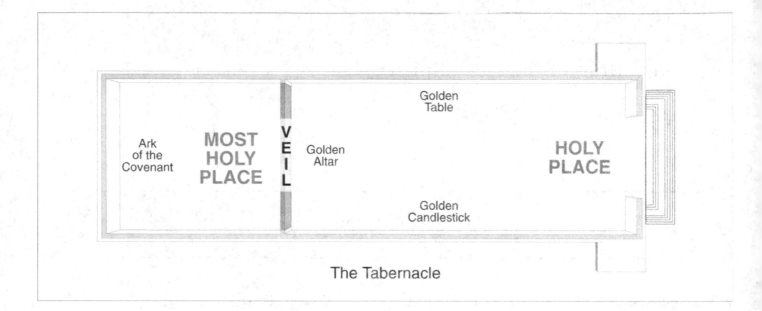

The Tabernacle

When we became the children of God (Gal. 3:26) we became temples in which God now lives and makes His home. Did you know that if you are a believer you are a temple? You are, for that's what 1 Corinthians 6:19 tells us: "Do you not know that your body is a temple of the Holy Spirit who is in you, whom you have from God, and that you are not your own?" Let this verse be a very important reminder to you. The Holy Spirit lives in you; He *indwells* you. He indwells every believer who lives during the Church Age, but it wasn't always so. How did it come about that God should choose to indwell us? Listen, and I will tell you.

God's Dwelling Place on Earth, the Old Sanctuary

Many hundreds of years ago, God planned a house which was to be His first dwelling place on earth. He had chosen the Jews to be His own special people, and now He wanted them to have a special place where they might come to worship Him with all their sins confessed and forgiven. God said to Moses, "And let them construct a sanctuary [a sacred building] for Me, that I may dwell among them" (Ex. 25:8). What does the word "dwell" mean? Yes, to live.

Where did the Israelites live in the days of Moses? They lived in the wilderness for forty years after God brought them out of Egypt, did they not? There they moved about from place to place, wherever the pillar of cloud led them. God's people lived in tents, and God's dwelling place on

earth was to be a very special tent called the Tabernacle. It was carried from place to place.

Who helped the builders of the Tabernacle to make it exactly as God wished it to be made? God the Holy Spirit. The Tabernacle had to be made according to God's plan, for it taught the Israelites many important lessons about the Savior and the work He was coming to do.

The Tabernacle was divided into two rooms. The larger room was the Holy Place; the smaller room was the Holy of Holies, or the Most Holy Place. There, inside the golden walls, God was pleased to dwell. When the Tabernacle was finished, it was set up right in the middle of the camp of the Israelites. Why? So that God could "dwell among" His people. How did they know He was really there? We are told that the sign of God's presence was the bright cloud which hovered above the Tabernacle, and that "the glory of the LORD filled the tabernacle" (Ex. 40:34).

The Tabernacle, and later the Temple in Jerusalem, was a sacred or holy place which only the priests could enter after they had made offerings for their sins and for the sins of the people. Once every year, the high priest went into the Holy of Holies to bring a special offering for the sins of the people. He brought the blood of a sacrifice and sprinkled it on the mercy seat, while the people waited outside in the outer court to see whether God would accept their offerings and forgive their sins (Heb. 9:7).

Do you wonder why the people had to stay in the outer court and could not come into the Tabernacle? The Lord Jesus Christ had not yet come to die for their sins. Until He came, the direct way to God was not open to just anybody (Heb. 9:8–9). In those days believers still needed go-betweens, priests, who prayed for them. When the Great Mediator, the Lord Jesus Christ, came, He would bring God and man back together again. Jesus Christ brought the perfect offering for sin—Himself. He became our own Great High Priest, who opened up the way into God's presence for us (Heb. 9:24; 10:20).

When the Holy Spirit came down on the day of Pentecost, He made a great change in the world for all believers. They need not go to the Temple any longer, for God had moved out; He had chosen for Himself a new dwelling place on earth. What place was that? Think of your memory verse, 1 Corinthians 6:19. Yes, every believer's body.

The New Sanctuary

Do you think that the Israelites deserved having the great honor of God's presence right in their midst? Certainly not! They had promised the Lord that they would keep all of His commandments (Ex. 19:8). Then they turned around and made themselves a golden calf to worship and sinned against the Lord. They did not deserve anything from God except punishment. Yet God loved them. In His grace He kept right on dwelling among them, showing them what He was like.

Now before you look down your noses on the Israelites and think, "I would never have done that," let me remind you that you and I do not deserve to be God's dwelling place on earth any more than they did, for we, too, have sinned (Rom. 3:23). But God in His grace has made a new and wonderful way whereby every believer may have his sins forgiven and thereby be able to worship God right inside himself, in his innermost being.

Would you like to know how God prepared us to be His new dwelling place, His temples on earth? The first step was for us to receive a new birth. When we believed in the Lord Jesus Christ, we were cleansed from all sin (1 John 1:7); we were made spiritually alive. God gave us eternal life and a human spirit which can have a relationship and fellowship with Him. Then all was ready, and God moved in. We were no longer plain men and women, boys and girls; we became temples of the Holy Spirit.

Do you remember what the sign of God's presence in the Tabernacle was? Yes, the bright cloud and the glory which filled the entire place. What do you think might be

the sign of His presence in the believer-temple? From the moment He indwelt us, the Holy Spirit has been at work making us more and more like the Lord Jesus Christ was when He was on the earth—holy, good, loving, and kind. Most people do not read the Bible, but when they look at a believer who loves the Lord and His Word, they will see something very wonderful: an inner beauty, the beauty of Christ produced by the Holy Spirit. Then they will want to know how they, too, can have Christ as their Savior.

What God Wants Me to Know

Many believers think that the church building in which they worship is holy because they think it's God's house even now. They tiptoe into the building and are very careful not to do anything displeasing to God while they are at church. Yet these same people will do things in their body which they would never think of doing in a church building. But what does the Word say? "Do you not know that you are a temple of God, and *that* the Spirit of God dwells in you? If any man destroys [dishonors] the temple of God, God will destroy [discipline] him, for the temple of God is holy, and that is what you are" (1 Cor. 3:16–17). Naturally, we will want to keep our church buildings neat and clean, for that is where we come together to learn God's Word and worship Him. But there is nothing sacred or holy about the building. We no longer call it a "sanctuary" but an "auditorium." Today, we are the sanctuaries or temples of the Holy Spirit. We sit on chairs and fill the auditorium. We are the temple that must be kept holy, for this is where God is.

I wonder, is the temple of your body a nice and clean place for the Holy Spirit to live? How can you keep it clean and make it a wonderful home for Him? God has given us a "miracle broom" to cleanse the dwelling place of the Holy Spirit. Can you think what it is? It is called 1 John 1:9. When we use it, it sweeps away all our sins.

But 1 John 1:9 cannot cleanse you and make you into a temple of God if you do not belong to the Lord Jesus. Only the salvation work of Jesus Christ can cleanse away your sins. What do I mean? The Bible says that without the shedding of blood, the salvation work of Christ, there is no forgiveness (Heb. 9:22). Jesus Christ died on the cross twice, first spiritually, then physically in His body. He died so that you may be born again. You already had your first birth—that's easy to see. God planned your body and made it. Your body is the house in which the real you lives. But God wants your body to be more than just a house for you; He wants it to be the temple of the Holy Spirit. Right now you can believe in Jesus and have the Holy Spirit indwell you.

Lesson Review

What have we learned about God's dwelling places on earth? Answer "right" or "wrong." The Holy Spirit chose the priests of the Tabernacle for His first dwelling place on earth. Wrong. His dwelling place was the Holy of Holies, in the Tabernacle. The church building is the Holy Spirit's dwelling place today. Wrong. He indwells the body of every believer. The Holy Spirit enters every believer when he prays for Him. Wrong. At the moment he believes in Christ. The indwelling of the Holy Spirit will never leave the believer. Right. Every believer may now worship God directly. Right. We keep the temple of our body holy by making use of 1 John 1:9. Right. Your body is your own, to do with as you wish. Wrong. The believer's body belongs to the Lord to do with as He wishes.

> ### *Memory Verse*
> "Do you not know that your body is a temple of the Holy Spirit who is in you, whom you have from God, and that you are not your own?" (1 Cor. 6:19)

LESSON TWO
THE STORY OF PETER

Our memory verse says "Do you not know that your body is a temple of the Holy Spirit who is in you, whom you have from God, and that you are not your own?" (1 Cor. 6:19). "Your body is a temple of the Holy Spirit," and "you are not your own" tell us that we are not only a dwelling place of God, we are His! We do not belong to ourselves, nor do our body-temples. Does that surprise you? Perhaps you always thought, "This is my body; I can do with it as I please!" But that is not so. God owns us twice—He made us, and He bought us. How did He buy us, you may wonder? Open your Bible to 1 Peter 1:18–19: "Knowing that you were not redeemed with perishable things like silver or gold from your futile way of life inherited from your forefathers, but with precious blood, as of a lamb unblemished and spotless, *the blood* of Christ." We were bought with the precious blood of Christ, His substitutionary spiritual death on the cross. Jesus Christ took our place on the cross.

If you go out and buy something, it's yours to do with as you wish. God bought us, so He can do with us as He wishes. The trouble is that you and I want our own way. We want to do only what we like. But God has created us for His pleasure. When we were born again, God made us new creatures in Christ for His glory (1 Cor. 6:20). God gave us volition so that we can choose whether we will live to please Him or live to please only ourselves. But remember, for those "smarty guys and girls" who think they can sin all they want to as long as they confess their sins, there is God's divine discipline. They won't get away with it. It is true that God is "faithful and righteous to forgive us our sins," but He is also faithful and righteous to 'spank' us when we have it coming to us. Sin dishonors the temple of God and grieves the Holy Spirit; yet He continues to indwell us (John 14:16).

The Purpose of the Indwelling

Now let's talk about another part of our memory verse—this part: "the Holy Spirit who is in you." Do you know why the Holy Spirit has come to indwell you and make you a temple of God? There are four reasons for the indwelling of the Holy Spirit. The four reasons can be found in the following verses. "He shall glorify Me; for He shall take of Mine, and shall disclose *it* to you" (John 16:14). "But when He, the Spirit of truth, comes, He will guide you into all the truth; for He will not speak on His own initiative, but whatever He hears, He will speak; and He will disclose to you what is to come" (John 16:13). "But you shall receive power when the Holy Spirit has come upon you; and you shall be My witnesses both in Jerusalem, and in all Judea and Samaria, and even to the remotest part of the earth" (Acts 1:8).

The first and most important reason for the indwelling Holy Spirit is to glorify God; the second is to teach believers the Word; the third reason is to guide us; and the fourth? Yes, to give us power. Now let us see the great difference the indwelling of the Holy Spirit made in the life of the disciple Peter.

The Manifestation of Indwelling

The disciples had walked and talked with the Lord Jesus for three years now. They had heard Him teach many great truths over and over, yet somehow they couldn't seem to remember them. All they were sure of was that Jesus was "the Holy One of God" (John 6:69b).

Peter was the one who had said those words. He was ready to go with the Lord Jesus anywhere at all, even unto death—or so he thought. Turn to Matthew 26:31–35. When the Lord Jesus and His disciples had finished the last Passover meal, they all went to the Mount of Olives. Again the Lord Jesus told them that He would have to die soon. In fact, that very night they would all have occasion to stumble or sin because of Him. He, their Shepherd, would be taken from them, and they, like frightened sheep, would scatter in all directions. But He would rise from the dead and go before them to Galilee.

Peter had listened to God's Word, for remember, the Lord Jesus is God. But Peter chose to ignore it. He said quite cockily, "*Even* though all may fall away because of You, I will never fall away" (Matt. 26:33). Peter had meant every word of what he said. So when he heard what Jesus told him next, that Peter would deny Him three times before the cock crowed the next morning, Peter shook his head and said bravely, "Even if I have to die with You, I will not deny You" (Matt. 26:35). When the other disciples saw Peter's courage, they, too, assured the Lord of their faithfulness to Him.

A little later that same evening, when the soldiers came to arrest Jesus, we find out who was right. In Matthew 26:56b we read that "all the disciples left Him and fled." Why? Because they were weak and afraid.

Do you know the sad story of Peter's denying three times that he even knew Jesus? Peter could so easily have spoken a word for the Lord at His trial; he might have said, "Really, this *is* the Christ, the Son of the living God!" But he didn't. Instead, Peter began to curse and say roughly, "I do not know the man!" (Matt. 26:74).

Oh, how miserable Peter was when he heard the cock crow! He wept bitterly over his own weakness and failure, as he remembered the Lord's words (Matt. 26:75). But now let's look at Peter and the disciples several weeks after this. Jesus had risen and ascended to heaven. The Holy Spirit had come to indwell every believer. What a difference there was now! Peter faced some of the same crowd who hated the Lord Jesus so much that they had cried out, "His blood *be* on us and on our children! Crucify, crucify Him!" (Matt. 27:25; Luke 23:21b). What is Peter saying to them? "Let it be known to all of you, and to all the people of Israel, that by the name of Jesus Christ the Nazarene, whom you crucified, whom God raised from the dead—by this *name* this man stands here before you in good health. 'And there is salvation in no one else; for there is no other name under heaven that has been given among men, by which we must be saved'" (Acts 4:10, 12).

Doesn't Peter know that they might do the same to him that they had done to Jesus? Oh yes, he knows it very well. He listens to their threats of what would happen if he ever spoke of Jesus Christ again (Acts 4:17–18). Then he answered calmly and unafraid, "We cannot stop speaking what we have seen and heard" (Acts 4:20). Peter is convinced that he must obey God's Word rather than be afraid of what man might say (Acts 4:19).

Look at the rest of the disciples. They have come out of hiding to witness for the Lord, too. All of them were imprisoned, beaten, threatened, hated, and most of them gave their lives for their Lord. What made the difference? What caused the great change in their lives that changed them from weak, fearful men without doctrine to strong, fearless men who knew and taught the Word of God? Jesus was no longer with them to give them courage and strength or to teach them doctrine, but He had sent someone in His place—the Holy Spirit. He had kept His promise that when the Holy Spirit would come to live in them, they would receive power to be His witnesses.

But there was something else the Holy Spirit did for the disciples. Jesus had told them what the Spirit would come to do: The disciples suddenly began to remember and understand the things Jesus had taught them (John 12:16). Watch what I mean! After the disciples had been with the Lord Jesus for three years, they still could not understand where the Lord Jesus was going after He died for the sins of the world. Jesus had just finished telling them that He would go to the Father and return to take them with Him, when Thomas asked, "Lord, we do not know where You are going, how do we know the way?" (John 14:5). Do you remember what Jesus answered him? "I am the way, and the truth, and the life; no one comes to the Father, but through Me" (John 14:6).

Yes, once the disciples could not even remember the way to heaven, but now Peter was speaking plainly of the one who could get them there—Jesus Christ. He said, "And there is salvation in no one else; for there is no other name under heaven that has been given among men, by which we must be saved." In the power of the indwelling and filling of the Holy Spirit, Peter and the other disciples became great preachers and witnesses for Christ. Some of the disciples wrote some of the books of the New Testament. They could have done none of these things in their own strength; they owed their changed lives to the presence of God the Holy Spirit. His power helped them from within to understand and remember and to be fearless and strong that the Lord Jesus might be glorified in them and through them.

What God Wants Me to Know

You and I did not have the privilege of seeing and hearing the Lord Jesus teach for three years as did the disciples, yet He left us all of His words—everything He wants us to know—in the Bible. Because He knew that we, like the disciples, could neither understand His Word nor remember it without the help of the Holy Spirit, we, too, have received the Spirit of God who teaches us all things (1 Cor. 2:12; 1 John 2:27).

If you are a believer in the Lord Jesus Christ, do not ever say that you don't read the Bible because you cannot understand it. Just give the Holy Spirit a chance to show you that you can. Listen when the Word is taught; read it yourself every day. The Holy Spirit will give you an understanding mind. As you learn the Word, the Holy Spirit will guide you day by day. He will remind you of the things you have been taught just like He reminded the Lord's disciples so long ago. You cannot do these things for yourself; that's why the Holy Spirit was given to you, so that you might *know* the things that are freely given to us (1 Cor. 2:12). After all, God knows all things, and He can do all things. What two words in the Essence Box tell us this? Omniscience and omnipotence.

Each member of the Godhead is omnipotent. Just think— the greatest power in heaven and earth is in you, believer! It is the power of the third person of the Trinity, God the Holy Spirit.

Now, why do you think God has given you this great power within you? The power He gave you is certainly not some kind of mysterious, magical power that will make people think that you are great! It is the power of the Holy Spirit, and it was given to you to do those things which will bring honor and glory to the Lord Jesus Christ. You are to glorify Him, to make Him great!

Take a last look at Peter. A great Roman officer had just dropped down on his knees before Peter. Would Peter accept such an honor? No, quickly he grabbed the officer's hands and pulled him up. "Stand up; I too am *just* a man," he said (Acts 10:26). Peter knew that greatness and honor and glory belong to the Lord, not to Peter. Peter was only there to point this officer to the Lord (Acts 10:42–43). That's the way to see and to use the power of the Holy Spirit!

Will every one of these wonderful things happen in your life through the indwelling of the Holy Spirit? They may,

and they may not. It all depends on one thing, and that is the filling of the Spirit. Next time, we will learn how to be filled with the Spirit so that we might use the great power within us as God intended.

I want to make sure you understand that the Holy Spirit indwells believers only. If you have never made your decision to accept Jesus Christ as your Savior, you are not a temple of God, and God the Holy Spirit does not indwell you. Once the Lord Jesus Christ said, "He who believes in Me, as the Scripture said, 'From his innermost being shall flow rivers of living water'" (John 7:38). What did He mean by that? Well, the Lord was speaking about the Holy Spirit, whom He would give to all who believed in Him (John 7:39). By the power of the Holy Spirit, blessing and power would flow out to others—the power to tell others about the life-giving Son of God. Would you like that power to tell the unbelievers about Jesus Christ? Would you like to bring glory to Him? Then why not believe right now that Jesus died to save you?

Lesson Review

Does the Holy Spirit indwell to glorify the believer? No, to glorify Christ. How was Peter changed through the indwelling of the Spirit? Before, he forgot the Word; after, he remembered the Word and taught it. Before, he was weak and afraid; after, he was strong and fearless. Before, he denied the Lord; after, he preached for the Lord.

The reasons for the indwelling of God the Holy Spirit are to glorify God, to teach the Word, to guide the believer, and to give power.

Memory Verse

"Do you not know that your body is a temple of the Holy Spirit who is in you, whom you have from God, and that you are not your own?" (1 Cor. 6:19)

Chapter Twenty-Six

The Filling of God the Holy Spirit

OVERVIEW

A. Subject: The Filling of God the Holy Spirit—Acts 6—7

B. Lesson Titles:
1. Lesson One: The Filling of the Spirit
2. Lesson Two: Stephen Glorifies the Lord

C. Story Objective:

The Holy Spirit indwells every believer for the purpose of glorifying the Lord Jesus Christ. Whether glorification is realized or not depends upon the filling of the Spirit. As was previously stated, the indwelling of the Holy Spirit is permanent (John 14:16) and wholly and entirely a work of God. The filling of the Spirit is temporary, dependent upon certain conditions in the life of the believer. Indwelling is once and for all, while filling is revocable (Acts 2:4). Ephesians 5:18 commands the believer to be habitually "filled with the Spirit."

Distinction must be made between the Holy Spirit's work at salvation—indwelling (1 Cor. 3:16; 6:19)—and His post-salvation work of filling (Rom. 8:10). We are said to "be indwelt," but we are commanded to "be filled." Vocabulary describing the filling of the Spirit includes: "walk" (Gal. 5:16); "put on" (Rom. 13:14); "be filled" (Eph. 5:18); "walk in the light" (1 John 1:7); "abides in the light" (1 John 2:10); "abide in Him" (1 John 2:27–28).

At any point in our lives we are either spiritual, filled with the Spirit, or carnal, out of fellowship (1 Cor. 3:1). In status spirituality, we cannot sin except through negative volition (Eph. 3:16–17; 1 John 3:9). Sin grieves the Holy Spirit (Eph. 4:30), and the production of human good quenches His power in us (1 Thess. 5:19). It follows, there-fore, that the hindrance to the filling of the Spirit is uncon-fessed sin in the life. Human good is a result of sin. Thus, to be filled with the Spirit, all known sins must be confessed (1 John 1:9). When we name or acknowledge our sin or car-nality to God, all sins—known and unknown—are forgiven and the Holy Spirit fills the soul and takes control instantly.

When the Spirit fills and controls, He produces the fruit of the Spirit which is the character of the incarnate Christ, and Christ is glorified in the believer's life (Gal. 4:19; 5:22–23; Phil. 1:20). Apart from the filling of the Spirit, no divine good—only human good—is produced in the Chris-tian life.

Spirituality and carnality are mutually exclusive; they are therefore absolutes. The spiritual believer is said to be "in the light"; the carnal believer is "in the darkness" (1 John 1:6–7). The spiritual believer imitates God (Eph. 5:1; 1 John 3:9); the carnal believer imitates the unbeliever (Gal. 5:19–21; 1 John 2:11; 3:4, 15). The Spirit-filled believer ac-complishes three objectives: imitates God and glorifies Christ (1 Cor. 6:20); produces the fruit of the Spirit—the character of the incarnate Christ (Gal. 4:19; 5:22–23; Phil. 1:20; 1 John 2:5–6) thereby magnifying Christ in his body (Phil. 1:20–21); and produces divine good—gold, silver, and precious stones. The carnal believer produces only wood, hay, and straw (1 Cor. 3:12). Apart from the filling of the Spirit, no divine good—only human good—is pro-duced in the Christian life.

D. Vocabulary and Doctrinal Concepts:
1. Vocabulary: carnality, council, covenant, customs, Gibeonites, Greek language, grieve, high priests, the Law, quench, spirituality, substitutionary

2. Doctrinal Concepts: Spirituality:
   a. Vocabulary describing the filling of the Spirit includes:
      1) "Walk" (Gal. 5:16).
      2) "Put on" (Rom. 13:14).
      3) "Be filled" (Eph. 5:18).
      4) "Walk in the light" (1 John 1:7).
      5) "Abides in the light" (1 John 2:10).
      6) "Abide in Him" (1 John 2:27–28).
   b. At any point in our lives we are either spiritual, filled with the Spirit, or carnal, out of fellowship (1 Cor. 3:1):
      1) Sin grieves the Holy Spirit (Eph. 4:30).

2) The production of human good quenches His power in us (1 Thess. 5:19).

E. *Source Book* Keywords: God the Holy Spirit (filling of, grieving, indwelling, quenching), Joshua, rebound, Stephen

F. Activities:
   1. Suggested Visuals: filling of God the Holy Spirit, Stephen
   2. Games, Songs, Worksheets
   3. Memory Verse: "For you have been bought with a price: therefore glorify God in your body." (1 Cor. 6:20)
   4. Opening and Closing Prayer

LESSON ONE
THE FILLING OF THE SPIRIT

When we learned about the indwelling of the Holy Spirit we found out that the greatest power in heaven and earth has moved into your life. I promised you then that we would learn how to make use of this power as God intended. That's what our lesson on "The Filling of the Spirit" will be all about. Today, I want to show you how this power can work for you. We will see how it actually worked out in the life of a New Testament believer.

To Use or Not to Use This Power

Before we talk about the power of the Holy Spirit within every believer, let's talk about another great power we all have serving us daily—the power of electricity. In our homes, electricity is furnished by the power plants in our city; it is ready to go to work for us at the flip of a switch or the plugging in of an appliance. Wouldn't it be stupid for any of us to say, "Since there is nothing more for me to do than flip a switch, and since I don't see how it can work, I just won't use electric power"?

You laugh? Would it surprise you to know that when it comes to the filling of the Holy Spirit or His power going to work in us, many Christians make no use of His power for much the same reason? What do I mean? Well, they simply do not see how merely confessing one's sins can turn on the Spirit's power in the believer's life. They think, or say, "But isn't there something else I ought to do? I just don't feel that the Holy Spirit is filling me with His power." Because of their unbelief in God's Word, the power supply is not restored.

Can you imagine how serious it would be if we had a total power failure in our city? Why, the whole city would be plunged into darkness. All machinery would stop immediately. We would have no water pressure to supply us with drinking water or water to put out fires. Hospitals could not function properly; elevators would stop; traffic would be all snarled up; and unless the power was restored quickly, all foods would spoil. In short, without electricity our lives would be dreadful.

Did you know that there are definitely times of power failure in the believer's life, when the power supply is cut off? Whose fault is this? The Holy Spirit's? Never. The Holy Spirit is God. He is all-power; He is immutable; this means that His power never changes. There is never more power, nor less power; it is all-power! Power failure is entirely the believer's fault. By sin we alone can cause the power within us to be shut off.

"Be Filled with the Spirit"

As we have learned, the body is only the house in which the soul, the real you, lives. We were all born with a sin nature (Rom. 5:12). When we believed in the Lord Jesus Christ, we were made spiritually alive; that is, we received a human spirit (Eph. 2:1). Immediately, God the Holy Spirit came to indwell us and make us temples of God (1 Cor. 6:19). When He came to indwell us, He also began to fill us with His power, even as He did the disciples on the day of Pentecost (Acts 2:4). How long will the Holy Spirit indwell believers? Forever. Even if a believer keeps on sinning? That's right, the Holy Spirit always indwells—that's 'forkeeps,' but He does not always fill. At any moment in our lives we are either filled or not filled with the Spirit. When are we not filled? The moment we sin, for sin shuts off the Spirit's power inside us every time.

We have just described a believer who is filled with the Spirit. That means the Holy Spirit controls his life. But now let's describe a believer who is not filled with the Spirit, one who is out of fellowship. Whose power controls this believer's life? Certainly not that of the Holy Spirit! The Holy Spirit has been crowded out of His rightful place. His power has been shut off and the sin nature has taken over. As long as this sin remains unconfessed, the Holy Spirit's power cannot go to work for the believer. Do you wonder why not?

Carnality Stands in the Way

We know that God, and that includes God the Holy Spirit, is absolutely holy and righteous. He cannot have fellowship with a sinful believer. The Bible tells us that sin in the believer's life both "grieves" and "quenches" the Holy Spirit. "To grieve" means "to make sad"; "to quench" means "to put out," like putting out a fire or a light. We are commanded not to do these things: "Do not grieve the Holy Spirit of God, by whom you were sealed for the day of redemption" (Eph. 4:30) and "Do not quench the Spirit" (1 Thess. 5:19).

When do we grieve or make the Holy Spirit sad, and when do we quench Him? Whenever you sin, you grieve the Holy Spirit. Whenever you try to please God or do a good work for Him without being filled with the Spirit, you quench Him. Any good thing you do when you are not filled with the Spirit is just your own kind of good, not God's. It comes from your sin nature just as sin does, and God cannot use it.

How the Power Can Be Restored

How can the power failure in your life be restored? By confessing your sins. Can you quote 1 John 1:9? "If we confess our sins, He is faithful and righteous to forgive us our sins and to cleanse us from all unrighteousness." To confess a sin is to name that sin to God. If a lie has broken your fellowship with God, you would simply admit to the Father that you have just lied. If you had disobeyed your parents, you would tell the Father so. Then you would be forgiven, cleansed immediately, and once more you would

be filled with the Spirit. Then, if you know what's good for you, I am sure you will go ahead and do what your mother and father wanted you to do in the first place. What does this tell us? That although sin stops the Spirit's power in us, His power can be easily restored. Sin must be confessed! That's all there is to it!

Suppose after you confessed, you still feel badly about your sin; suppose you do not feel as if you are filled with the Spirit. You may even want to make it up to God for having sinned, or perhaps pray and ask the Father to fill you with the Spirit. Well, we must never depend on our feelings. They will trick us as sure as anything. We must depend on what the Word of God says! Confess it and forget it!

To explain what I mean, listen to what happened when Joshua, who led the Israelites after the death of Moses, trusted his feelings rather than God's Word. Before the Israelites entered the Promised Land, God commanded them to cast out by force the people who lived there before them and worshiped false gods. "You shall make no covenant with them or with their gods. They shall not live in your land, lest they make you sin against Me" (Ex. 23:32–33).

Now the day came when the Israelites got ready to take the land and divide it among themselves. For a time they obeyed God's Word. The news of their strength and victory was soon known everywhere. The Gibeonites wondered what to do (Joshua 9:1–9). They had an idea. They would send messengers to Joshua. The messengers would wear old, torn clothes and worn-out shoes. They would carry dry, moldy bread in old sacks and pretend they had come from a far country to make a friendship pact with the Israelites. They would pretend that they had come because of the great things they had heard about the Lord God.

And would you believe it? When Joshua heard their words and saw how tired and worn-out they looked from their 'long' journey, he asked no questions. He trusted his feelings, not the Word of God. He made peace with them and agreed to let them live in the Land. Three days later Joshua found out he had been tricked. These men were from a nearby city with which God had said that the Israelites should make no agreements (Joshua 9). Don't you think Joshua regretted that he had not trusted God's Word and obeyed it? Let that be a lesson to you never to act according to how you feel, but according to what God says in His Word.

What does God say about your being filled with the Spirit? Ephesians 5:18*b* says "but be filled with the Spirit." How are you filled with the Spirit? When all known sins in your life are confessed. And when you are filled with the Spirit, some wonderful things will happen in your life—mainly that you will glorify God in your body!

What God Wants Me to Know

Everything we have said and learned in this lesson is for the believer only. If you have never believed in the Lord

Jesus Christ, you cannot be filled with the Spirit. You cannot produce anything that counts for God in your life because you do not have the Spirit living in you. In God's sight, the only good thing you can 'do' is to believe on His Son and be saved (John 6:28–29). Only then can you have the Holy Spirit working in your life to glorify God.

Lesson Review

Filled or indwelt? Listen to the statements I will make, think them over, and tell me whether I am speaking about the indwelling or the filling of the Spirit. The believer will always be this. Indwelt. When the Holy Spirit does this in the life, the Lord Jesus is glorified. Filling. The Holy Spirit does not always do this. Filling. The Holy Spirit will do this for us when we confess our sins. Filling. We are told that we are this, but we are commanded to be that. We are

told we are indwelt; we are commanded to be filled. Grieving and quenching will stop this work of the Holy Spirit in the believer's life. Filling. First Corinthians 6:19 tells us about this. Indwelling. First Corinthians 6:20 tells us about this. Filling. "For you have been bought with a price: therefore glorify God in your body" (1 Cor. 6:20). Our purchase price is the blood of Christ, His substitutionary spiritual death on the cross (1 Pet. 1:18–19).

Memory Verse

"For you have been bought with a price: therefore glorify God in your body." (1 Cor. 6:20)

LESSON TWO
STEPHEN GLORIFIES THE LORD

*W*ouldn't it be a lovely thing to see a believer whose life is constantly filled with the Holy Spirit—one out of whose innermost being "flow rivers of living water" (John 7:38)? Remember, I don't mean real water, but power and blessing through the filling of the Holy Spirit. In such a believer's life, the Lord Jesus Christ would be glorified all the time. Wouldn't it be great if you were that believer? You know, you could be! The Lord Jesus said that when the Holy Spirit came He would not speak of Himself, but "He shall glorify Me" (John 16:13–14). "To glorify" means to show how wonderful and marvelous someone is; to make that someone great; to praise and honor him before others. But how can the Holy Spirit do that? Where does He live? Yes, inside every believer. So His work is an 'inside job.' He glorifies Christ in and through believers on earth. Whether or not Christ is glorified depends on what? Right! That depends on whether you are or are not filled with the Spirit. How can you make sure you are filled with the Spirit? By confessing your sins.

We saw that God commands us to "be filled with the Spirit" (Eph. 5:18). If you could read this in the Greek language, you would see that it actually says, "Be constantly and repeatedly filled with the Spirit!" Why? So that you might constantly and repeatedly glorify Christ.

The Book of Acts tells of a man who was constantly filled with the Spirit. Would you like to see how his life

and even his death glorified the Lord Jesus Christ? Let us turn to Acts, chapters 6 and 7.

Stephen Introduced, Acts 6:5–8

Stephen was one of the first seven deacons or church officers chosen in the early church in Jerusalem. He was a wonderful man in the Lord's sight, for the Bible says of him that he was "a man full of faith" or grace (Acts 6:5*a*). To be

full of grace is to recognize that although you deserve nothing from God, He has given you everything (1 Cor. 15:10*a*). Because you know that God treated you in grace, you treat others with the same love and kindness, no matter what they do to you. How was Stephen able to be so full of grace? Look at verse 5*a*. "They chose Stephen, a man full of faith and of the Holy Spirit" (Acts 6:5). Stephen was not only full of faith, he was also filled with the Holy Spirit. It was the filling of the Spirit which gave Stephen power to be that kind of a person who is full of grace. Let's see for ourselves how Stephen's life and death glorified the Lord. In the filling of the Spirit, Stephen is a man of wisdom (Acts 6:3). He is trustworthy, and his life shows grace and power. "And Stephen, full of grace and power, was performing great wonders and signs among the people" (Acts 6:8).

Stephen and His Enemies, Acts 6:9–12

As Stephen went about doing his work as a deacon, blessings flowed from his life to the lives of others. He told many people about the Lord Jesus Christ, for in the power of the Holy Spirit Stephen was a faithful witness to his Lord (Acts 1:8). As will happen so often, many of the Jews did not believe what he said, even as boys and girls may not listen to your telling them God's way of salvation. They began to argue with Stephen, but they were not getting anywhere because of the great wisdom the Holy Spirit had given him (Acts 6:10).

Yes, Stephen had his enemies, and they were planning to get rid of him. First they found men who, for money, would be willing to lie about him and accuse him falsely. Do you know what these men said? "We have heard him speak blasphemous words against Moses and *against* God," they lied (Acts 6:11*b*). This caused Stephen much trouble, for the leaders of the Jews had Stephen grabbed roughly and brought to them for trial (Acts 6:12).

It is not always easy to stand up for the Lord Jesus. Often Satan tries to make us timid and afraid. But we should always remember a promise found in God's Word, in 1 John 4:4: "You are from God, little children, and have overcome them; because greater is He who is in you than he who is in the world." Believe what it says: that the Holy Spirit who is always in us is greater than Satan. Just look at the courage He gave Stephen.

Stephen Accused, Acts 6:13–15

The false witnesses repeated their lies about Stephen, and even added to them before the council or court of law. "This man incessantly [never stops] speaks against this holy place, and the Law [God's Word, the Old Testament]; for we have heard him say that this Nazarene, Jesus, will destroy this place [the Holy Temple] and alter [change] the customs which Moses handed down to us" (Acts 6:13*b*–14). That part about the customs being changed was true. Remember, a new age—the Church Age—had begun. But all the rest were terrible lies. If you would like to know what the Lord Jesus had really said, turn to John 2:19 and 2:21: "Destroy this temple, and in three days I will raise it up . . . But He was speaking of the temple of His body."

What would you have thought and done if someone had told awful lies about you, lies that might cost you your life? Would you have tried to defend yourself? Would you have screamed that this was not true? Would you have been hateful and angry? Would you have cried and run home? I can tell you how you would have acted if you were filled with the Spirit—this would not have bothered you one bit (Acts 20:24). You would have remained calm, with no anger or hatred in your mind, and the Lord Jesus Christ would have been glorified. So it was with Stephen.

The whole council was staring at him to see whether they had frightened him. Far from it. Stephen was so continuously filled with the Spirit that it showed right through the expression on his face. What did the men see in Stephen's face? "And fixing their gaze on him, all who were sitting in the Council saw his face like the face of an angel" (Acts 6:15). Yes, it seemed to them that they were looking into the face of an angel (Acts 6:15; cf. Ex. 34:35).

Stephen's Defense and Accusation Acts 7:1–60

"Are these things so?" asked the high priest (Acts 7:1*b*). Now what should Stephen do? Should he take the easy way out and perhaps save his life, or should he tell them about the Lord Jesus? Because Stephen was filled with the Spirit, this was an easy decision to make. When you and I are filled with the Spirit, we cannot help witnessing for our Lord! Starting with the story of Abraham, and going all through the Old Testament, Stephen told them about the Lord's glory and grace. He reminded them how they had kept saying "No" to God's Son until at last they had killed Him. And as for the Holy Temple, well, he reminded them that God no longer lived in temples made with hands.

All the time Stephen was speaking, everyone in the court of law had listened quietly. The Holy Spirit was showing them their need of the Savior. Stephen could tell by their angry faces that they knew exactly what he was talking about. They would never receive the Lord Jesus as their Savior. "You stubborn, stubborn people, why do you fight against the Holy Spirit?" he said sadly (Acts 7:51).

When Stephen told them that they were the ones who were sinners because they would not receive the Savior, the people in the courtroom became furious. How dare this man accuse them! He was the one who had been accused, not they! They bared their teeth at him, much like a growling, snarling dog would do, and showed their hatred openly.

Have you noticed the difference between Stephen and the council? When they said Stephen was guilty and they lied about him, the Holy Spirit made his face shine like that of an angel. When Stephen said they were guilty, their faces twisted with rage. They could not control their tempers, for the Holy Spirit was not in them.

Stephen paid no attention to their anger, but "gazed intently into heaven" (Acts 7:55). He kept his mind on the Lord Jesus, and suddenly the Lord Jesus opened up heaven and let Stephen see Him in all His glory. What a sight that must have been! Stephen called out joyfully, "Behold, I see the heavens opened up and the Son of Man standing at the right hand of God" (Acts 7:56). Usually we read of the

Lord as seated "at the right hand of God" (Heb. 10:12), but here He stood up as if He had risen to welcome Stephen. Would this change the minds of these unbelievers about the Lord Jesus Christ? No! They screamed and yelled and stuck their fingers in their ears, for they refused to hear another word out of Stephen. They mobbed him, ran him out of their city, and began to throw stones at him (Acts 6:57–58).

What strength the Holy Spirit gave him, for Stephen did not cry out in anger or complaint! Instead he kept on praying. Sharp and jagged rocks cut and bruised him, but still Stephen spoke to His Lord: "Lord Jesus," he called, "receive my spirit [into your presence]!" (Acts 7:59). Then he knelt down, and with the last strength that was left in him, he cried out for all to hear, "Lord, do not hold this sin against them!" And when he had spoken these words, "he fell asleep" (Acts 7:60). Stephen's body had died.

Does this remind you of someone else who was cruelly treated and put to death? Yet, when He hung on the cross He could still cry out, "Father, forgive them; for they do not know what they are doing" (Luke 23:34). That was the Lord Jesus Christ. The filling of the Spirit had made Stephen like the Lord. God the Son had glorified God the Father in His life and in His death (John 17:1, 4). Stephen had glorified the Lord Jesus Christ in his life, but what is more, he glorified Christ in his death. Thus he was an even greater witness for the Lord in his death than he had been in his life.

People fear and panic at the thought of death. Many will deny the things they believe rather than face death. Peter did once, remember? When someone sees a person who has no fear of death, who can even forgive them as he is dying, it does more than all the talk in the world to show them the love and power of the Lord Jesus Christ to save sinners. One of the reasons why the Lord allows believers to die is that sometimes a person can glorify Christ more by his death than by his life.

What God Wants Me to Know

Stephen was not afraid to die. He knew that God's Word says that to die simply means going home to heaven, and who is afraid of going home? Stephen knew and loved the Lord so dearly, he was thinking only of Him, even as the stones crushed out his life. There was a man watching him die. He had agreed that Stephen should be put to death, but he never forgot what he saw and heard that day (Acts 22:20). His name was Saul, who later became the great Apostle Paul. I am sure that Stephen's Spirit-filled life had a great influence in Paul's life.

The Lord Jesus needs boys and girls who will let the Holy Spirit fill them and therefore control their lives. He can use them for His glory. Do you remember to keep your sins confessed as soon as you realize you have sinned in order that you might be constantly filled with the Spirit? When you do, the Holy Spirit has complete freedom to work in and through you and to make you like Christ.

When an unbeliever sees your clean and pure life, he sees the glory of the Lord Jesus. When we let the Holy Spirit use our tongues to speak for Christ, some unbelievers will believe and be saved. Would you be willing to let the Lord use you? Then be sure to obey His command to "be filled with the Spirit" (Eph. 5:18), and He *will* glorify God in your body!

What a difference there was between brave and faithful Stephen and those wicked, hateful unbelievers who put him to death! Yet, did you know that "all have sinned" (Rom. 3:23)? The main difference between Stephen and his enemies was that Stephen was a saved sinner, while his enemies were lost sinners. Yes, all have sinned, including you. But thank God all may be saved! And that includes you, too. If you have never accepted God's free offer of salvation, may I ask you what are you waiting for? There will never be a better time for you to decide for Christ than now. Just as in the filling of the Spirit, God commands the believer to be filled with the Spirit but leaves the choice up to him, so in salvation His command to the unbeliever is that he should believe in His Son (1 John 3:23). Yet God leaves the choice to you. What will it be?

Memory Verse

"For you have been bought with a price: therefore glorify God in your body." (1 Cor. 6:20)

Chapter Twenty-Seven

Promotion

OVERVIEW

A. Subject: Promotion—Isaiah 28:10; Ephesians 4:13; 2 Peter 3:18

B. Lesson Title: Growing in Grace and Knowledge

C. Story Objective:

The spiritual life of every Christian, regardless of physical age, should show the marks of a steady growth pattern toward maturity. There are no set "plateaus" in the Christian way of life, but rather a constant "reaching forward to what *lies* ahead . . . of the upward call of God in Christ Jesus" (Phil. 3:13*b*–14), an ever-continuing advance "to the measure of the stature which belongs to the fulness of Christ" (Eph. 4:13*b*). There must be further intake of doctrine; there must be growth, or else the spiritual life declines and becomes stunted and unproductive.

This chapter will serve the following purposes: It will review and tie up the lessons on the persons of the Godhead or Trinity; it will show our Lord's own growth cycle; and finally, it will plant the good seed which someone else will water so that God will cause "the growth" (1 Cor. 3:6).

D. Vocabulary and Doctrinal Concepts:
1. Vocabulary: architect, exalt, foundation, manger, swaddling clothes, synagogue
2. Doctrinal Concepts:
   The Christian growth cycle:

a. "Grew . . . in favor both with the LORD and with men" (1 Sam. 2:21*b*, 26).
b. Jesus grew, strong in wisdom and spirit (Luke 2:40, 52).
c. The Teacher of the Word (John 14:26; 16:13; 1 Cor. 2:12; 3:6).
d. "Grow up in all *aspects* into Him" (Eph. 4:15).
e. "Be strong in the Lord" (Eph. 6:10).
f. Keep on pursuing, "press on" (Phil. 3:12–14).
g. "Your faith is greatly enlarged" (2 Thess. 1:3).
h. "Continue in the things you have learned . . . which are able to give you the wisdom that leads to salvation" (2 Tim. 3:14–15).
i. "That by it you may grow" (1 Pet. 2:2).
j. "Grow in the grace and knowledge" (2 Pet. 3:18).

E. *Source Book* Keywords: Christ (boyhood, obedience of Christ), grow in grace, promotion

F. Activities:
1. Suggested Visuals: none
2. Games, Songs, Worksheets
3. Memory Verse: "But grow in the grace and knowledge of our Lord and Savior Jesus Christ." (2 Pet. 3:18*a*)
4. Opening and Closing Prayer

LESSON
GROWING IN GRACE AND KNOWLEDGE

*P*romotion day is always a special day, whether it is in school or in Bible class. Do you know what I would like to be able to do today? I would like to look right into your mind to see how much you have learned and how much of it you can still remember. God wants you to grow in the grace and knowledge of our Savior, not just grow in size. He wants you to grow spiritually as well as physically, to move on and up. He never intended time or life on earth to stand still.

Look at all the growing things around you. The little acorn becomes a tall tree; the egg will someday be too small for the baby chick inside it. When the right time comes, the shell will crack and make room for the chick to climb out of it. Then the day comes when the chicken will lay her own eggs, or if it turns out to be a rooster, will crow heartily. Time does not stand still; seconds become minutes, hours, days, weeks, months, and years. Once you were a helpless baby, but look at you now.

"A Little Here, a Little There"

I shouldn't be surprised that you know more of God's Word and doctrine than many grown people. How did you come by this knowledge? You came by it the Bible way—"Order on order, order on order, Line on line, line on line, A little here, a little there" (Isa. 28:10). An order is a written commandment from the Word. Lesson after lesson the stories added knowledge to knowledge that you might be "built up" into strong Christians (Col. 2:7).

Think of all those huge skyscrapers in large cities. How did they get to be that way? Little by little. First there was only a hole; then a foundation was poured. Next the steel framework was put up. There it stood like an enormous skeleton. But slowly, slowly, concrete was added; brick by brick was 'fed' to it until the skeleton was covered and the building took on shape. At last, the outer shell was ready. Now other workmen came to take over and finish the job. Today these skyscrapers are busy places, housing many offices and stores and people. They are doing the very thing for which the architect designed them.

God designed you to grow to "be to the praise of His glory" (Eph. 1:12*b*). You, too, can become a giant of faith, grace, and knowledge, no matter what your age or height may be. Let's pretend you are one of those skyscrapers we just talked about. Of course, I can speak only of those who have believed in the Lord Jesus Christ, as they are the only ones who have the right kind of foundation upon which to build the Word (1 Cor. 3:11).

The One Who Works from Within

Your teachers can only be the 'outside' workmen. Teachers add line upon line in Bible class, a little here and a little there. But the teacher who really counts is the one who works from within—God the Holy Spirit. He takes the things you hear from us and makes them 'stick.' When you begin to learn about God you have a foundation, your faith in the Lord Jesus Christ, and a few bricks of knowledge. You already know what God is like, His essence. We made sure this had really stuck with you before we added the many doctrines you have learned about the persons of the Trinity.

What were some of these? Yes, you learned that God is the Great Three-in-One, the Trinity. God the Father, God the Son, and God the Holy Spirit are three persons, yet one God. You learned that the Father is the planner of all things, the Son works out the Father's plans, and the Holy Spirit shows them to us. You learned that God the Father is not only the Father of our Lord Jesus Christ but also the Father of whom else? All believers. You learned that God the Son is different from the Father and from the Holy Spirit in that He is also man. We called Him the God-man-Savior and heard how He came into the world—and why? To be God's 'show and tell' to the world. We found out how much God loved us to give up His only Son for our sins. Jesus Christ became the man-in-the-middle when He died on the cross. What was the new word you learned that told us Jesus brought God and men back together again? Mediator.

See how your skyscraper of knowledge has grown? Can you think of where we went from here? What came after the cross? Yes, the Lord's burial, resurrection, ascension, and session. And after that? Right! We found out that He will return twice more: the first time to the clouds at the Rapture when He comes to take us home with Him, and the second time? Yes, to the earth, to judge and to rule.

In the Power of the Holy Spirit

Now let me see whether you can remember your lessons about God the Holy Spirit. He has promised to remind you of all things you have learned from God's Word. First of all, we learned who the Holy Spirit is. Can you tell me? He is the third person of Trinity. We learned of His work in the days of the Old Testament, and how He came down from heaven on the day of Pentecost. He came to indwell all believers and stay in them forever to teach and guide them, to be their power and to glorify the Lord Jesus Christ. We learned that He can only fill us when we keep our sins confessed. He can only teach us when we are in fellowship with God.

And so we have come to the end of the pile of bricks which were to be added to your skyscraper. Looks as if you have come a long way, doesn't it? But don't get self-satisfied; you've got a long, long way to go yet, and so have I—all the way until we have reached "the measure of the stature which belongs to the fulness of Christ" (Eph. 4:13). We can only wonder, "Will we *ever* get there?"

The Lord Jesus Christ came to earth to show us we can, but only in the power of the Holy Spirit. Let's look at Christ's growth as a human being, shall we? Then we will find out how we can become like Him.

The Promotion of Our Lord Jesus Christ

When God sent His Son to be the Savior of the world, eternal God became a tiny baby (John 1:14). Mary took that baby and wrapped Him in swaddling clothes and laid Him in the manger (Luke 2:7). At Christmastime, people like to talk of the Baby in the manger, but they forget about Him the rest of the year. They forget that He did not stay in the manger very long. In fact, just eight days later Mary and Joseph brought Him to Jerusalem, to the Temple to present Him to the Lord God (Luke 2:21–24).

The next time we read about the Lord Jesus, we find that He was about two years old. He lived in a small house in Bethlehem where the wise men found and worshiped Him (Matt. 2:9, 11). That tells us our Lord Jesus grew and had birthdays just as you and I. We are told that He grew, not only in body, but also in His human spirit, as He learned new things daily (Luke 2:40). God the Father was well pleased with His Son, and so were the people who knew Him (Luke 2:51–52).

Even as a boy, the Lord Jesus loved to go to synagogue or church. He listened with great interest as the Old Testament was taught and read, and He always knew the right answers. The teachers were amazed at Him! Jesus would have loved to stay at church all the time (Luke 2:46–49). Yet He knew that He must obey Mary and Joseph and do as He was told while He was still a child (Luke 2:51; cf. Col. 3:20). He knew that He must obey His heavenly Father and go to the cross so that you and I could be saved.

Then came the promotion of the Lord Jesus. What do I mean? Turn with me to Philippians 2:9–11: "Therefore also God highly exalted Him, and bestowed on Him the name which is above every name, that at the name of Jesus EVERY KNEE SHOULD BOW, of those who are in heaven, and on earth, and under the earth, and that every tongue should confess that Jesus Christ is Lord, to the glory of God the Father." Because of the perfect obedience of Jesus Christ, God the Father raised Him from the dead and seated Him at His own right hand in heaven. He gave Him a name which is above every name (Acts 4:12). And now comes the most amazing thing of all! What is it?

What God Wants Me to Know

God offered to 'promote' anyone to a place in His family. Would you like to become a son or a daughter of God? "But as many as received Him, to them He gave the right to become children of God, *even* to those who believe in His name" (John 1:12). Right now you can be born again. You can begin to grow in the knowledge of God by taking in His Word.

Another promotion waits for all who belong to God already (Gal. 3:26). God's plan is that you be made over to be just like His Son (Rom. 8:29). Do you have to work at it? Do I? No, God knew we could never do it in our own strength; that's why He gave us the Holy Spirit. Little by little, as we are in fellowship, the Holy Spirit changes us as we begin to apply God's Word to our lives, as we do what God's Word says. Yes, we do have a long way to go until we reach the Lord Jesus' measurements. But we must be filled with the Spirit; then, we can learn and do God's Word. We can continue in the things we have learned, and we can be sure of our promotion (Phil. 3:14; 1 John 3:2). Someday we will be exactly like Him, for we shall see Him as He is! But until then, "Grow in the grace and knowledge of our Lord and Savior Jesus Christ" (2 Pet. 3:18).

Memory Verse

"But grow in the grace and knowledge of our Lord and Savior Jesus Christ." (2 Pet. 3:18*a*)

Chapter Twenty-Eight

Thanksgiving Multiplies God's Grace

OVERVIEW

A. Subject: Thanksgiving Multiplies God's Grace—John 1:1–14

B. Lesson Title: The Thanksgiving of the Lord Jesus

C. Story Objective:

Thanksgiving is commanded in Scripture (Ps. 105:1; 107:1; Col. 3:15) and stems from orientation to God's grace (1 Cor. 15:10) and from knowledge of doctrine (Ps. 34:1–4; 35:27). It should always include the person and work of our matchless Savior, the Lord Jesus Christ, who has done and continues to do so much for us! In giving thanks, the believer acknowledges his dependence upon God for all that he is and has (Ps. 103:1–2).

The supreme example of thanksgiving is the God-man-Savior Himself. In His humanity, Jesus Christ put prayer above every activity in His life. Prayer was as natural as breathing to Him. As He sought out the Father, He demonstrated His dependence on the Holy Spirit and His compatibility with the will of the Father. His prayers of thanksgiving shall furnish the background for this lesson. Paramount among them is, of course, His thanksgiving for the "bread" and the "cup" (Matt. 26:26–27) which pictured His death on the cross. This prayer shall be woven into the application for the unsaved child, while the Lord's prayers of thanksgiving supply the Bible background to be taught.

God always honors the thankful believer. Many wonderful things have been brought about through true thanksgiving, for the thanksgiving of many multiplies God's grace for His glory (2 Cor. 4:15).

D. Vocabulary and Doctrinal Concepts:
  1. Vocabulary: dungeon, jailor, stocks

2. Doctrinal Concepts:
  a. Thanksgiving commanded:
    1) To men and angels (Ps. 103:1–2, 19–21).
    2) "Let everything that has breath praise the LORD" (Ps. 150:6).
    3) For all things (Eph. 5:20).
    4) In everything (1 Thess. 5:18).
    5) For all men (1 Tim. 2:1).
    6) Acknowledge thanks (Heb. 13:15).
  b. Times of thanksgiving:
    1) Morning and evening (1 Chron. 23:30)
    2) In assembly worship (Ps. 35:18)
    3) Any time (Ps. 92:1)
    4) At midnight, alone (Ps. 119:62)
    5) Before meals (Luke 9:16; 24:30)
    6) Always (Eph. 5:20; 2 Thess. 2:13)
  c. The multiplication of grace through thanksgiving:
    1) Daniel's deliverance (Dan. 6:10, 23)
    2) Jonah's deliverance (Jonah 2:9–10)
    3) Paul's and Silas' deliverance (Acts 16:25–26)
    4) In principle (2 Cor. 4:15)
  d. The thanksgiving of Jesus Christ:
    1) For spiritual progress of new believers (Matt. 11:25; Luke 10:21)
    2) For the bread and cup; His death (Matt. 26:27; Luke 22:19)
    3) For the loaves and the fishes (John 6:11)
    4) For answered prayer (John 11:41)
    5) Before a meal (John 21:13; cf. Luke 24:30)

E. *Source Book* Keywords: Christ, Daniel, Jonah, thanksgiving

F. Activities:
  1. Suggested Visuals: none
  2. Games, Songs, Worksheets

3. Memory Verse: "He who offers a sacrifice of thanksgiving honors Me." (Ps. 50:23*a*)
4. Opening and Closing Prayer

LESSON
THE THANKSGIVING OF THE LORD JESUS

Can you find the last Psalm in your Bible? What is it? Psalm 150. Let's read the first sentence of verse 1 and the last sentence of verse 6: "Praise the LORD!"; "Praise the LORD!" To "praise" the Lord means to be thankful to Him for what He is like and for all He has done for us. Our memory verse for this special lesson says, "He who offers a sacrifice of thanksgiving honors Me [God]" (Ps. 50:23*a*).

Actually, we all should praise and be thankful for our wonderful God. Psalm 150:6 says, "Let everything that has breath praise the LORD." Are you breathing today? You are, or else you would not be alive and with us here. Breathing seems to come naturally to you; you do it all day long, all night long, day in, day out. God gave you the ability to breathe just as He gave you all you are and have. Have you thanked Him for it? You had not thought of it? Why, don't you know your next breath depends on Him (Dan. 5:23)?

Thanking the heavenly Father is a sign that we know how very much we need Him. It should come naturally to us—as naturally as does breathing! It is always a pleasure to meet thankful people, I mean truly thankful people! Unhappily, there are too few of them. We are so quick to ask the heavenly Father to do things for us but slowpokes about thanking Him, if we thank Him at all! We should all be thankful, and after today's lesson I trust we will have more thanksgiving and praises to offer to God and to glorify Him.

Did you know that some wonderful things happen when believers are really thankful? It's just like working out a multiplication problem with God giving you all the answers you need. Watch it as we begin our lesson!

Results of Thanksgiving

Let's take the first three problems, two from the Old Testament and one from the New Testament to show you what I mean. Problem number one is a law against prayer. The king Darius has signed the law against prayer, and breaking it means death in the lions' den. A man named Daniel had to solve this problem, and he knew just how— he prayed three times a day just as he had always done before, right in front of his open window. Daniel thanked God even when it might have cost him his life. And what did God do? He honored Daniel's faithfulness and answered his prayers by His grace. Although Daniel was thrown into the lions' den, no harm came to him (Dan. 6:10, 23) and God was glorified.

Problem number two: A great fish had swallowed up the disobedient prophet Jonah. After Jonah confessed his sin of disobeying God's Word, he began to give thanks in the belly of the fish. And what did God do for Jonah? He honored Jonah's confession of sin and He spoke to the fish, and the fish vomited out Jonah upon dry land (Jonah 2:9–10). Again, thanksgiving had glorified God!

Problem number three: Two men lay in a dungeon. Their feet were in the stocks, and there was no way for them to escape, not even from the rats that tried to nibble at their toes and their bruised, beaten backs. What an awful situation for God's servants Paul and Silas to be in! It was midnight. Paul and Silas were praying, and of all things— praising and thanking God! I wonder, how many of us would have complained? Do you know what happened then? God sent a great earthquake to shake the prison foundation. Every single door opened, and all prisoners were free. And as if that were not enough, the jailor and his entire family were saved and thanked and praised God (Acts 16:25–26, 34). See what God does for thankful believers?

The Lord Jesus Gives Thanks

We have learned about God the Son. Do you think He was thankful? Or did He even need to thank God, since He is God Himself? As God, He does not pray to or praise God, but as the man Jesus Christ He most certainly did. Prayer and praise came to Him like breathing, as it should come to us. Someday, when you want to read the Gospels—Matthew, Mark, Luke, and John—take your pencil and mark every verse you find about the Lord Jesus praying to His Father in heaven. We will look for His prayers of thanksgiving.

Thanksgiving for Other Believers

The Lord Jesus Christ had sent out seventy helpers to tell others about God's plan of salvation. Now the seventy men had come back happy. They were glad to serve their Lord, glad that His name was so great and powerful that even the bad angels could not hurt them. The Lord Jesus praised and thanked His heavenly Father for having shown these things to His group of helpers (Luke 10:21).

Thanksgiving for Answered Prayer

And then there was the time when the Lord's friend Lazarus had died. Already Lazarus had been dead and buried three days. But now the Lord Jesus stood before the place where Lazarus was laid. He was praying. What did He say? Open your Bible to John 11:41: "And so they removed the stone. And Jesus raised His eyes, and said, 'Father, I thank Thee that Thou heardest Me.'" He thanked God the Father for having heard Him! Nothing had happened yet; what was He so thankful for then? God knew, did He not? For John 11:44 tells us that Lazarus came forth out of the grave, alive once more.

Thanksgiving before a Meal

Do you pray before you eat or drink? Sometimes? When you remember to? Does God remember to supply your food? Or do you think your parents do that? In a way they do. Your father goes out and earns a living for the family; your mother cooks the meal. True, but God gave them strength and health, a job and knowledge, didn't He (Deut. 8:17–18)? In fact, God supplies all our needs "according to His riches in glory in Christ Jesus" (Phil. 4:19).

The Lord Jesus never once forgot to thank the Father for food or drink. So well did His disciples remember the way He gave thanks before a meal that they recognized Him by the way He praised God after He rose from the dead (Luke 24:30). Let me tell you how His thanksgiving for food multiplied God's grace supply one day.

Five Barley Loaves and Two Little Fishes

The twelve disciples had a problem. "How can we feed a crowd of five thousand men, not counting their women and children [perhaps 14,000 people altogether]?" They were in the 'back of beyond' with no grocery stores for miles around. Between them, they had about thirty-four dollars, which would hardly buy each more than a crumb! Yet the Lord Jesus had told them, "You give them *something* to eat!" (Luke 9:13).

Perhaps the disciples looked so puzzled, not knowing how to solve this great problem, that the Lord finally said, "How many loaves do you have? Go look!" (Mark 6:38). Well, here was something they could do. Surely, some of the people there would have brought along something to eat. They came back with long faces. Andrew, Peter's brother, was the only one to report, "There is a lad here who has five barley loaves and two fish" (John 6:9*a*). But Andrew had his doubts about how helpful that would prove to be. He added sadly, "but what are these for so many people?" (John 6:9*b*).

After all the people had been told to sit down on the grassy ground, the Lord Jesus took the loaves and the fish which the boy had so cheerfully given Him. He held them in His hands and thanked the Father for having provided them. I wonder what the disciples thought when they watched Him. Did they grumble under their breath, "Thanks for what? For that bit of nothing?" Do you think it worthwhile to thank God for a steak but not for a peanut-butter and jelly sandwich?

I think the disciples' eyes and mouths must have popped open with surprise when the Lord's thanksgiving began to multiply the loaves and the fish. Everyone had more than enough to eat, and twelve baskets full of pieces of bread and fish were left over—one for each of the disciples to carry home as a reminder of what God can do. I rather think they felt a bit sheepish, don't you (John 6:11–13)?

And what did the people think? Many of them knew that Jesus is God and believed in Him (John 6:14). And the boy who gave his supper? I am sure he never forgot that day. I should not wonder but that he remembered to give thanks before every meal from that day on. Certainly, the Father was glorified.

What God Wants Me to Know

Perhaps we should be made to carry about a basket full of all that God does for us every day and for which we have not even begun to be thankful. Surely, then we would remember to offer praises and glorify Him. We should always be thankful, not just for the good and nice things that come along but for all things and in all things. You can wake up giving thanks and go to sleep giving thanks. In fact, when you are in fellowship with God, you cannot help but be thankful!

Just think of it: The God-man-Savior, our Lord Jesus Christ is thankful for you! You are His joy (Heb. 12:2)! He died for you! You cannot begin to thank Him enough for that alone! But you have so much else for which to be thankful! Be a grateful believer from now on, will you?

And now we have come to the last thanksgiving picture of the Lord Jesus that we want to see today. The day of the Lord's last Passover on earth has come. He takes the bread and the cup into His hands, the same hands which will soon be pierced by nails. He looks up to heaven and thanks the Father (Luke 22:19–20). This is no ordinary thanksgiving prayer before a meal. Do you know for what He is thanking the Father? Listen to what He says to His disciples: "This is My body which is given for you . . . This cup which is poured out for you is the new covenant in My blood." Yes, He actually thanks the Father for letting Him die for your sins and mine! Imagine that! Even when He knew who would and who would not believe on Him!

Not to believe on the Lord Jesus Christ is to turn away thanklessly from God's greatest gift—His Son. Still, "He [God] Himself is kind to ungrateful and evil *men*" (Luke 6:35*b*). He is allowing you to be here to learn of His grace. He is ready to accept you today if you will only believe in the Lord Jesus Christ (Eph. 1:6). Think it over carefully; because the Lord Jesus prayed and thanked God and went to the cross, our blessings for now and eternity are multiplied. Will you make your decision today and be truly thankful? Then "Believe in the Lord Jesus, and you shall be saved" (Acts 16:31). Then you, too, can join us in saying, "Thanks be to God for His indescribable gift!" (2 Cor. 9:15).

> ### Memory Verse
> "He who offers a sacrifice of thanksgiving honors Me " (Ps. 50:23a)

Chapter Twenty-Nine

Christmas: God Prepares for His Son

OVERVIEW

A. Subject: Christmas: God Prepares for His Son—Luke 1 and 2

B. Lesson Title: The Unfolding of God's Plan of Redemption

C. Story Objective:

God's great plan of redemption was set into operation when Adam sinned. All through the Old Testament, the Jews looked forward to the coming of a Savior, as revealed through the sacrifices, feasts, etc. But God must make extensive preparation for the coming of His Son into the world. When He came, there must be no doubt as to who He was. Step by step the preparation went forward. Little by little the great plan unfolded, until by the time the Old Testament was completed all the pieces fit together into a complete picture of the Son of God.

God separated unto Himself a new nation through which the Savior would come. He gave this nation a kingdom which would be established forever; He prepared a mother through whom the Son of God would be born, and He also prepared a body for His Son. He planned a birthplace, in Bethlehem, where Jesus should be born—a stable, the appropriate place for a Lamb to be born. He also prepared a name—Jesus, Savior, to tell the people why He had come.

The preparation all completed, the Lord Jesus came into the world as the God-man-Savior. There was no excuse for not recognizing Him; yet "He came to His own, and those who were His own did not receive Him" (John 1:11). The majority of the Jews were not ready or willing to receive Him. They wanted a King, not a Savior. But to as many as did or will receive Him, He gives power to become the sons of God.

D. Vocabulary and Doctrinal Concepts:
   1. Vocabulary: inn, stable
   2. Doctrinal Concepts:
      a. The Savior first promised (Gen. 3:15).
      b. God begins a new nation (Gen. 12:1–3).
      c. God establishes David's throne forever (2 Sam. 7:12–16).
      d. God prepares a mother to bear His Son and tells who He will be—Immanuel, meaning "God with us" (Isa. 7:14; Matt. 1:23).
      e. God chooses a city (Micah 5:2).
      f. God prepares a body (Heb. 10:5).
      g. God prepares a name (Matt. 1:21).

E. *Source Book* Keywords: Christ (birth, Lamb without spot, royalty of Christ), Christmas

F. Activities:
   1. Suggested Visuals: none
   2. Games, Songs, Worksheets
   3. Memory Verse: "You shall call His name Jesus, for it is He who will save His people from their sins." (Matt. 1:21*b*)
   4. Opening and Closing Prayer

LESSON
THE UNFOLDING OF GOD'S PLAN OF REDEMPTION

*P*erhaps you have had a new little baby in your home. Did your father and mother do anything to get ready for his coming? The new baby must have a home to live in, a bed to sleep in, and clothes to wear, mustn't he? For nearly a year your parents put together all the things that would be needed.

In the Bible we read of a very special little baby who was to be born into the world. This baby was God's own dear Son. And because He was so very special, it took not one year but many thousands of years to prepare for His coming.

When Adam and Eve sinned way back in the Garden of Eden, they lost their fellowship with God. They could no longer have a relationship with God, for sin stood in the way. God must punish them because they disobeyed Him. Their punishment for sin would be death—not just the death of their bodies, but spiritual death and eternal separation from God in the lake of fire. Yet in spite of their sin and disobedience, God still loved that first man and woman whom He had created. He wanted to have a relationship with them again, so He made them a promise. "I will send Someone to take your punishment for you. I will send a Savior to die for your sins that you may go free," God promised.

The Old Testament tells us how God kept His word. We read how He worked out a wonderful plan before His Son could come into the world. Everyone must know who the Savior was and why He had come. He must come in such a special way that there could be no doubt that this was the very One God had promised Adam and Eve so long ago.

God the Father Prepares a Nation

Do you remember why many of the early settlers left their old countries and came to America? They wanted to be able to worship God in the way they believed was right. They started a new nation and set up our government on principles according to the Word of God.

Now, God the Father, too, needed a new nation which would worship Him correctly and which belonged to Him in a special way. God spoke to one man and told him he was to be the father of a new nation. Through this new nation God was preparing, His Son would come into the world, and all the world would be blessed. Abraham believed God. He left his old country to live in the new country God had showed him.

God Prepares a Kingdom

In only a few hundred years, Abraham's family had become a very large nation of thousands and thousands of people. God called this new nation "Israel." Then God chose a king who loved and trusted Him with all his heart to rule over God's nation. Do you know who he was? Yes, David.

David knew the Word of God and taught it to the people. One day God spoke to David and said, "Your kingdom shall endure before Me forever" (2 Sam. 7:16*b*). You see, God's Son was not only to be from the Jewish race, but from the family of King David. One day He would sit upon David's throne and rule the world forever. Like David's kingdom, the kingdom of the Lord Jesus Christ would be a righteous kingdom, established or set up upon the Word of God.

God Prepares a City

David was born in a small city called Bethlehem (1 Sam. 16:4; 20:6). God planned that in this very same city the Savior would be born (Micah 5:2). Then God let His people know where His Son would come into the world so that there would be no mistaking Him when He did come.

God Prepares a Mother

Many years before she was born, God told the Jews that He would also prepare just the right mother for His Son. He even described her; she would be a young woman, never married, and would have descended or come from the family of King David.

Finally, when nearly all the preparations were made for the coming of the Savior, God sent an angel to a young woman named Mary. The angel told Mary the wonderful news, that she was the one whom God had chosen to be the mother of His Son. Mary was everything God said she would be: young, unmarried, of the family of David, sweet and pure. Mary was amazed, even troubled at the news that she was to have a son who would "be great, and will be called the Son of the Most High" (Luke 1:32*a*). "The Lord God will give Him the throne of His father David," the angel had said (Luke 1:32*b*). "How can this be?" Mary wondered, since she was not yet married (Luke 1:34).

God Prepares a Body

The angel reminded Mary that "nothing will be impossible with God" (Luke 1:37). The Holy Spirit would perform or work a miracle in this lovely young woman whom God had prepared and chosen. He would cause a baby to grow in her. "The Holy Spirit will come upon you, and the power of the Most High will overshadow you; and for that reason the holy offspring shall be called the Son of God," the angel told her (Luke 1:35). Now Mary understood and nodded, "Be it done to me according to your word" (Luke 1:38b).

Since all babies should have a father, God also prepared a human father to take care of His Son while He was growing up. Mary was engaged to marry a carpenter named Joseph. He, too, was of the family of King David (Matt. 1:6, 16). The angel appeared to Joseph one night and explained that the Baby's real father was God, but that Joseph must look well after Mary and the son she was going to have.

God Prepares a Name

All babies must have a name, and so must the Son of God. Six hundred years before God's Son was born, God told His people what this miracle baby would be called. His name would be very, very important, for it would tell the people who He was. His name would be "'IMMANUEL,' which translated means 'GOD WITH US'" (Matt. 1:23). Although this baby was a true human being, He was also truly God. The angel told Mary that God had prepared a human name for His Son which would tell us what He would do. "You shall call His name Jesus," the angel had said, "for it is He who will save His people from their sins" (Matt. 1:21). The name "Jesus" means "Savior." This is exactly what Jesus came to earth to do—to be our Savior.

God Prepares a Birthplace

Do you know where Mary lived? That's right, in Nazareth. Had God forgotten that He had prepared another birthplace, the town of Bethlehem, for His Son? Oh, no, God knew that Mary and Joseph must travel to the city of David just at the time when Jesus was about to be born.

It was part of God's plan that there would be no room for them in the inns of Bethlehem. All through the Old Testament God had taught that His Son would be the "Lamb of God" who must be the real sacrifice on the cross. When He had died for the sins of the world, the Jews no longer needed to offer lambs upon their altars. Lambs are not born in inns or taverns, but in stables. That's why God had prepared a stable for His dear little Lamb, again reminding us that Jesus is the "Lamb who has been slain" (Rev. 13:8b).

So it was that when all the preparation was completed, Mary "gave birth to her first-born son; and she wrapped Him in cloths, and laid Him in a manger, because there was no room for them in the inn" (Luke 2:7). This Baby was born into the Jewish race, of the family of David, in the city of Bethlehem, of the virgin Mary, in a stable with the lambs. And Mary called His name Jesus, just as God had prepared for her to do.

Could there be any doubt as to who this Baby was? Could there be any excuse for not knowing, not recognizing Him? The shepherds and wise men believed and rejoiced in the coming of the Savior and King. Do you?

What God Wants Me to Know

Even though God chose a special people, even though He told them of His great plan, most of them were not prepared for Him when He did come. They did not seem to understand what we have already learned, that when Jesus came the first time it was to die on the cross for the sins of the world—for their sins, for your sins, and for mine. Many people wanted Him to come the first time as a great and glorious king, to set up His kingdom, and to give them important places in His kingdom. They did not like to be told that they were sinners and needed a Savior.

All through the Old Testament times, the Jews had offered up animals while they waited and longed for the coming of their Savior who would be offered up for them once and for all. But when He came at last, they did not recognize Him as God's Lamb. They kept right on sacrificing animals and turned away from God's Son. How sad to think that "He came to His own [people], and those who were His own did not receive Him. But as many as received Him, to them He gave the right to become children of God, *even* to those who believe in His name" (John 1:11–12).

Jesus has come and has died on the cross for your sins. Will you believe that He has done this for you and receive Him as your Savior? You have learned that someday He is coming back in great power and glory to set up His kingdom, but the only way you can be in His kingdom is first to believe that He died on the cross for your sins.

Although Jesus is not yet the ruler of this earth as God has promised He will be, He wants to be "King" in the lives of everyone who has trusted in Him. He wants to rule our lives day by day; that means He wants to have His way in our lives. Too many of us want to rule our own lives. We want our own way. But, did you know that your own way is the way of the sin nature? When God is not controlling your life, the sin nature is, and the sin nature can only get you into trouble. There is just one way of putting Christ on the throne of your life—and that is by the filling of the Spirit (Gal. 5:16). We are filled with the Spirit when we confess our sins, and then we must learn God's Word to keep us from sinning (Ps. 119:11).

That is God's way. You can be sure that God, who plans so perfectly, always has the very best plan for our lives. Will you ask Him to help you want His Word and His way?

Memory Verse

"You shall call His name Jesus, for it is He who will save His people from their sins." (Matt. 1:21b)

Chapter Thirty

Easter Story: The Resurrection

A. Subject: Easter Story: The Resurrection—Matthew 27:59—28:15; Mark 16:1–11

B. Lesson Title: The Empty Tomb

C. Story Objective:

Over the centuries, tombs and the artifacts found in them have taught us many lessons concerning the way of life and death and the beliefs of early peoples the world over. But there was one tomb that was remarkably different in that it taught eternal lessons, not because of what was found in the tomb, but because of what was not found in it—the body of Jesus. When the angel rolled away the stone from the opening of the tomb of the Lord Jesus Christ, the tomb was found to be empty! Jesus Christ had risen from the dead, even as He had promised. The lessons of the empty tomb are not preserved for us in museums, but on the pages of the Word of God.

The resurrection of Jesus Christ was necessary to complete our salvation (1 Cor. 15:3–4). His death on the cross took care of the salvation of our souls; His resurrection guarantees the yet future salvation of our bodies. Resurrection provided victory over death and the grave, and His resurrection assures the believer that he shall be raised also (1 Cor. 15:51–57).

D. Vocabulary and Doctrinal Concepts:
1. Vocabulary: barge, decay, embalm, memorial, prime minister, resurrection, Sabbath, tomb
2. Doctrinal Concepts:
   a. After death, what (Job 14:14)?
   b. The certainty of the Resurrection (Job 19:26).
   c. No corruption for the Holy One (Ps. 16:10).
   d. "I will be satisfied with Thy likeness when I awake" (Ps. 17:15).
   e. The two resurrections: of life and of judgment (John 5:29; cf. Matt. 25:41).
   f. The Resurrection chapter (1 Cor. 15).

E. *Source Book* Keywords: cross (burial, resurrection, ascension, and session), resurrection

F. Activities:
1. Suggested Visuals: none
2. Games, Songs, Worksheets
3. Memory Verse: "I am the resurrection and the life; he who believes in Me shall live even if he dies." (John 11:25)
4. Opening and Closing Prayer

LESSON
THE EMPTY TOMB

*E*aster is the special Sunday we set aside to talk about the resurrection. Do you remember what the word "resurrection" means? That's right, "rising from the dead." But it is more than that—it is rising from the dead in a new body that will never die again.

People have always wanted to know what happens to a person after he dies, and they have asked, "Is there really life after death?" Open your Bible to Job 14:14. The Book of Job is one of the oldest books in the Bible. Probably Moses wrote it. He tells us that Job was sure he *would live again*. He answers for us this question, "If a man dies, will he live *again*?" Then he says, "All the days of my struggle I will wait, Until my change comes." There was no doubt in Job's mind that even though his body would be put in a grave where it would turn back into dust (Gen. 3:19*b*), he would see God in his own, new body (Job 19:26).

Where did Job learn this? From God. Down through the ages God has let His people know that there would be a resurrection. But as people forgot God and turned away from the Son of God, their beliefs about God got all mixed up with their own ideas. Yet the knowledge of some kind of resurrection was not completely lost. How do we know this?

We know this from scientists who have learned many things about people who lived long ago by discovering their graves. From these graves, and what was found in them, we can tell how ancient peoples lived and died and what they believed. Most of them believed in some kind of life after death, either spirit life or life in a body. The way they buried their dead showed this belief.

Some early people burned the bodies of their dead. They thought this would help the spirit to get away to the next world. In India they build great heaps of wood on which to burn the bodies. The Teutons, ancient northern Europeans, placed their dead warriors on a barge with all the weapons that had once belonged to them and sent it flaming down the river.

The Egyptians believed that only by keeping the body from decaying could the dead have life after death. So they learned how to keep the body from turning back into dust for many years. The more important the person who died, the more care was used in preserving his body. The Egyptians began to build huge pyramids for their Pharaohs or kings. Joseph had been Egypt's prime minister, and although he was not an Egyptian, he was shown a great honor when he died. His body was embalmed, and he was put into a coffin in Egypt (Gen. 50:26). More than four hundred years later his body was brought back to his own homeland to be buried at last (Joshua 24:32).

The Egyptians thought that the dead would need many things for life after death, so many objects were buried along with them. The kings, especially, were buried with many valuable treasures of gold, silver, and jewels, even furniture. But the Egyptians finally had to stop burying their kings in pyramid tombs because these tombs were always robbed. They began to dig tombs out of the cliffs and mountains and roll large stones over them. These tombs were sealed to guard them from thieves.

One Pharaoh, King Tut or Tutankhamen, was discovered in one of those cave tombs with some of the greatest treasures ever found. All these things are kept in museums today, where you can see them, even King Tut's wonderfully preserved body. But, even though great care had been taken in trying to keep the bodies of the dead from turning back into dust, no one can ever stop the body from decaying eventually. God had said this would happen to our bodies after death because man had sinned.

The kind of tomb a person was buried in—not only in ancient times, but often in our day, too, depended on how great and important he was in life. Some tombs of great people, such as kings and presidents, are large and beautiful buildings. Maybe you have heard about the Taj Mahal in India built by a king as a memorial for his queen.

In Arlington National Cemetery, there is the Tomb of the Unknown Soldier. It was built to honor all soldiers who gave their lives for our country. All tombs, the famous as well as the unknown, are just alike in one way—they all have in them at least one dead body, rotting away. But there is one tomb that was different—the *empty tomb* near Jerusalem. Let's hear about that tomb.

The Extra Special Tomb

The empty tomb near Jerusalem was very special, for some very remarkable things were found in it. There were the burial wraps, which had been tightly wound around a dead body, still in the shape of that body, but empty! There was the napkin, folded neatly, and there were the angels. But what really made the tomb extra special was what was *not* found in it—the dead body!

What Became of the Body?

Shall we do some detective work and learn what became of the body which had definitely been buried there? Turn to Matthew 27:59: "And Joseph took the body and wrapped it in a clean linen cloth." The body of the Lord Jesus Christ, who had just died on the cross, who had given His precious life for your sins and mine, had just been prepared for burial. Nicodemus and Joseph of Arimathea had wrapped the body of Jesus in linen strips and spices (John 19:39–42). Now they laid Him to rest in Joseph's new tomb which had been cut out of a rock. Joseph rolled a large stone in front of the opening to protect the body from robbers (Matt. 27:60).

Since robbing graves was very common in those days, the evil men who had sent Jesus to the cross thought that the Lord's disciples might try to come and steal His body and claim He had risen as He said He would. They must make sure this would not happen. So they hired soldiers to watch the tomb day and night (Matt. 27:62–66).

There was no doubt that Jesus had been buried. The Bible describes how Jesus was buried and reports that many people had seen His body placed into the tomb. After the tomb was sealed, the people went home—some very sorrowful, some not caring, some glad that Jesus was out of the way. Only the soldiers stayed. They had a job to do and they did it; but for all their watchfulness and weapons, for all His enemies' plans to keep the body where it was, they were helpless against God's plan for His Son's resurrection. They looked for robbers, but not for God's promise: "Neither wilt Thou allow Thy Holy One to undergo decay [decay of His body]" (Ps. 16:10).

Sad to say, neither did Jesus' friends look for God's promise (Mark 16:10). They had heard Jesus say, "After three days I am to rise again" (Matt. 27:63). They knew that the Old Testament taught the resurrection of the Savior after the third day. They had heard Him tell Martha and Mary, "I am the resurrection and the life; he who believes in Me shall live even if he dies" (John 11:25). Didn't they believe it? Not really, or they would not have given up all hope (Mark 16:11).

The Resurrection, Matthew 28

Well, we found out this much: The body *had* been buried! Sometime, just before this Matthew chapter 28 begins, Jesus' body rose from the dead and came through the tomb—through the stone, without a sound. The guards heard and saw nothing. Three days and nights had passed, and God's promise had come true. He had risen as He said. Then a dazzling figure like lightning appeared suddenly between the guards and the tomb. A great earthquake shook the ground. So frightened were the soldiers that they fainted. The angel rolled back the heavy stone from the door of the tomb.

When the soldiers awoke from their faint, they could see that the tomb was open—and *empty*. Quickly they ran to tell the men who had hired them to watch the tomb what had happened. They were paid large sums of money to tell a lie—that Jesus' body had indeed been stolen (Matt. 28:11–15).

Was the stone rolled away so that Jesus could get out of the tomb? No, Jesus as God is omnipotent or all-powerful. The stone need not be rolled away for Him, but for *us*! It had to be rolled away to teach a lesson no other tomb could

teach—the resurrection from the dead. God knew that the women who were on their way to the tomb could never move away the heavy stone even an inch. As was the custom, after the Sabbath or Saturday, three women came to visit the tomb and cover the body with spices. As they walked along toward the burial place, they wondered who would roll back the stone for them (Mark 16:3).

They did not have to wonder long, for when they arrived at the tomb, the stone had already been moved aside. Amazed and a bit fearful, the women peeked inside the tomb. A bright and shining angel sat as if he were waiting for them. The women trembled, but he spoke to them: "Do not be afraid; for I know that you are looking for Jesus who has been crucified. He is not here, for He has risen, just as He said." He invited them to come and see where the Lord's body had lain; then they were to run quickly and make the good news known to the Lord's disciples. They would meet the Lord Himself along the way (Matt. 28:5–7).

And then—what do you think? Why, as they went to do as the angel had told them, Jesus, seeming to come from nowhere, suddenly stood beside them. They were so glad to see Him, they fell at His feet and worshiped Him.

What God Wants Me to Know

The lesson of the empty tomb is there for all to see—and *believe*. There could be no doubt: A dead body had been placed there, and there was no doubt it had been raised; but what was and what was not found can never be put on display in a museum. You just cannot put an angel or the risen Savior in a glass case. Yet the things found, the Person *not* found, and the lesson of the tomb are plain to see in the pages of God's Word. We read of it today; others will read of it in years to come, or will hear of it. What remains now is to believe! While on earth, our Savior said, "I am the resurrection and the life; he who believes in Me shall live even if he dies" (John 11:25). Will you believe the lesson of the empty tomb? It tells us that all who believe in the Lord Jesus Christ will someday have a resurrection body just like His, one which will never wear out, die, or decay.

If you will not believe in Him, there is another resurrection waiting for you—the "resurrection of judgment" (John 5:29). God *will* raise you up from the dead, yes, but only to cast you away from Him forever (John 3:18). You must make the decision. Which will it be: the resurrection unto eternal life, or the resurrection unto everlasting fire? "Believe in the Lord Jesus, and you shall be saved" (Acts 16:31).

There is more to our salvation than Jesus' death on the cross. If Jesus had only died there would be no salvation. Only a risen Savior can save. The whole Gospel is found in the words of 1 Corinthians 15:3–4: "For I delivered to you as of first importance what I also received, that Christ died for our sins according to the Scriptures, and that He was buried, and that He was raised on the third day according to the Scriptures." The Resurrection shows us that God the Father accepted what Jesus Christ did for us on the cross. Now because Jesus rose from the dead, our bodies, too, will rise, never to die again. Our salvation is complete. His death saved our souls; His resurrection saved our bodies. Never again need we fear death, for Jesus Christ won a victory over death (1 Cor. 15:57). Even though our bodies may be laid in a grave someday, we shall live because He lives! Death cannot keep us in the grave forever. Isn't this something to talk about? Isn't it worth sharing with others?

Tell them of our living, risen Lord, that they, too, may be resurrected unto life everlasting!

Memory Verse

"I am the resurrection and the life; he who believes in Me shall live even if he dies." (John 11:25)

VISUAL AIDS

ABRAHAM

ADAM AFTER THE FALL

ALTAR

ARK OF THE COVENANT

ANGEL OF THE LORD

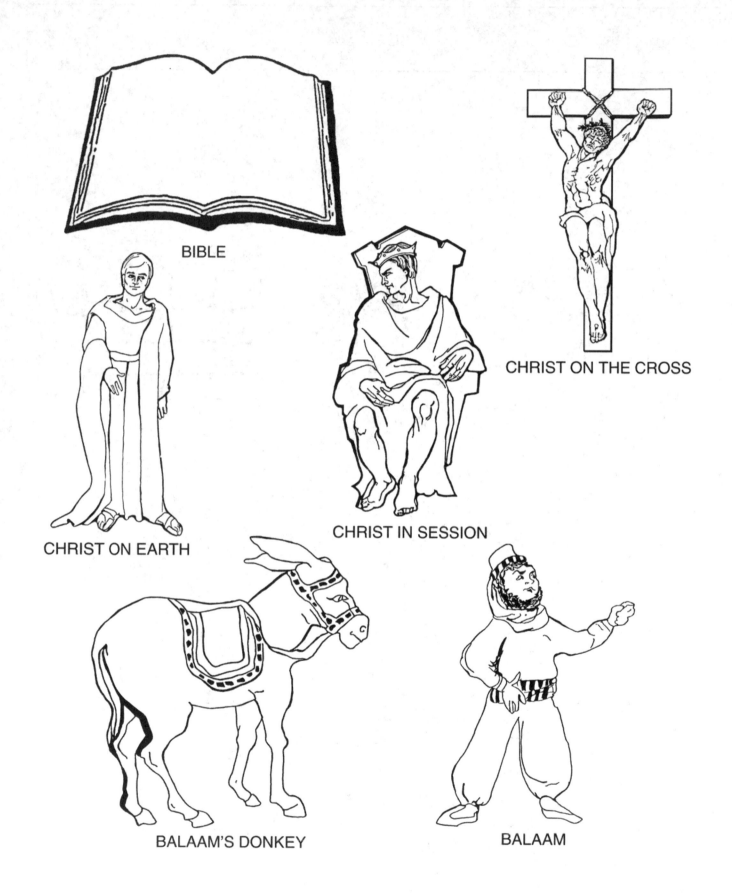

BIBLE

CHRIST ON THE CROSS

CHRIST IN SESSION

CHRIST ON EARTH

BALAAM'S DONKEY

BALAAM

CHRIST AT SECOND ADVENT

DAVID AS KING

CHRIST ASCENDING

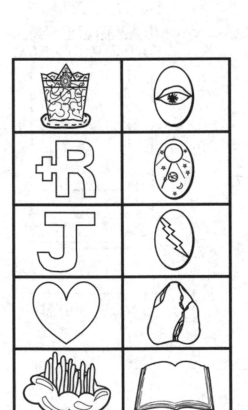

ESSENCE BOX

CHRISTIAN SOLDIER

CAMEL

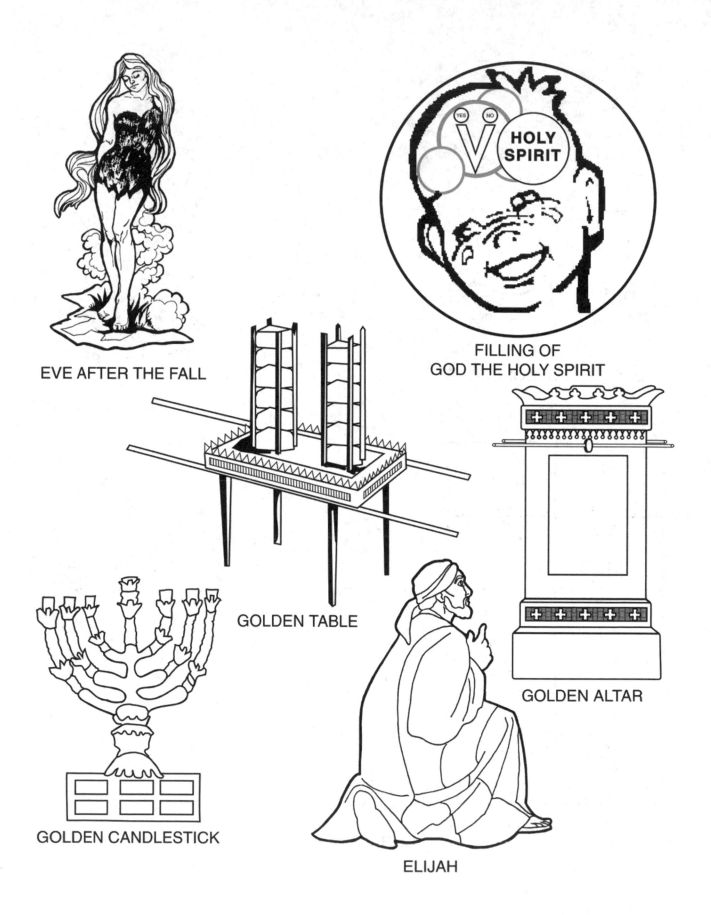

EVE AFTER THE FALL

FILLING OF
GOD THE HOLY SPIRIT

HOLY
SPIRIT

GOLDEN TABLE

GOLDEN ALTAR

GOLDEN CANDLESTICK

ELIJAH

INNER HAPPINESS PALACE

INDWELLING OF
GOD THE HOLY SPIRIT

HOLY
SPIRIT

JOSEPH

ISAAC

JOSHUA

JOHN THE BAPTIST

NICODEMUS

PETER

RAVEN

PRODIGAL SON AND FATHER

KING SAUL

STEPHEN

TOMB SEALED

FATHER

GOD

SON

HOLY SPIRIT

TRINITY

SHEEP

SHEPHERD

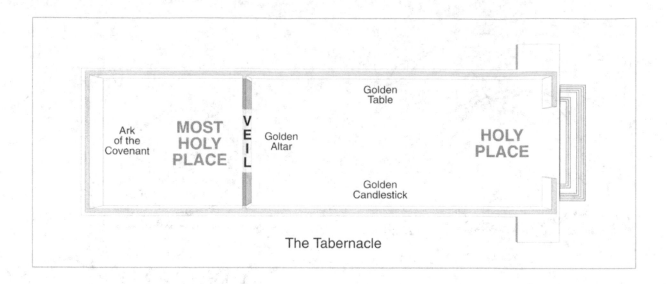

The Tabernacle

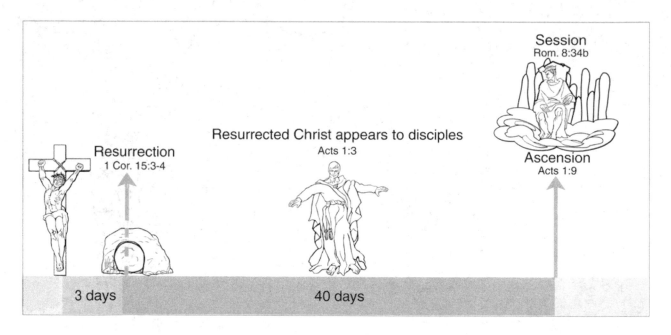

CHRIST'S TIME LINE

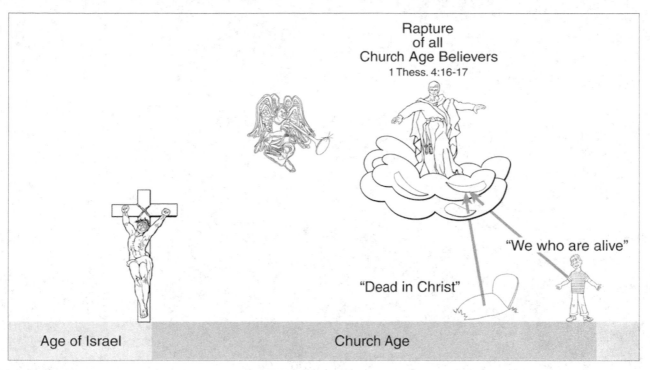

RAPTURE TIME LINE

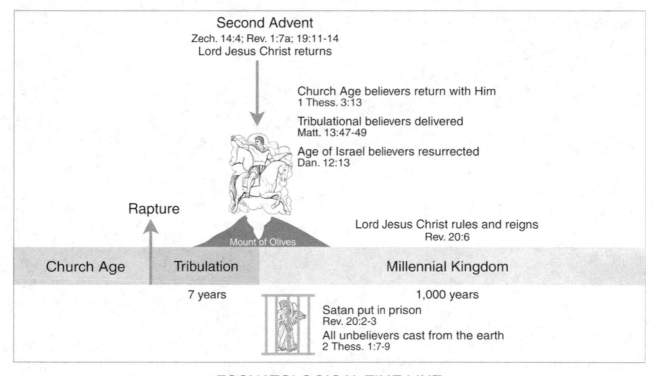

ESCHATOLOGICAL TIME LINE